Beasts of the Modern Imagination

Beasts of the Modern Imagination

Darwin, Nietzsche, Kafka, Ernst, & Lawrence

Margot Norris

The Johns Hopkins University Press

Baltimore and London

This book has been brought to publication with the generous assistance of the Andrew W. Mellon Foundation.

The Johns Hopkins University Press, 701 West 40th Street,
Baltimore, Maryland 21211
The Johns Hopkins Press Ltd, London

The paper in this book is acid-free and meets the guide-lines for permanence and durability of the Committee on Production Guidelines for Book Longevity of the Council on Library Resources.

Library of Congress Cataloging in Publication Data

Norris, Margot.
  Beasts of the modern imagination.

  Includes index.
  1. Literature, Modern—20th century—History and crit-icism. 2. Man—Animal nature. 3. Anthropomorphism. 4. Animals in literature. 5. Mimesis in literature. 6. Darwin, Charles, 1809–1882—Influence. 7. Art, Modern—20th century. 8. Literature and science. 9. Psychoanalysis and literature. I. Title.
PN56.M25N67   1985   809'.93384   84-21320
ISBN 0-8018-3252-7 (alk. paper)

Frontispiece: Max Ernst, from *Une Semaine de bonté,* 1934

Der Mensch ist durch seine Irrtümer erzogen worden: er sah sich erstens immer nur unvollständig, zweitens legte er sich erdichtete Eigenschaften bei, drittens fühlte er sich in einer falschen Rangordnung zu Tier und Natur, viertens erfand er immer neue Gütertafeln und nahm sie eine Zeitlang als ewig und unbedingt, so dass bald dieser bald jener menschliche Trieb und Zustand an der ersten Stelle stand und infolge dieser Schätzung veredelt wurde. Rechnet man die Wirkung dieser vier Irrtümer weg, so hat man auch Humanität, Menschlichkeit und "Menschenwürde" hinweggerechnet.

[Man has been cultivated through his errors: to begin with, he always saw himself only incompletely; secondly, he endowed himself with fictitious attributes; thirdly, he felt himself in a false hierarchical relationship to animal and nature; fourthly, he invented ever new tables of virtue that, for a time, he deemed eternal and unconditional, so that eventually this or that particular human drive or condition took first place and became ennobled as a result of this valuation. But if one discounts the effects of these four errors, one has also done away with humaneness, humanity, and "human dignity."]

Friedrich Nietzsche, *Die fröhliche Wissenschaft*

Contents

Acknowledgments

This book was written over an eight-year period with invaluable help from many sources, here cited chronologically.

Thomas Staley, of the University of Tulsa, made available to me the Max Ernst materials of the Cyril Connolly library before it was even cataloged by the University of Tulsa Library. As a result I first discovered Ernst's collage novels in the form of autographed copies with little birds drawn around the signature.

The American Council of Learned Societies gave me a study fellowship, which enabled me to spend a year at the University of Heidelberg reading modern German philosophy.

A University of Michigan Rackham Summer Fellowship gave me a much needed summer's freedom to do the research on Charles Darwin.

Balz Engler, of the University of Basel, made it possible for me to spend a year teaching there on a faculty exchange. My chapter on *Ecce Homo* gained much by being written in the city where Nietzsche himself taught and wrote. Ejner Jensen and John Knott supported the exchange from the American side, where it was sponsored by the University of Michigan Department of English Language and Literature.

Earlier versions of chapters 3, 5, and 6 appeared in the December 1980, April 1978, and April 1983 issues, respectively, of *MLN*, Modern Language Notes. An early draft of chapter 7 appeared in the first issue of *Structuralist Review* in Spring 1978. I wish to thank the following individuals and institutions for permission to reproduce the works of Max Ernst: Kunstsammlung Nordrhein-Westfalen, Düsseldorf, for "After Us—Motherhood"; the Solomon R. Guggenheim Foundation for "The Attirement (Robing) of the Bride," from the Peggy Guggenheim Collection, Venice, Solomon R. Guggenheim Museum, New York; the Société de la Propriété Artistique et des Dessins et Modèles and Visual Artists and Galleries Association, Inc., acting on behalf of the estate of Max Ernst for permission to use the pictures from the collage novels, and "The Blessed Virgin Chastises the Infant Jesus" © S.P.A.D.E.M., Paris/V.A.G.A., New York, 1984; and Claude Hersaint for his kind permission to reproduce "Oedipus Rex." The College of Literature, Science, and the Arts of the University of Michigan helped defray my costs for permission fees.

Abbreviations

Frequently cited works are indicated in parentheses in the text by the abbreviations listed below.

DARWIN

A   *Charles Darwin's Autobiography,* ed. Sir Francis Darwin (New York: Henry Schuman, 1950).

DM   *The Descent of Man, and Selection in Relation to Sex* (London: John Murray, Albemarle Street, 1890).

EE   *The Expression of the Emotions in Man and Animals* (Chicago: University of Chicago Press, 1965).

Gruber   Howard E. Gruber, *Darwin on Man: A Psychological Study of Scientific Creativity,* together with *Darwin's Early and Unpublished Notebooks,* transcribed and annotated by Paul H. Barrett (New York: E. P. Dutton & Co., 1974).

JR   *Journal of Researches into the Natural History and Geology of the Countries Visited during the Voyage of H.M.S. Beagle Round the World, Under the Command of Capt. Fitz Roy, R.N.* (New York: D. Appleton & Co., 1896).

O   *The Origin of Species* (New York: New American Library, 1958).

V   *The Variation of Animals and Plants Under Domestication,* 2 vols. (New York: D. Appleton & Co., 1896).

NIETZSCHE

All citations from Nietzsche's work refer to *Friedrich Nietzsche-Werke,* vols. 1–5, ed. Karl Schlechta (Frankfurt am Main–Berlin–Wien: Verlag Ullstein GmbH, 1976). In the text, each abbreviated title is preceded by its volume number in this edition.

AC   *The Antichrist (Der Antichrist)*

BGE   *Beyond Good and Evil (Jenseits von Gut und Böse)*

BT   *The Birth of Tragedy (Die Geburt der Tragödie)*

EH   *Ecce Homo*

GM   *The Genealogy of Morals (Zur Genealogie der Moral)*

GS   *The Gay Science (Die fröhliche Wissenschaft)*

NCW   *Nietzsche Contra Wagner*

PW	Posthumous writings from the 1880s, including the letters of 1861–1889 ("Aus dem Nachlass der Achtzigerjahre")
TI	*Twilight of the Idols (Götzen-Dämmerung)*
Truth	"About Truth and Falsehood in the Extra-moral Sense" (*Über Wahrheit und Lüge im aussermoralischen Sinn*)
UM	*Untimely Meditations (Unzeitgemässe Betrachtungen)*
Z	*Thus Spake Zarathustra (Also sprach Zarathustra)*

KAFKA

All citations from Kafka's stories refer to *Sämtliche Erzählungen,* ed. Paul Raabe (Frankfurt am Main: Fischer Bücherej, 1970).

Deleuze Gilles Deleuze, *Masochism: An Interpretation of Coldness and Cruelty,* trans. Jean McNeil (New York: George Braziller, 1971).

HA	"A Hunger Artist" ("Ein Hungerkünstler")
PC	"In the Penal Colony" ("In der Strafkolonie")
RA	"A Report to an Academy" ("Ein Bericht für eine Akademie")

HEMINGWAY

DA	*Death in the Afternoon* (New York: Charles Scribner's Sons, 1932).
GHA	*Green Hills of Africa* (New York: Charles Scribner's Sons, 1935).

All translations from the German in this book are mine unless otherwise indicated.

Beasts of the Modern Imagination

1
Introduction:
The Biocentric Tradition

Beasts of the Modern Imagination explores a specific tradition in modern thought and art: the critique of anthropocentrism at the hands of "beasts"—writers whose works constitute animal gestures or acts of fatality. It is not a study of animal imagery, although the works I explore do present us with apes, horses, bulls, and mice who appear in the foreground of fiction, not as the tropes of allegory or fable, but as narrators and protagonists reappropriating their animality amid an anthropocentric universe. These beasts are finally the masks of the human animals who create them, and the textual strategies that bring them into being constitute another version of their struggle. The focus of this study will then be a small group of thinkers, writers, and artists, who create *as* the animal—not *like* the animal, in imitation of the animal—but with their animality speaking. I will treat Charles Darwin as the founder of this tradition, as the naturalist whose shattering conclusions inevitably turned back upon him and subordinated him, the human being, the rational man, the scientist, to the very Nature he studied. Friedrich Nietzsche heeded the advice implicit in his criticism of David Strauss and used Darwinian ideas as critical tools to interrogate the status of man as a *natural* being. He also responded to the implications of his own animality for his writing, by transforming his work into bestial acts and gestures. The third, and last, generation of these creative animals includes Franz Kafka, the Surrealist artist Max Ernst, and D. H. Lawrence.

There are, of course, others who might plausibly have been included in this tradition: the biologist George Romanes; vitalists like Henri Bergson; other Surrealists, such as Masson, perhaps; the *Blaue Reiter* painter, Franz Marc; and, of course, Sigmund Freud, the great cartographer of the libido. But I decided to develop my explorations around producers of the self-reflexive animal metaphor for philosophical as well as organizational reasons. In keeping with the biocentric spirit of my subjects, I did not wish to use the animal as a mere pretext: the discarded basis of more abstract speculation, the victim of a seemingly inevitable cultural drift into the realms of idealism, rationalism, or metaphysics. I wanted to maintain a zoocentric perspective and to keep animal life central to my study. But following this rationale led me into curious problems while exploring the feasibility of including American producers of animal imagery in my study. Ernest Hemingway, the experiential writer, the denizen of the wilderness, the hunter and advocate of power and aggression, turned out, upon careful scrutiny, to be a "ringer," an aesthete masked as a beast, who actually subordinates life to art and Nature to representation. In the end, I do conclude my study with *Death in the Afternoon* because it seemed that Hemingway's prose would serve as an instructive counterpoint to biocentric writing. But I decided to defer study of other American writers such as Jack London and the poet Robinson Jeffers until I can extend my historical background beyond the Continental philosophies that form the basis of the tradition I delineate here.

Like Kafka in his tales, which often begin with a statement whose ultimate retraction is the major burden of the story, I will eventually have to concede that this "tradition" is no tradition at all. In a conventional sense, Darwin does influence Nietzsche and make his work possible; and Darwin and Nietzsche together inspire the disanthropic and misanthropic visions of Max Ernst, Franz Kafka, and D. H. Lawrence. But their intertextual relations do not reflect the smooth, linear transmission of ideas that founds our notions of intellectual tradition on models of continuity such as familial genealogy and legal inheritance. Without recourse to the Freudian anxiety of influence that propels Harold Bloom's model of a literary tradition founded on poetic *méconnaissance*, I would suggest a similar circularity in the intertextual relations of Darwin, Nietzsche, and Lawrence. Nietzsche misunderstands, rejects, and reappropriates an alienated version of Darwin's most radical thinking, as Lawrence does also with respect to Nietzsche. But Nietzsche's *méconnaissance* of Darwin (and Lawrence's of Nietzsche) is grounded not in personal and psychological necessities, but in ontological ones, in the need to erase the anthropomorphic interventions of pedagogy, mimesis, and intellectual influence itself in the execution of the bestial gesture.

In exploring these modern philosophers of the animal and its instinctual life, I inevitably *re*biologize them even in the face of contemporary momentum (manifested in Jacques Lacan's neo-Freudianism, for example) to debiologize thinkers whose works can be studied profitably for their models of signification. For, although the negative and critical aspect of this tradition (its disanthropic, deconstructive, antianthropocentric revolution) is my major focus, I also consider the vitalistic, biocentric, zoomorphic energy that propels this Nietzschean *Anknüpfung,* this suture over the great cleft produced in our human being by the repression of the animal and the living body. But the biocentricity of this tradition—its valuation of the body and the body's effusion of power, its instinctual epistemology, its celebration of unmediated experience—renders its writings at war with themselves, hostile to art, impervious to representation, inimitable. As a result the short-lived tradition ends in a cul-de-sac, and one finds little evidence of it after the 1930s.

The biocentric understanding of the ontological nature of the animal evolved dialectically out of its difference from the exclusively human aspects of culture, culture as the product of *homo significans.* As a result, the biocentric critique of anthropocentrism is aimed at the human being as a cultural creature, as implicated in the Symbolic Order.[1] While Darwin collapsed the cardinal distinctions between animal and human, arguing that they exhibit intellectual, moral, and cultural differences in degree only, not in kind, Hegel made the function of the "other" in human desire the cornerstone of the symbolic life that marks the radical distinction between Nature and culture.[2] But art is, of course, implicated in complex ways in the subject's exchanges with the "other": by functioning as a putative repository of meaning, by embodying authority, by distributing status and prestige to authors, audiences, and representations, and so on. Biocentric thinking cannot, therefore, be accommodated by traditional art and will require modes that further frustrate communication, that negate their authority, that rupture representation and rebuff interpretation. The art produced by a biocentric discourse consists, consequently, of tormented generic and rhetorical experiments that have suffered an evolutionary disadvantage, as it were, with respect to reception by a wide public.

The value of observing the contrast between Darwin's and Hegel's premises is that they generate a distinction between animal and human, and between creatural and cultural man, that reverses the structural premises upon which such distinctions have been traditionally founded. The animal's putative inferiority to the human is conventionally ascribed to a lack, a deficiency in reason, speech, soul, morality, a higher nature, while in contrast to the animal the human being is viewed as complete, perfect, fulfilled. But the biocentric thinkers treat the animal (including the human as animal), as they do Nature, the realm of the biological, the real: as a plenum. It is cultural man, rather, who is engendered by an imaginary lack that gives birth to desire, language, intersubjectivity, social life, that is, the entire Lacanian Symbolic Order that is governed by the "other." The result is a difference in natural and cultural ontology: the animal's desire is direct and appropriative while the human's is mediated and directed toward the recognition of the "other"; the animal's natural power is sufficient for its kind while the human's biological power is inadequate to capture recognition and achieve prestige and must be supplemented by signifiers and symbols; the animal is autotelic and lives for itself in the fulness of its being while the cultural man lives in imitation of the desire of the "other," driven by his *manque-à-être*; the animal surrenders to biological fate and evolutionary destiny while the human disregards the physicality of what is and reads his fate in the gaze of the "other."

By identifying these distinctions, we can better sort out the ambiguous ontological status of man as the human animal. In place of the traditional binary opposition of mind and body, there emerges a new system whose distinctive criteria are structural: for example, present and absent, direct or mediated, original or representational, spontaneous or calculated, autotelic or instrumental. As a result, the traditional oppositions are replaced by false doubles. Two kinds of desire, two kinds of power, two kinds of violence must be distinguished on the ground of their origin (instinct or self-consciousness), their process (direct or mediated), and their end (autotelic or instrumental) in order to determine which is creatural and which is cultural. This new system of formulating the difference between Nature and culture is enormously useful in exploring modern writers intent on creating new ontological alternatives for man, such as the *Übermenschen* or instinctual aristocrats in Nietzsche and Lawrence. Nietzschean and Lawrencian heroes are predators, but not Hegelian Masters; they are cruel, but they are not sadists; their aggression is a pure discharge of vitality and power, which does *not* have as its aim the domination of the minds and souls of others. These distinctions begin to clarify for us the vexing question of Nietzschean and Lawrencian "fascism." We can explain, for example, why the premises their philosophies share with the later Nazi, Fascist, and Falangist ideologies do not result, in Nietzsche and Lawrence, in a similar political program. Their antihumanistic, antidemocratic, supramoral sentiments are also antisocial and antiideological. Nietzschean and Lawrencian heroes want no more homage from their victims than lions do from lambs, and they therefore abjure the demagogic capture of the masses.

The salient difference between Nature and culture in this new way of formulating their distinction is the "political" function of mediation and, by extension, mimesis. I say "political" because for biocentric thinkers mediation functions to insert a lack or an absence into the play of natural power. For example, the predator simply overcomes and appropriates his victim by natural force, while the demagogue relies on the mediation of his polemic to persuade others to relinquish their power and surrender to him. The demagogue lacks the natural force to subdue others directly, and he therefore uses the supplement of a mediated object ("I want you to desire what I desire") for his victory. The demagogue depends upon a mimetic response from the masses, demonstrating the politicizing of mimesis that prevails also in the "identification" of son with father in psychoanalytical oedipal development, as well as in the politics of religious worship. The Antichrist in Nietzsche's work signifies, among other things, a rejection of the mystical program of imitating Christ, saints, and prophets, as demonstrated in Zarathustra's rejection of disciples.

For biocentric thinkers, then, mimesis acquires a negative value as inimical to the animal's power and to the body's life. Mimesis is the negative mark, the mark of absence, castration, and death, an insight that required artists to reevaluate the ontological status of their media as negative being, as mere simulacra of life. Nietzschean antipathy to mimesis, which can be traced in the progressive devaluation and virtual disappearance of the Apollonian in his philosophy, contributes to spawning pervasive antiart sentiments and practices in early twentieth-century art. This movement has two major, related consequences: a subversive interrogation of the anthropocentric premises of Western philosophy and art, and the invention of artistic and philosophical strategies that would allow the animal, the unconscious, the instincts, the body, to speak again in their work. These biocentric practices have in common the outflanking of reason and submission to fate, an aim apparent in the gamut of their experimental practices, from the improvisations and automatic writing of the Surrealists to Kafka's logical erasures of his own fictions.

The experiential, spontaneous, gestural, performative aspect

The Biocentric Tradition

of biocentric art made it inherently unsuitable for transmission from one generation of artists to another and therefore militated against its formation of a tradition. This resistance to tradition operated on several levels. Deliberately or inadvertently, these writers discouraged disciples, by their misanthropy, hermitry, or itinerancy. Just as they attempted to deny the influence of their predecessors, that is, their imitation of other writers, so they refrained from becoming Masters, from exerting influence and capturing the recognition of followers. Nietzsche's aim is often to assault rather than to persuade. Lawrence is less the evangelist the critics make of him than the schoolteacher who rejected the very premises of pedagogy. And Kafka is the extreme case of the writer who resisted publication throughout his life and, at its end, sought to frustrate his artistic heirs utterly by attempting to wipe his works off the face of the earth. Furthermore, they created styles that were largely inimitable by virtue of either their multiplicity (Nietzsche and Ernst) or their singularity (the libidinal force in Lawrence's writing, the nihilism of Kafka's). And they made themselves dangerous to imitate by implicating any prospective followers in their own fundamental cultural subversion. Contemporary fiction reflects, rather, the influence of James Joyce, the master parodist, the genius of imitative form, the consummately domestic writer, who, in spite of his coziness with the libido, never ventures into the ontological wildernesses of the biocentric thinkers.

Historically, I trace the biocentric tradition to Charles Darwin, and particularly to his break with eighteenth-century rationalism. Darwin's implicit nemesis was not Hegel, but Descartes, philosophically transplanted into the contemporary "argument from Design," whose deistically useful application of a mechanistic model of creation made possible the wedding of natural science and natural theology in the early nineteenth century. "If, as Paley put it, we find a watch, we necessarily infer a watchmaker; therefore, the contrivances of nature are conclusive evidence for the existence of their Creator" (Gruber, 52). Darwin replaced this cybernetic model of Nature as a machine with his theory of natural selection, which removed intelligence (and, by inference, a rational Creator) altogether as the source of life and put in its place innumerable, dispersed, trivial organic forces operating unconsciously and irrationally, on an ad hoc basis, subject to chance, over time. Darwin thereby liberated biology from its Enlightenment enthrallment to physics. In place of a rational cause, he gave Nature an organic cause; in place of an extrinsic teleology, he freed Nature from its mediated instrumentality and made it autotelic. With his theory of natural selection, *physis* triumphed over *technē*. And, in the very bloom of the Industrial Revolution, the machine and the rational intelligence that designs it become philosophically inimical to the burgeoning vitality of Nature and of living things.

The machine, as the emblem of the rational, obsesses the thinkers of the biocentric tradition and becomes the perennial target of their critiques. The dominant theme states both the inverted causality formulated by Darwin, that reason is the product, not the producer, of Nature, and its perilous and ironic consequence, that reason is enthralled to the organic, the unconscious, the irrational, and that, for all of the anthropocentric claims and prerogatives it has traditionally validated, it is deployed by the libido. Even Darwin's contemporary, the witty Thomas Huxley, recognized as much when (only partly in jest) he imputed instinctual and predatory motives to the learned scientific debate over evolution itself. His clever animal metaphors contain a serious residue, a covert reminder that the scholars' aggressive behavior will betray its own atavism. "And as to the curs which will bark and yelp, you must recollect that some of your friends, at any rate, are endowed with an amount of combativeness which (though you have often and justly rebuked it) may stand you in good stead. I am sharpening up my claws and beak in readiness."[3]

Darwin wrote in his *Autobiography*: "The old argument of design in nature, as given by Paley, which formerly seemed to me so conclusive, fails, now that the law of natural selection has been discovered. We can no longer argue that, for instance, the beautiful hinge of a bivalve shell must have been made by an intelligent being, like the hinge of a door by man."[4] But where Darwin's abjuration of the mechanical model of Nature bore down most heavily on theology, Nietzsche's critique of Descartes exposes its limiting and reductive effect on our concept of living (animal and human) creatures: "With respect to animals, it was Descartes who first dared, with admirable boldness, to conceive of the animal as *machina* [*sic*] . . . what is grasped at all about man today extends only to understanding him as 'machinal' [*sic*]" (3, *AC*, 620).[5] The Cartesian model produces a vitalistically castrated animal and a mechanical man who thinks like a robot with a computer, "an unliving and yet uncannily active concept and word factory. . . . I am guaranteed only empty 'being', not the full and green life; my original perception guarantees me only that I am a thinking, not a living creature, that I am not an *animal* [*sic*], but, at best, a *cogital* [*sic*]" (1, *UM*, 280). In the semantically paradoxical qualification of "at best" ("höchstens"), Nietzsche implies the deficiency of the *cogito*: that Cartesian consciousness presents us to ourselves only as a partial object, not as a complete organism.

Nietzsche's structural approach to analyzing the history of the body / mind relationship usefully focuses the hidden assumptions behind anthropocentrism, particularly when it assumes a diachronic dimension as well. In trying to discover why the animal is traditionally negatively marked and construed as lacking that which makes the human complete, he notes that not only is rational consciousness regarded as a tessera, an essential part needed to complete the whole, but that the Cartesian dictum grants it logical priority as well, allowing us to say of ourselves only "*cogito, ergo sum,* but not *vivo, ergo cogito*"(1, *UM*, 280). Ultimately, Nietzsche uses Darwinian notions to defeat the Cartesian logical priority of consciousness with a historical argument (disguised as fable) for the ontological priority of living Nature.

> Once upon a time, upon a star in some remote corner of the universe glittering and bestrewn with innumerable solar systems, clever animals invented knowledge. It was the most arrogant and untruthful moment in the "history of the world"; but it lasted only a minute. Nature had just taken a few breaths when the star petrified, and the clever animals died. One could invent such a fable and still not illustrate sufficiently how pitiful, how insubstantial and ephemeral, how purposeless and arbitrary the human intellect appears in the context of nature. For eternities it did not exist; and when it is once more extinct, nothing will have changed. For this intellect has no broader mission that would extend beyond human life. It is human, only, and only its possessor and inventor treats it as seriously as if the axis of the world revolved inside it. But if we could communicate with the mosquito, we would discover that it sails through the air with the same empathy and feels inside itself the flying center of the world. (3, *Truth,* 1017)

We can live without thinking (in the *Rausch,* for example), Nietzsche seems to be implying, but we cannot think without living. Vital nature precedes, and survives, the advent of human consciousness and reason, which, set against the immense backdrop of evolutionary history, constitute rational man as a mere ephemerid.

But Nietzsche, who treats intellectual forms as being as temporal, mutable, and contingent as biological forms, regards them as adaptations produced to compensate for bodily and instinctual weaknesses. He therefore explains why, historically, intellectual and spiritual ascendancy is coupled with repression of the sensual and passionate body, and why human cultural evolution has favored the survival of effete intellectual traditions (Christianity, democratic socialism, Romanticism, rationalism) at the expense of Dionysian modes of behavior (the militarism of Caesar and Napoleon, chthonic religions, the immorality of the Borgias, and so forth). Nietzsche's model of the birth of rational consciousness therefore complements Hegel's by giving human desire (for the desire of the "other") a causal lack (libidinal enervation) and thereby inversely relating animal and human desire.

Since Nietzsche regards rational consciousness as a compensation for instinctual deficiencies, the elision of the libido in Cartesian rationalism (evident both in the mechanical conception of the animal and in the primacy of the *cogito*) constitutes the human being as a eunuch. Both Freud, who in his essay on "The Uncanny" explores the relationship of mechanistic science and machines (automata) with fears of castration,[6] and D. H. Lawrence, who treats the *cogito* as a partial object, a fetish, elaborate the psychosexual implications of Nietzsche's critique. In place of the traditional mind / body opposition, a far more sophisticated structural model of their interaction emerges in which a libidinal and a symbolic economy interact. In this economy a libidinal deficiency, which may be either real (the physiological enervation of Nietzsche's theory) or imaginary (the Lacanian threat of castration, for example), requires compensation. The human organism generates substitutions that always take the form of symbolic objects or fetishes. These acquire their symbolic value because libidinal energy is attached (cathected) to them, and they thereby assume phallic significance, that is, they come to stand for desirability itself.

This new model of the libidinal exchanges between natural and cultural life has its most disturbing consequences in connection with the redefinition of human violence. Violence has traditionally been attributed to the beast and the repression of the animalistic in man justified as the containment of violence necessary to permit the flourishing of a rational, ideal, humanistic culture. However, in biocentric thought, animal violence is restored to its amoral Dionysian innocence: it functions as a discharge of power for its own sake, as an expenditure of superfluous, opulent energy and strength, and it is therefore simply appropriative, destroying its victims without malice or hatred, in the simple fulfillment of its biological destiny. In humans, this is the militarism and barbarism of Nietzsche's *Übermenschen* and Lawrence's lords of creation, and the attitude of both Nietzsche and Lawrence toward this natural human cruelty is a fatalistic assent. "Blessed are the powerful, for theirs is the kingdom of earth," writes Lawrence. "Even Attila, the Scourge of God, who helped to scourge the Roman world out of existence, was great with power."[7] And Nietzsche writes in his *Nachlass,* "I rejoice in the military development of Europe, as well as its internal anarchic conditions; the time of peace and chinoiserie predicted by Galiani for this century is over. Personal, masculine capability, corporeal capability [*Leibes-Tüchtigkeit*] is becoming valued again, values are becoming more physical, nutrition more carnivorous. . . . The barbarian, as well as the wild animal, is affirmed in each of us" (4, *PW,* 27).

Implicit in this assent to animal (and human animal) violence is a critique of the myriad forms of cultural cruelty that are justified in the interest of civilization: the sanctions of morality, discipline, punishment, execution, repression, ideological persecution, and so on. Nietzsche's deconstructions of morality in *The Genealogy of Morals* and *The Birth of Tragedy* expose culture's fatuous claim to have abolished the bestial. "Virtually everything we call 'higher culture' rests on the spiritualization and sublimation of cruelty [*Grausamkeit*]—that is my proposition; the 'wild animal' has not been exterminated at all; it lives, it thrives, it has only become—deified" (3, *BGE,* 139). But Nietzsche's critique has a complex teleology: his outrage at civilization's hypocrisy and self-deception is motivated less by the violence it does to truth than by the violence it does to life. The civilized strategy against animal aggressiveness is both illogical and subversive: it multiplies rather than negates violence by repressing biological force with rational force, and, because it is motivated by the resentment of the weak against the strong, its aim is not the conservation and defense of life but its diminution and enervation in vital, potent, creatures. D. H. Lawrence represents this effete cultural righteousness in the figure of the castrating eunuch.

Beasts of the Modern Imagination

Nietzsche's exploration of the perversity of cultural violence, in both its logical self-contradiction and its bizarre libidinal circularity, paves the way for the biocentric indictment of the cultural figures of the priest, the scientist, and the artist. These are regarded as inimical to life because they sacrifice the interests of the animal and the living body on the altar of ideology, to reason, spirit, ideals, virtues, beauty, form. In excoriating the figure of the priest for sadism, Nietzsche deliberately uses the metaphor of the *Tierbändiger* to evoke the ironic interplay of means and ends (cruelty fighting cruelty) and the perverse exchange of roles as the "priest" becomes a more monstrous version of the very beast he tames. "Morality is a menagerie; its premise, that iron bars are more useful than freedom, even for the captive; its other premise, that there are animal tamers who do not shrink from frightful means, who know how to handle red-hot iron. This horrific species, which accepts battle with the wild animal, calls itself 'priest'" (4, *PW,* 399). Other versions of these sadistic animal tamers occur in Kafka's work, and, without critique, in Hemingway's, such as the matadors in *Death in the Afternoon.*

The critique of pornology (the hypocritical investment of libido in cultural forms) is extremely difficult precisely because pornology speaks a devious discourse that purports to repress eroticism and violence while promoting and indulging it in a cultural guise. We therefore find quite different strategies at work in the critiques of different biocentric thinkers. Nietzsche and Lawrence practice a direct and brutal polemic, extruding pornological thought as an alien and "other" cultural form from which their own natural ontology and animality set them apart. Franz Kafka and Max Ernst, in contrast, are themselves deeply implicated in pornological modes, and they therefore pose as pornologists in order to invite the audience's complicity. When, upon first reading, we admire the hunger artist or applaud Kafka's ape for his successful human evolution, we become unwitting victims of a critique conducted in the form of a trap. I include a limited study of Hemingway precisely to serve as an instructive contrast, since his is uncritical pornology, naïve about its own hypocrisy. As a thoroughly anthropocentric writer superficially camouflaged as an advocate of life and power, Hemingway serves as a perfect foil for biocentric thinkers.

Hemingway's work is particularly useful for displaying the artist as sadist, and he thereby inadvertently helps to demonstrate the two antithetical kinds of violence (natural and cultural, predatory and sadistic). He further unwittingly reveals them to be related and continuous, as the matador literally creates "art" out of torture and killing, thereby transforming an act of cruelty into a cultural event. Kafka seemingly does the same thing as he presents us with great cultural achievements in the guise of macabre performances: torture and killing ("In the Penal Colony"), suicide ("A Hunger Artist"), oppression and degradation ("A Report to an Academy"). But the difference lies in Kafka's technique of slyly repealing the representation, by de-signifying the event, stripping it of symbolic meaning, rendering its justifications absurd, reducing it to the order of the real, until the putatively transcendent heroes end like dead animals thrown into ditches and garbage dumps (Gregor, the officer, the hunger artist, and Josef K). Hemingway encodes atrocity as cultural performance; Kafka decodes cultural performance as atrocity. This antirepresentational strategy is a major weapon in the biocentric critique of an anthropocentric art in the service of human (as opposed to animal) desire.

The differences between biocentric and anthropocentric art correspond to the models of animal and human desire and the opposition they engender between creatural and cultural man. The end of biocentric art is autotelic—not the production of a representation, an artifact, a form, an ideal, but the creative process itself, the discharge of energy and power. "Art reminds us of conditions of animal *vigor* [*sic*]; it is sometimes an excess and effusion of burgeoning corporality in the world of images and wishes; at other times, an arousal of animalistic functions through images and wishes of intensified life, a heightening of the sensation of life and its stimulant" (4, *PW,* 128). Nietzsche gives these physiological metaphors of art as the ultimate aphrodisiac (*als grösstes Stimulans des Lebens* [4, *PW,* 344]) an increasingly literal twist; he describes artists as powerful animals (*Krafttiere, sensuell*) and equates their artistic productivity with their sexual prowess "with artists creativity ends with reproductive capability [*Zeugungskraft*]" (4, *PW,* 348). Yet it is on the question of art's erotic power that a structural distinction of Nature and culture can serve to avoid a potential confusion: neither Nietzsche's nor Lawrence's aphrodisiac art is allied to pornography precisely because of its biocentricity, its animal atavism, its primitiveness. It stimulates the body ("All art serves as suggestions to the muscles and senses, which are primordially active in naïve artistic peoples" [4, *PW,* 345]), not the cultural imagination.

Anthropocentric art, formulated according to the Hegelian model of human desire, follows the triangular structure of all social and cultural mediations. The art consists of representations, whose function is to serve as tokens of cultural exchange and as media of social communication, that is, as mediated objects in the intersubjective relations between artist and public, who constitute a reciprocal "other." This explains the significance and prestige of art, which is not intrinsic in the material but is invested in it by a subject seeking validation from an imaginary "other." For example, if I "know" or "understand" a great work of art, I achieve a particular prestige because I have ostensibly appropriated the hidden "meaning" bestowed upon it by an "other" with the power to signify, for instance, God, the Author, Philosophy. Nietzsche reserves particular scorn for artists he deems the handmaidens of morality, philosophy, and religion, precisely because he detects in their practice the politics of the sycophantic panderer (3, *GM,* 289) whose power is derivative, cast from the shadow of an imaginary "other." "At the least they always require a shield, a reserve, an already established authority: the artists never stand for themselves; independence goes counter to their deepest instincts" (3, *GM,* 289). But in those cases where independence is claimed for art, *l'art pour l'art,* Nietzsche devises an even more subtle twist to the anthropocentric model of art. "If we subtract from the lyric in tone and word the suggestion of this intestinal fever, what remains of lyric and music? . . . Perhaps *l'art pour l'art*: the virtuoso squawking of cold-blooded frogs, despairing in their swamp" (4, *PW,* 344).The subtraction of the intestinal fever (here, the physiological effect of being in love) marks the cold objectivity of *l'art pour l'art* as the site of a castration, the symptom of a missing passion.

In this second case, where no apparent external authority guarantees the significance of the anthropocentric work of art, the ulterior mechanism behind its idealization becomes more easily discernible. Since the physiological impulse appears to be lacking, that deficiency or lack becomes itself the source of an effete art whose function is that of a fetish, an arbitrary object invested with phallic significance in order to deny castration. Nietzsche, like Lacan in this century, seems to recognize that all idealization (and idealism) is psychologically grounded in symbolic castration (Nietzsche calls the idealist the *Ideal-Kastrat,* [4, *PW,* 171]) and that the overestimation of the ideal is no more than displaced libidinal energy in the form of phallic signifi-

The Biocentric Tradition

cance. The very prestige of art is consequently a symptom of its divorce from living vitality that betrays the status of its representations as mere simulacra of life. Nietzsche is therefore able to call the art of various ages (New Attic comedy, modern literature) counterfeit and the functions of various artists (Hugo, Wagner) charlatanism, without succumbing to the naïveté of the ancient charge that actors are liars and that the stage purveys untruths. But in Nietzschean psychology, the deficiency of life engenders hatred and resentment (*ressentiment*) in the weak, who fear the power of the strong as a threat to their survival. Idealism therefore has as an ulterior motive a hatred (*dédain*) for life and "natural things" (4, *PW,* 173), which prompts it to devalue Nature as its opposite. This *dédain* of the natural world constitutes the hidden cultural violence embedded in idealism, which Nietzsche finds represented in the figure of the castrato. "The voice of the castrato does *not* nauseate [*degoutiert*] us either despite the grisly mutilation that is its necessary condition: it has become sweeter" (4, *PW,* 171).

Their mediated status renders the representations of anthropocentric art suspect on two related grounds: they lie, and their falsehood prompts and perpetuates a devaluation of Nature and of life. Nietzsche's critique of representation therefore proceeds from a psychological analysis of the metaphysical presuppositions of such abstractions as form, species, law, idea, purpose—all fictions with a false reality slipped under them (4, *PW,* 117). The function of these philosophical concepts is precisely to make living Nature intellectually tractable; to render its eternal changing, its infinite variety, its illogical procedures, its shape-shifting *becoming* intelligible to the rational imagination. Abstractions make it possible to freeze Nature in time, to fix it and make it hold still like a butterfly on a pin, to make objects equal to each other in order to create a "world of identical cases" that is "calculable, simplified, comprehensible, to us" (4, *PW,* 118). Abstractions are therefore more valued than Nature, Nietzsche argues, not because they are truer, or because they represent a truer world, but because they are useful for domesticating the world for our easier consumption. "*Form* counts as something permanent and therefore more valuable; but form is merely invented by us" (4, *PW,* 117). But it is the violence representation does to life, rather than to truth, that Nietzsche most thoroughly excoriates.

A nonartistic example does as well to illustrate the cultural overestimation of the abstract at the expense of the natural. The young Darwin who kills the curious, intent Chiloean fox in order to have it stuffed and displayed in the museum of the Zoological Society (*JR,* 280), values its cultural representation, its abstract function as a scientific model or "specimen," more highly than its unique, vivid, creatural existence. But Darwin, whose theories were not yet fully developed at the time of the *Beagle* voyage, is participating here in a scientific representational mode that he himself will render obsolete. After the discovery of evolution, the zoological museum, with its atemporal, discontinuous representations that virtually adumbrate a sytem of Platonic preexisting forms, is no longer adequate to represent the salient characteristics of biological form: its contingency and mutability. For Darwin himself revolutionized the concept of form, demonstrating that Nature produces form, not vice versa, and that form is engendered by force and desire rather than by mind. Specifically, it is natural selection and sexual selection that give the elephant her trunk and the stag his horns.[8] Visual representation can communicate only the effect and symptom, never the organic process itself, unless the representation attacks the representation itself, as Surrealist art does when it hybridizes and mutates human and animal forms.

Given the two kinds of art engendered by natural and cultural perspectives, biocentric art confronts the challenge of producing a physiological or aphrodisiac art, an art that stimulates rather than persuades, that communicates viscerally rather than intellectually, that is transmitted animal to animal, organism to organism, like an infection rather than a philosophy. Of course, the paradox implicit in this caveat, of producing an art *within* culture that is not *of* culture, is only imperfectly resolvable in practice. All aspects of the work of art—its production, reception, and mechanisms—would need to escape cultural appropriation at the same time that books are written, printed, and sold in the usual way. But the philosophical model of culture I have been using, which delineates its distinctive features as mediation and enthrallment to the "other," does indeed suggest practical ways for biocentric art to preserve its bestial, autotelic aims. It would have to be produced unselfconsciously, without the motive, overt or covert, of aggrandizing the artist's ego, reputation, or social condition; its aim must be neither to impress nor to persuade, and the artist must be indifferent to misunderstanding; it must rely on techniques that circumvent reason but that speak to blood and bowels in those whose instincts are not yet atrophied.

The Biocentric Tradition

Because of the implication of representation in anthropocentric art (its abstraction, overestimation, and displacement of Nature), biocentric art turns to an antirepresentational mode best deployed in the form of the critique. A more logical recourse for biocentric artists might appear to be the total abolition of representation and the invention of a nonrepresentational mode. But the purely formalistic concerns of much abstract art (of synthetic cubism, for example) suggest that such a strategy might have exacerbated the problem by simply producing more abstraction. Instead, their technical solution lay in the skillful use of the critique, which invokes representation only to dismantle it, and thereby accommodates both an affective and an intellectually destructive (and deconstructive) aim. Nietzsche's program for philosophizing "with the hammer"[9] presents a suitable metaphor for those complex functions, as the critical act becomes an exercise in both power and aggression, and the destruction of the idols of culture by de-signifying and demythifying them (that is, using the "hammer" to sound the hollowness at their center) reveals their meanings as a lack and their prestige as founded on a void. This antirepresentational mode takes heterogeneous forms in different artists, including the representation of violence *to* representation, the de-signification of the figure of the animal, and rhetorical experiments with animal point of view.

The Surrealism of Max Ernst demonstrates best the biocentric attack on representation. I remember the first time I ever looked at Ernst's collage novels. I sat in the college library with the volume held at arm's length, taking quick, squinty peeks at the page, then snapping the book shut after each plate, as though in recoil from an assault. At the time I attributed my revulsion to the representations *of* violence in the works (hangings, beatings, stabbings, and so forth). But later I concluded that I was as repelled by the monstrous and fragmented figures in whom violence was, at best, a matter of inference rather than representation, and that my visceral shock had been triggered as much by the violent distortions of form as by the content of the scenes, that is, by the violence *to* representations, rather than *in* them. Ernst assaults one's Platonic notions of form as something unified, ideal, permanent, and normative by inserting into his representations the Darwinian disruptions of form: time, mutability, variability, and chance. A post-Darwinian bird-headed man therefore produces a double shock in the viewer: the destruction of species as a normative category and the realization that, given the evolutionary play of time and chance, the creature represents a biological possibility. Ernst also occasionally represents his assault on representation narratively or pictorially, as in *Une Semaine de bonté*, where cultural monuments and classical figures are infested by vermin and teeming animal life, and where animals appropriate cultural roles (as in "The Lion of Belfort") and practice cultural forms of cruelty.

Although Ernst's art constitutes a radical questioning of the metaphysical presuppositions that govern our thinking about form and representation, it is Lawrence who specifically uncovers the *dédain* for life and natural things concealed in much literary practice and who devises a biocentric poetics to combat it. When I first began this study out of a more or less idle curiosity about the prominence of "animal imagery" in modern art, it was with utter naïveté about the vexed and oxymoronic nature of that term. *Imagery* presupposes the use of the concrete to express the abstract, and indeed, it seemed that nowhere in literature were animals to be allowed to be themselves, to refer to Nature and to their own animality without being pressed into symbolic service as metaphors, or as figures in fable or allegory (invariably of some aspect of the human). This poetic practice has ancient philosophical roots; Nietzsche, in an argument echoed and elaborated in Derrida's discussion of "white mythology,"[10] suggests the empirical foundations, the experiences of the body, effaced in such metaphysical concepts as "being."[11] This widespread tendency to subordinate our perceptions of the natural world to cultural uses is generalized by Karl-Heinz Fingerhut in his careful and compendious study of Kafka's *Tierfiguren*[12] into the postulate of a universal human instinct, an *Anthropomorphisierungstrieb*. The hidden assumption behind this thinking— that the animal and Nature do not signify—is, of course, literally true, and biocentric thinking would neither dispute nor wish to reverse it. But the practical consequence of this assumption, the devaluation of Nature *as* Nature and the contempt of all that is animal, renders the cultural bias of literary practice pernicious and dangerous from the biocentric point of view.

Lawrence, who, like Nietzsche, seems to measure human strength by the ability to dispense with meaning, implicitly critiques the confusion of signification with value. He consequently treats the encoding of the animal as symbol, metaphor, or allegory, as an impoverishment and a denigration, and, in a maneuver that challenges the traditional anthropomorphic functions of figurative language itself, he restores the animal qua animal to literature by liberating it from its tropological enslave-

The Biocentric Tradition

ment to the human. "And this is the result of making, in our own conceit, man the measure of the universe. . . . Do you imagine the great realities, even the ram of Amon, are only *symbols* of something human? Do you imagine the great symbols, the dragon, the snake, the bull, only refer to bits, qualities or attributes of little man? It is puerile. The puerilty [*sic*], the puppyish conceit of modern white humanity is almost funny."[13] Lawrence's practice, like Ernst's, is to insert aspects of Darwinian living form, such as temporality, mutability, and susceptibility to chance, into literary conventions, thereby transforming character into multiplicitous and fluid "allotropes," eschewing novelistic closure, propelling events by irrational mechanisms of impulse, nostalgia, and free association that Lawrence often cloaks in the language of animism, as magic or spells. Lawrence's rich figurative language continually repeals its representational function by recalling its literal (ergo concrete or natural) residue, a technique that echoes the dream's literal decoding of idiomatic language. St. Mawr, the great stallion, is finally reclaimed as a symbol of a horse, a horse in the power and glory of his animality.

Lawrence effects the dissolution of culture in his works with various strategies aimed at neutralizing the effects of the "other" on the individual. The thematic divestiture of cultural artifacts and attributes (houses, careers, ambition, marriage, even speech and memory) follows, in Lawrence's fiction, upon an ontological shift in the protagonist, for whom the entire social realm becomes unreal, and, therefore, dispensable. Lawrence portrays this ontological shift through a system of visual metaphors that correspond to representation and invisibility. Before the social world becomes wholly transparent and fades out of the protagonist's imagination like a mirage or a hallucination, its unreality is first signaled through various attributes of representation: two-dimensional, miniaturized, synecdochic, fetishistic, abstract. Implicit in Lawrence's sense of the social realm as mimetic theater—a *tableau vivant,* a charade, with houses and *meubles* as theatrical props—is the dominance of an illusory "other" that makes us play self-consciously for its approval. Lawrence's "other" functions like an ocellus, a false eye (I) or an illusory consciousness, like the circles on butterfly wings that frighten predators away, or the portraits of Jesus in which the eyes seem to follow one about the room. Lawrence contrasts human enthrallment to this false eye (I), this illusory consciousness of the social world, with human disregard for the real eye of the animal: people utterly negate the animal as a perceiving consciousness by acting as though animals do not see them, and yet society's ocelli make them self-conscious, afraid, ashamed, gratified. In *St. Mawr,* the animal eye, or "third eye," ultimately reclaims the protagonist to Nature as it reclaims the novella's point of view. The voice that speaks of the feral landscape at the end of the work speaks for Nature and its creatures (including human creatures) and places them beyond the reach of the "other." Impervious to human judgment, admiration, and significance, Lawrence's is not a Romantic wilderness.

Beneath the striking surface dissimilarities, Lawrence and Kafka share a philosophical "deep structure" grounded in their common interplay with Nietzsche's biocentric premises. This common ground is a similar grasp of the ontological relationship of the animal to culture, the common impetus behind their experiments with cultural divestiture and its implications for narrative perspective. For Lawrence, for example, this divestiture is portrayed as an enormous leap that defies novelistic plausibility; beginning with maximal cultural representation (in *St. Mawr,* an Edwardian heroine of rank and wealth, with a house in Westminster), he ends with the greatest practicable ferity (a stripped-down, natural existence in an unconquerable wilderness) with its threat to individualism, sanity, and survival preserved. Kafka practices his cultural divestiture over time, with a gradual shedding of his figures' bourgeois attributes (beginning with Gregor Samsa), so that in his last published story only the minimal cultural representations of the remnants (or rudiments) of Josefine's rodent society remain to be divested. But if Lawrence divests greater quantities of cultural appurtenances, Kafka divests culture more absolutely. Not only is Josefine stripped of her artistic semiological functions, but also the narrator abdicates his role as an "other" by dismantling and destroying his own discourse. His narration cancels itself in the act of telling; his argument retracts itself after every point. The animal point of view, in Kafka, turns out to be no point of view at all, but rather a comportment toward others that negates itself because it is marked by a lack of judgment, by a lack of otherness, by profound indifference. Kafka, in "Josefine, the Singer or the Mouse Folk," produces the most radical and most brilliant solution to the technical paradox of biocentric art.

By experimenting with alternative ontologies, biocentric artists were inevitably confronted with the metaphysical presuppositions underlying literary modes and genres. The rationalistic assumptions of conventional realism (including a logical subject,

The Biocentric Tradition

cause and effect, the relationship of part and whole, "plausibility," noncontradiction) could scarcely accommodate the exploration of organic, feral, natural life. Biocentric art therefore eschewed realism in favor of new, experimental modes that are easily confused with the visionary, the allegorical, or the satirical, if we consider only their representations and disregard the destructive rhetorical strategies aimed at those representations. The novel, likewise, is historically and conventionally grounded in the social or Symbolic Order, and, although later generations of postmodern writers have indeed deranged the relationship between subject, world, and "other" in complex ways, the experiments of modern novelists are difficult to push, hermeneutically, beyond the point of mere subversion. However antirational, anti-institutional, and misanthropic their purpose, *Women in Love* and *The Trial* seem finally to explore the fate of cultural man in society without giving more than incidental voice to the animal. For these reasons, biocentric art tends to flourish in the minor works of major authors, in loose, short, informal, fictional genres without clear traditional functions or conventional expectations, such as sketches, short stories, novelettes, dramatic monologues, and travelogues. But because it requires a philosophical reeducation of the reader, generic and modal experimentation invariably has a decisive (and usually negative) impact on the reception of the literary work. In the case of Kafka, for example, allegorical readings have tended to prevail[14] over rhetorical readings of the works (perhaps because translation renders Kafka's rhetorical nuances uncertain and elusive to the American readership that constitutes such a crucial element in his international market), and the incomplete and inconclusive novels take precedence, as major works, over the brilliant animal narratives that are the product of his literary maturity. I would argue that the canonical triumph of the novels lies precisely in their vestigial anthropocentrism, which blunts the reader's confrontation with Kafka's radical animal ontology.

The reception of the biocentric tradition has been such that one might think its art had been designed to frustrate communication and thereby ensure its own obscurity and ephemerality. And so, in a sense, it has, although less from perversity than from philosophical necessity. Once a text abdicates its anthropocentric functions of meaning, of representing its author, and authorizing, its cultural relationship to the reader becomes disturbed and ceases to operate along conventional lines. Although texts accomplish this in the variety of ways I have been discussing, Kafka's critique in "Josefine" serves as a uniquely radical example of an antirepresentational and anticultural text. By calling up representations only to repeal them, making statements only to recant them, Kafka's text achieves an interplay between presence and absence (like a word that is crossed out, or an order that is cancelled) that serves as an exemplar for the Derridean antimetaphysical concepts of the trace, or, more specifically, for "writing under erasure," *sous rature*.[15] How then do we read texts *sous rature,* texts that rebuff us, that withdraw their meaning from us, that abdicate authority? Since the psychoanalyst performs a similar role in therapy, we may use this situation as a model, and it suggests that such texts force us to read ourselves, to reflect upon our own enthrallment to the "other," to listen to the voice of our own beast.

These self-reflexive metaphors of recognizing the animal in oneself have acquired a glibness in the post-Darwinian age that belies the scandal produced by biocentrism. In recounting the three great shocks inflicted upon the human ego by science—the Copernican revolution, Darwinism, and psychoanalytic theory—Freud reveals modern man as displaced from the center of his universe three times over, from cosmos, earth ("biological research destroyed man's putative priority in creation and relegated him to a descent from the animal kingdom, and to an ineradicable animal nature"),[16] and the human mind itself. But it was a Victorian lady who revealed even more clearly the dimensions of human vanity threatened by evolutionary theory. "It is said, that when the Bishop of Worcester communicated the intelligence to his wife that the horrid Professor Huxley had announced that man was descended from the apes, she exclaimed, 'Descended from the apes! My dear, let us hope it is not true, but if it is, let us pray that it will not become generally known.'"[17] The good lady minds less being an animal, than being seen or regarded as an animal, a comportment that, in fact, proves her humanity (in a Hegelian sense) by revealing her primary enthrallment to the "other." The anguished cry of the "Elephant Man" (in the recent Lynch film production), "I am not an animal!" is precisely a proclamation to the "other" of his consciousness, his function as a subject, his power to signify, claims that alone can guarantee him the social prerogatives of the human (freedom from abuse, enslavement, and reification). The point I wish to emphasize is that the question of the status of the animal has meaning only in the context of the social realm, the Symbolic Order, in which it is negated as a value, and

The Biocentric Tradition

in which it enjoys only negative prestige. To biocentric thinkers like Lawrence, the concerns of the bishop's wife constitute the primordial scandal: the scandal of being scandalized. In the Lawrencian biocentric universe there would be power and splendor in proclaiming, "I *am* an animal," although in that asocial realm, with its negation of the "other," that ontological proclamation would be superfluous.

The question of the psychological enactment of biocentrism, that is, What exactly does one do about it? inevitably raises concomitant questions about the fate of culture. The fictional program of biocentric thinkers evades this dilemma to some extent by isolating biocentric protagonists from culture, like Zarathustra on his mountain top, Lawrence's heroes on their exotic voyages, and Kafka's animal protagonists, whose *milieux* become increasingly feral until all traces of culture are effaced. This lends a certain naïveté to the most direct solution to the biocentric dilemma, namely that what is called for is not doing but undoing, that for humans, becoming the animal entails becoming what one already is, a reclamation produced not by acts of consciousness but by acts of forgetting. This ontological shift would not constitute a nihilistic act but a Dionysian affirmation of the body, the animal, and vitalistic nature. The "highest state a philosopher can achieve: a Dionysian standing in *Dasein*—my formula for this is *amor fati*" (4, *PW*, 426). Presumably the mutability and diversity of organic life would produce many versions of biocentric behavior, including aggressive carnivores like Nietzsche and vegetarian herbivores like Kafka.

Careful to avoid the anthropomorphizations of Nature and natural man implicit in Romanticism, Nietzsche elaborates and complicates this model of natural reclamation to keep it consistent with biocentric objectives. Although he claims that domestication is superficial and reversible (thereby contesting its putative Darwinian formulation), Nietzsche rigorously hedges the "return to Nature" with qualifications. Nature is not a lost Eden or a privileged origin, and a simple return is impossible because "there has never been a natural humanness" (4, *PW*, 208). Rather, the process entails a struggle against *un*natural values, and its result is better described in the metaphor of recuperation and convalescence as a "healing" of Nature "from" culture (4, *PW*, 334). The result of this process is not Rousseau's noble savage but the wild man, who, culturally speaking, is *der böse Mensch*. Furthermore, Nietzsche considers Darwinian Nature inimical to the "higher type" of human organism, the lucky accident, producing instead a human creature constituted of adaptation and compromise, the average type of the *Nivellierten* (4, *PW,* 221). "I find the 'cruelty of Nature,' of which one speaks so much, in a different quarter: she is cruel to her lucky ones [*Glückskinder*], she preserves and protects and loves *les humbles* [*sic*]" (4, *PW,* 341). The return to Nature is therefore complicated by the "great question" posed in Darwinian metaphors, "where has the plant '*Mensch*' grown most splendidly before now?" (4, *PW,* 439)—that is, under what optimal conditions can a higher type of wild man, a barbarian of the heights (4, *PW,* 438) be produced? Without actually presenting a program, Nietzsche suggests that *Übermenschen* will not thrive in Nature but must be carefully bred and nurtured like hothouse plants. This eugenic proposal is saved from the anthropocentric implications of its agricultural metaphor only by Darwin's own reminder that the breeder is not a creator, that he does not control natural process but merely interferes with its directions, and that from the point of view of the organism, his function is analogous to that of chance.

Nietzsche no more produces a political program than do the other biocentric thinkers, even though the political ramifications of his ideas are by no means benign, and even though his ideas are, and have been, misappropriated. These misappropriations not only result from the hermeneutical challenges that biocentric thought poses to readers, but are indigenous to any translations from Nature to culture that disregard the role of the "other" as the key to distinguishing natural and cultural systems. Without analysis of its rhetorical strategies and the crucial manipulation of the "other" at the heart of propaganda and spectacle, the Third Reich may indeed be misconstrued as a biocentric dystopia. But the tasks of distinguishing biocentrism from its cultural parodies, and of distinguishing the myriad false doubles created by the insertion of the lack and the "other" into the libidinal realms, are not easily mastered. Biocentrism, with its affirmation of the animal and, by possible extension, physical prowess, genetic constitution, and racial destiny, has therefore undergone intellectual repression along with fascist ideology in the aftermath to World War II. But given its own aspirations to the status of an intellectual trace, as well as its dangerous vulnerability to ideological misappropriation, the disappearance of the biocentric tradition need not be mourned.

Biocentrism is inevitably reanthropomorphized when it is

24

translated into cultural practice, in its benevolent versions no less than its malevolent. The democratic extension of recognition and protection to natural, organic, unconscious life—Nature, land, animals, and (in a curious ideological misalliance) prenatal life—is as much a false double of biocentrism as fascism. Undoubtedly biocentric impulses propel many of these concerns, for example, wilderness and wildlife conservation and animal liberation. But their effectiveness as political objectives depends upon justifying them on traditional humanistic grounds, as exemplifying rational and ethical human behavior, particularly behavior in relation to property, an argument that demonstrates Nature's appropriation into the Symbolic Order. The concept of responsible stewardship that informs much of the rhetoric of these movements actually reasserts the anthropocentrism implicit in the Biblical hierarchy of creation. Only a radical variant of these philosophies, one that essentially advocated returning the earth to a feral state, would approximate a genuine biocentric vision.

Since biocentrism has no real practical effects, the outcome of a study of biocentric thought and art should be, strictly speaking, an experience *sous rature*: something recognized, forgotten, and yet insistent still in affects, instincts, and dreams, like a faint nostalgia for our own infantile and presocial past. But in my own case, the forgetting and fatalism of biocentrism did not entirely heal the strange pain of having once seen through animal eyes. Instead of feeling enriched, like Tiresias, who lived two lives and enjoyed double vision, I felt scarred, like one discovering a hidden kinship with the most brutally oppressed creatures upon the earth. The gaze of wild animals in a zoo still makes me feel diffident and ashamed, as do, at times, the eyes of degraded household pets. And although I recognize it as no more than a humanistic compromise whose residue of virtue is corrupted at the outset, I try to protest the more egregious cultural appropriations of sensate life in food production, sport, clothing manufacture, and scientific experimentation. I try (however imperfectly) to maintain a vegetarian diet; to eschew fur and (when possible) leather clothing; to protest the genetic debilitations of wildlife by commercial and trophy hunters, and after once listening to the anguished bellow of a trapped wild boar in the German Odenwald, the unimaginable cruelties of trapping. I also pledge ten percent of my proceeds from this book to support the Animal Protection Institute in its fight against scientific experimentation upon live animal bodies. But my philosophically inconsistent and confused response is not intended to serve as a model for anyone else. The biocentric vision speaks with no strictly homogeneous voice, and everyone will hear a different call in the wild cry of the beasts of the modern imagination.

The Biocentric Tradition

2

Darwin's Reading of Nature

In his recapitulation and conclusion to *The Origin of Species* Darwin writes, "Nothing at first can appear more difficult to believe than that the more complex organs and instincts have been perfected, not by means superior to, though analogous with, human reason, but by the accumulation of innumerable slight variations, each good for the individual possessor" (*O,* 426). In this sentence Darwin quietly announces a new reading of the Book of Nature that inaugurates an intellectual and philosophical scandal to complement the emotional shock produced by his theories. The spatial metaphors of deanthropocentrism—man toppled from the pinnacle of creation or displaced from the center of the universe—inadequately reflect the radical shift of reason from producer to product of nature. The resulting crisis is one of Authorship. As model and analogue of human reason, God is abolished along with the fiction of the subject as the origin of the text. Nature is transformed from a mimetic text, a representation of divine thought, to a self-referential and self-reflexive text, disclosing only its own origin in unconscious, involuntary, mathematical processes ("accumulation" and selection) that are as dispersed ("innumerable"), trivial ("slight"), arbitrary ("variations"), and autotelic ("good for the individual possessor") as the play of differences that constitute language itself.

The semiological aspect of Darwin's method was recognized as early as 1877, when Dean Goulburn of Norwich opened his preface to Sir Frederic Bateman's *Darwinism Tested by Language* with a reproof to Darwinians for their misprision of differences.

> There are two contrary intellectual tendencies, which characterize minds of different orders, and, when indulged to excess, become intellectual vices. The one is the tendency to see a distinction where there is no real difference. This is the snare of cultivated (or perhaps of over-cultivated) minds, whose constitution may never have been robust, and what vigour they once had has been refined away by speculation. . . . Opposed to this is the tendency to ignore real differences; to bring rapidly under the same category two cases which have

one or more superficial features of resemblance, but which are
so fundamentally unlike that they cannot with any justice be
classed together.[1]

Goulburn charges Darwinians, in effect, with confusing "'-etic"
and "'-emic" orders of linguistic signification.[2] Bateman's book
was written in outraged response to Darwin's collapse of the
cardinal differences (physiological, intellectual, emotional,
moral, and even to some extent cultural) between humans and
higher animals in *The Descent of Man*. Bateman, a specialist in
aphasia, used the anatomical researches of Broca and Gall,
together with his own clinical experience at La Salpêtrière and
the Eastern Counties' Asylum for Idiots, to salvage *language* as
the final, incontrovertible difference in kind between man and
animal: "Language is our Rubicon, and no brute will dare to
pass it."[3] Although Bateman's arguments have, in their gross
form, prevailed and only recently come under challenge by
zoosemioticists, the modern philosophy of language has gradually eroded the religious agenda he intended to buttress.

> He aims at illustrating the truth in 'the grand old book,' that
> 'God made man in his own image; in the image of God
> created he him;' and with this view he shows that (just as in
> the precinct of the Divine Nature the Word, or Second Per-
> son, represents the Father, and reveals the Father to the crea-
> tures, so) the word is man's distinguishing characteristic, rep-
> resents him, is the great medium whereby he throws into
> other minds the thoughts conceived in his own. Language is
> unquestionably the great outcome of Reason; indeed it *is* the
> Reason.[4]

Goulburn lays the foundation for Bateman's privileging of
language as the analogue (and even locus) of the human soul[5] by
revealing in his substitutions ("the Word, or Second Person"),
synonyms ("Language . . . *is* the Reason"), metaphors, and
analogies a logocentric system of belief in which God functions
as a transcendent Signified, an immanent Meaning. The heresy
of Darwinian thought was the implicit transformation of the
theomorphic premise of this formulation (man created in the
image of God) into a theanthropic explanation of theological
thinking (God as a deduction from a model of human reason
and intelligibility). Perhaps the simultaneous outrage of the Victorian religious and scientific establishments was inspired by
Darwin's parricide of their common ideological ancestor: the
Enlightenment rationalism that engendered both physics and

Darwin's Reading of Nature

natural theology and thereby yoked science and religion together upon the same model of textual intelligibility. God wrote the Divine Book, whose alternate versions could be read either by the cleric as Scripture or by the scientist as Nature, a dual ambition to which the youthful Darwin aspired before embarking on the voyage of HMS *Beagle*.

While Darwin was at sea upon his naturalist's adventure, the eight "Bridgewater Treatises on the Power, Wisdom and Goodness of God as Manifested in the Creation" appeared in England. Their philosophical enterprise was the argument from Design, according to which the complicated contrivances of Nature presuppose, and therefore prove, the existence of a Creator. "Natural Theology in the eighteenth and early nineteenth centuries flourished in an age when the behavior of deterministic machines, such as clocks and music boxes and Babbage's calculating engine provided the only comprehensible physical analogies of complex behavior. For the Natural Theologian the seeming music-box perfection and precision of complex instincts was a source of wonder and pleasure, and a testament to the existence of the designing hand of the greatest Mechanic of all" (Gruber, 231). The argument from Design transforms the Book of Nature into a performative text, a text that verifies the truths that Holy Scripture (a constative text) can only state. Its function as demonstration is similar to that of miracles in Biblical times in its attack on the incredulity and skepticism of the faithful. But its status as proof or testimonial reduces Nature to a mediated object with an abstract function in God's polemical struggle for the faith of mankind. Nature's materiality becomes ontologically unimportant, and its study becomes reduced to a kind of primitive cybernetics.

Bateman's references to Disraeli's *Lothair* betray the emotional impetus behind the argument from Design: "Nothing can be more monstrous than to represent a Creator as unconscious of creating."[6] The odium of the monstrous, with its connotations of the alien, the abnormal, the unfamiliar, reveals how powerfully the normative and the conventional governed intellectual possibilities in nineteenth-century thought. Bateman, like Disraeli, cannot imagine an unconscious creator (let alone creation dispersed among numerous unconscious factors) because their favored paradigm of creation (and I am using *paradigm* here in a Kuhnian sense)[7] presupposes anthropomorphic rational activity. The affective motive behind the argument from Design was to make the world (and its Creator) familiar

Beasts of the Modern Imagination

and tame by founding it upon those analogies to the self, reason and human will,[8] that assure the existence of control over Nature's power and the domestication of Nature's otherness. Even Sir John Herschel, whose *Introduction to the Study of Natural Philosophy* Darwin much admired (*A*, 33), and whose methodological influence might first have suggested to him the function of force as the *vera causa* of natural phenomena, anthropomorphized natural force in terms of the human personality, as force of will, "if not man's, then presumably God's."[9] Darwin's discoveries required an intellectual leap that was ontological before it became methodological: he was able to imagine a nonanthropomorphic model of the self by divorcing law from reason, force from will, and creation from invention.[10] He was able to recognize that madness was not the only alternative to reason and that chaos does not logically follow the abolition of conscious design. In short, he rehabilitated the organic body, both animal and vegetable, with its unconscious interplay of form, function, and force, as model of natural creation and design.

Darwin's contemporaries understood perfectly the philosophical implications of a deanthropomorphized universe. Bateman cites with alarm the modern scientific creed, "I believe in Law, but no Lawgiver; in the life-giving power of Force and Substance; Intelligence from Non-Intelligence, without conscious Author."[11] Whether or not Darwin recognized the logocentric nature of the metaphors that dominated natural science and natural theology in his day, he liberated both language and Nature from the Subject—the *auctor* (Latin, originator), Author, Authority—by making language analogous to natural life in its developmental and evolutionary processes.

> Languages, like organic beings, can be classed in groups under groups; and they can be classed either naturally according to descent, or artificially by other characters. Dominant languages and dialects spread widely, and lead to the gradual extinction of other tongues. A language, like a species, when once extinct, never, as Sir C. Lyell remarks, reappears. The same language never has two birth-places. Distinct languages may be crossed or blended together. We see variability in every tongue, and new words are continually cropping up. (*DM*, 90)

Modern philology not only gave Darwin evidence of the historicity, variability, and mutability of language, but also allowed him to assume the independence of its structure and function from

Darwin's Reading of Nature

conscious thought and human invention. "It certainly is not a true instinct, for every language has to be learnt. It differs, however, widely from all ordinary arts, for man has an instinctive tendency to speak, as we see in the babble of our young children; whilst no child has an instinctive tendency to brew, bake, or write. Moreover, no philologist now supposes that any language has been deliberately invented; it has been slowly and unconsciously developed by many steps" (*DM*, 86).

If Nature has no Author, then who (or what) speaks it? Is it even intelligible, and can it be considered, even metaphorically, as a text? Darwin seems to have grasped that the concept of the Author is as much a prosopopoeia as Nature itself: a fictive individualization of the multiple, dispersed processes and functions that constitute any production, whether material or intellectual.

> It has been said that I speak of natural selection as an active power or Deity; but who objects to an author speaking of the attraction of gravity as ruling the movements of the planets? Every one knows what is meant and is implied by such metaphorical expressions; and they are almost necessary for brevity. So again it is difficult to avoid personifying the word Nature; but I mean by Nature, only the aggregate action and product of many natural laws, and by laws the sequence of events as ascertained by us. (*O*, 88)

Michel Foucault not only analyzes the convergences of myriad functions that constitute the fiction of the Author, but has given the phenomenon itself a historical character. "The coming into being of the notion of 'author' constitutes the privileged moment of *individualization* in the history of ideas, knowledge, literature, philosophy, and the sciences."[12] In nineteenth-century science this privileged moment collapsed even at the level of attribution as the honors for the discovery of evolution were dispersed among Alfred Russel Wallace, Darwin, and numerous other contributors of odds and ends to the theory, including Robert Chambers's *Vestiges* and Patrick Matthew's "complete but not developed anticipation" of evolution, which had appeared in a work on naval timber.[13] But Darwin further abolished the individualization of the Author at the levels of metaphor and analogy by substituting the many for the one, the dispersed for the unitary, the gradual for the instantaneous, the trivial for the portentous, and the oxymoron of unconscious choice for the anthropomorphism of deliberate decision. "I have said Natural Selection is to the structure of organised beings what the human architect is to a building.''[14] Darwin skillfully undermines the "Deification of Natural Selection" by two shrewd rhetorical maneuvers. He first constructs a deliberately unparallel analogy (Natural Selection//s the human architect) and then proceeds to correct it, not by personifying Nature once again but by dismantling the human architect down to the natural processes of his own production. "The very existence of the human architect shows the existence of more general laws; but not one, in giving credit for a building to the human architect, thinks it necessary to refer to the laws by which man has appeared.''[15]

As the son of a physician, and himself an erstwhile Edinburgh University medical student with a local summer clinic "practice" (*A*, 120), Darwin had no doubt derived his grasp of semiology in its medical form of symptomatology. Quite likely the comparative habits required for the analysis of the oblique and secondary indications of medical symptoms would have sharpened Darwin's hermeneutical skills more than the simplistic and arbitrary decoding procedures of contemporary physiognomists and phrenologists. Darwin was almost rejected for the *Beagle* voyage because Captain Fitz Roy, "an ardent disciple of Lavater," read lassitude into the shape of Charles's nose. "I think he was afterwards well satisfied that my nose had spoken falsely" (*A*, 36). But Darwin continued throughout his life to attend to the "speech" of inorganic structures and animal bodies, geological strata and coral reef formations, bird beaks and wing markings, human male nipples and stag horns—all spoke their origins and functions and the web of relations in which they are embedded. In the great diabole at the end of *The Origin of Species*, the body's powers of historical utterance, however metonymic, become immense and exalted. "We possess no pedigrees or armorial bearings; and we have to discover and trace the many diverging lines of descent in our natural genealogies, by characters of any kind which have long been inherited. Rudimentary organs will speak infallibly with respect to the nature of long-lost structures. Species and groups of species which are called aberrant, and which may fancifully be called living fossils, will aid us in forming a picture of the ancient forms of life" (*O*, 448). Darwin's later work on *The Expression of the Emotions in Man and Animals* (1872), although largely appropriated by ethologists and behavioral scientists, continues his semiological interest in the nonverbal language of the body and of the inarticulate impulses, sensations, and emotions, in humans and animals.

The abolition of the subject and the consequent collapse of the intentional fallacy in the study of Nature may have followed rather than preceded Darwin's recognition that the burden of signification resides, in any event, with the reader rather than with the author. Perhaps thanks to his Whig upbringing and the easy (if imperfect) erosion of his ethnocentrism, for which the abolitionist fervor of his Wedgwood relatives had prepared him, Darwin learned early of the opacity of ideology and its devious role in interpretation. Here is Darwin's account of his famous quarrel with Captain Fitz Roy over slavery: "We had several quarrels; for instance, early in the voyage at Bahia, in Brazil, he defended and praised slavery, which I abominated, and told me that he had just visited a great slave-owner, who had called up many of his slaves and asked them whether they were happy, and whether they wished to be free, and all answered 'No.' I then asked him, perhaps with a sneer, whether he thought that the answer of slaves in the presence of their master was worth anything?" (A, 37). The anecdote admirably suited the requirements of Fitz Roy's hidden agenda. Wishing to be both Christian and imperialistic, he was able to trick slavery out in moralistic garb, as the generous accommodation of a perverse savage nature and as an institution whose spiritual locus lay not in the politics of the master's force but in the sublimity of the slave's desire. The anecdote only required affirmation by a skeptic that the slaves spoke the truth, that they uttered a true statement rather than performed an obedient act, and that they could be identified as the proper subjects of their speech. As the better reader, Darwin discerned that it was not the slaves, but their master's force, that spoke their "No," a force that caused them to mimic their master's desire for their voluntary submission. To this invidious display of human logic and reasoning, Darwin's sneer, an animal gesture derived from wolves and dogs that bare their teeth in warning (EE, 248), was the fitting response.

"If man had not been his own classifier, he would never have thought of founding a separate order for his own reception" (DM, 150). The success of Darwin's hermeneutical approach to Nature depended upon the dismantling of his own anthropocentrism, a psychological process that, I believe, preceded its conscious emergence in his theories, and whose crucial role in his methodology is too often overlooked in the contemporary debate over the "new ways of thinking" that he inaugurated. The advent of the theories of Thomas S. Kuhn (*The Structure of*

Discovery) has begun to place the question of scientific methodology within the greater social context of the behavior of scientific communities. But although for the study of Darwin this has
resulted in the production of thorough and fascinating documentation of his intellectual and social influences, the approach
itself is too tainted with anthropocentrism to account adequately
for Darwin's unique emotional engagement with Nature.

> One can, in a sense, regard the voyage of the *Beagle* as a
> romantic interlude. One can point out that every idea Darwin
> developed was lying fallow in England before he sailed. One
> can show that sufficient data had been accumulated to enable
> a man of great insight to have demonstrated the fact of evolu-
> tion and the theory of natural selection by sheer deduction in
> a well-equipped library. All of this is doubtless true. Yet it is
> significant that the two men who actually fully developed the
> principle of natural selection, Charles Darwin and Alfred Rus-
> sel Wallace, were both travelers to the earth's farthest reaches,
> and both had been profoundly impressed by what they had
> seen with their own naked eyes and with the long thoughts
> that come with weeks at sea. It cannot be denied, however,
> that both had the additional advantage of literary counsel.[16]

Eiseley never tells us the significance of Darwin's travels, perhaps
because historians and philosophers of science have no good way
of assessing their role in disrupting Darwin's ontological and
metaphysical preconceptions. Yet I would argue that Darwin's
five-year journey halfway around the world constituted an imaginative adventure that invaded him with a sense of otherness, a
spirit of the wild, a feeling of alienation, or at least separation,
from culture that allowed him to imagine the seeming impossi-
bilities that became his theory.

True, Darwin's antianthropocentrism flourishes not in the
early accounts of the *Beagle* adventures but in the later *Descent
of Man,* and in the final studies of orchids, climbers, insectivo-
rous plants, lythrum, and earthworms conducted by the most
domesticated, sedentary, and reclusive of English country
squires. This aspect of Darwin's thought—his abjuration of an
anthropocentric coign of vantage—which I believe responsible
for the most radical aspects of his work, tends to elude scientific
commentators while falling quite naturally within the purview
of the literary critic sensitive to the philosophical ramifications of
point of view. Stanley Edgar Hyman therefore draws a delight-
fully eccentric (if slightly ridiculous) picture of the aged

Darwin's imaginative engagement with his flora and fauna. "In this imaginative design, Darwin is himself a kind of insect: he imitates the proboscis of an insect by pushing 'very gently a sharply-pointed common pencil into the nectary,' or 'I imitated this action with a bristle'; 'Accordingly I imitated the action of a retreating insect'; once, carried away, 'The walls of this cavity have a pleasant nutritious taste.' Even acting and thinking like an insect, Darwin cannot fertilize some flowers and cannot figure it all out."[17] The prophetic shades of Gregor Samsa in this passage are not purely accidental; Kafka had read Darwin and Ernst Haeckel as a young man, and his animal narrations ("Researches of a Dog," "The Burrow," "Josefine, the Singer or the Mouse Folk," and the explicitly Darwinian "Report to an Academy") constitute metaphysical elaborations on Darwin's own zoocentric play. Hyman only gives a playful nod to the methodological significance of these imaginative incursions into animal consciousness and instinct. "Darwin discovered these values in the earthworm by his usual processes of empathy and identification. . . . Sometimes Darwin played worm with them; as he wrote to Romanes in 1881, 'I tried to observe what passed in my own mind when I did the work of a worm.'"[18] But the Darwin who emerges from this stylistic analysis is a researcher secure and comfortable with highly unconventional procedures, a very different portrait from Peter Vorzimmer's impotent and obsolete old naturalist, devastated by the just attacks of his critics upon his logical and methodological inadequacies.[19]

It is tempting to attribute Darwin's success as a naturalist to his failure in classics, that is, to his timely escape from the influence of what D. H. Lawrence (echoing Nietzsche) called "the anthropomorphic Greeks." But perhaps his truly great gift was the ability to combine a capacity for immense wonder with a powerful tendency to demythify. His mimetic response to the schoolboy text *Wonders of the World* was both the wild desire to travel to the ends of the earth, and disputation "with other boys about the veracity of some of the statements" (*A*, 17). Homeric metaphors express his amazement. "The day was glowing hot, and the scrambling over the rough surface and through the intricate thickets, was very fatiguing; but I was well repaid by the strange Cyclopean scene. As I was walking along I met two large tortoises, each of which must have weighed at least two hundred pounds. . . . These huge reptiles, surrounded by the black lava, the leafless shrubs, and large cacti, seemed to my fancy like some antediluvian animals" (*JR*, 374). But while

encountering worlds scarcely less fantastic than those of his fictional precursors (Odysseus, Gulliver, Candide, among others),
he is endowed with the critical capacity to explore the literal
residue of his own hyperbole, to wonder if the giant turtles are
not indeed "living fossils" of prehistoric times. I take issue with
Hyman's emphasis on the Apollonian nature of Darwin's
response to the "poetry of the landscape" in the *Journal of
Researches*, as though he perceived Nature purely visually, aesthetically, and superficially. Darwin's emphasis on the ferity of
the landscape ("None exceed in sublimity the primeval forests
undefaced by the hand of man; whether those of Brazil, where
the powers of Life are predominant, or those of Tierra del Fuego,
where Death and Decay prevail" [*JR*, 503]) suggests an ontological response to the wilderness not unlike that of D. H. Lawrence
many years later, in which the perceptive subject is negated
and Nature can be imagined in the absence of a romantic
imagination.

The process of demythifying becomes for Darwin the collapse
of metaphorical thinking. "The terms used by naturalists, of
affinity, relationship, community of type, paternity, morphology, adaptive characters, rudimentary and aborted organs, &c.,
will cease to be metaphorical, and will have a plain signification
(*O*, 447)." His procedure reverses that of Goethe, who anthropomorphized chemical properties to make "elective affinities" a
metaphor for human passion. Darwin demythifies sexual selection at length in *The Descent of Man* by discovering the biological exigencies and their enabling mechanisms (the organic passion behind the emotional passion, the genetic choice behind
the situational choice) of pairing, mating, and reproduction. By
reading Darwin's work on sexual selection largely through
Freudian spectacles, Hyman obscures both the essential contribution of Darwin's deanthropomorphic approach to sexuality
and the philosophical (and hermeneutical) implications of the
discoveries themselves. Reading Darwin's ostensible fascination
with male breasts as a "fantasy of the male mother" consistent
with his "Oedipal identification,"[20] Hyman makes of the work
on sexual selection a map of Darwin's personal erotic obsessions
and repressions. Yet the male nipple, like its hypothetical counterpart, Eve's belly button, or, for that matter the mammalian
navel per se, was the bugbear of the argument from Design,
God's little practical joke, a lie or red herring ("Were they created bearing the false marks of nourishment from the mother's
womb?" [*O*, 445]) whose function could only be that of a lure to

Darwin's Reading of Nature

misprision. In the light of special creation, the Book of Nature becomes a deliberate hoax in which the anatomical features of reproduction that serve as metonymic figures of connection and descent become the "deceptive marks" of "a mere snare laid to entrap our judgment" (*DM, 25*).

Darwin's passion for collecting, which began in early childhood and which he believed to be innate ("None of my sisters or brother ever had this taste" [*A, 14*]), evolved into the Baconian method of collecting facts "on a wholesale scale" and "without any theory" (*A, 53*) in adulthood. This tendency almost proved Darwin's undoing by making of him a kind of Bouvard and Pécuchet[21] whose mania for totalization and completeness in the face of infinitude delayed the publication of *The Origin of Species* for twenty years.[22] It even then led him to consider his work only in synecdochic terms, as an abstract of an unwritten greater work, a hypothetical compendium of such supererogatory documentation that, he conceded, "very few would have had the patience to read it" (*A, 57*). Darwin's salvation was his distraction from the Baconian inventory (which would have transformed the Book of Nature into a mere lexicon) by the fragments, disjunctions, paradoxes, and anomalies that surfaced as soon as he regarded his phenomena as a network of relations, as a text, rather than as a statistical table. The faith in plenitude and continuity (which formed the ripened residue of the eighteenth-century idea of the Great Chain of Being)[23] crumbled for Darwin as his increasing preoccupation with problems of relation and their significance (differences, variations, disjunctions, absences, traces) led him to abandon the empiricist road for the nonpositivistic paths of hermeneutical thinking. David Hull points out that at least one of the difficulties Darwin's evolutionary theory encountered in gaining acceptance by contemporary philosophers of science lay in its rejection of metaphysical belief in essences. "Why not evolution? The answer can be found at a deeper level in a belief which Whewell shared with Aristotle, Bacon, Herschel, and Mill, a belief in the existence of natural kinds definable by a single set of necessary and sufficient conditions, a belief in essences. Empiricists wanted to eliminate so-called 'occult qualities' from science and yet they retained that element in earlier philosophies which contributed the most to the prevalence of metaphysical entities—essentialism."[24]

Darwin is not quite an empiricist (nor does he share the empiricist's metaphysical assumption of "presences") because what he construes as "facts" are neither observable phenomena nor demonstrable forces but rather the relations between them. "Facts" are able to "speak" or signify precisely because they are differences; when Darwin writes at the conclusion of *The Descent of Man*, "It is incredible that all these facts should speak falsely" (*DM*, 607), his syntactic antecedents show the "facts" to be similarities, affinities, distributions, and successions. Darwin sounds like a protostructuralist when he writes, "The great principle of evolution stands up clear and firm, when these groups of facts are considered in connection with others" (*DM*, 607). Ostensibly, the difference between the savage and the scientist is, to Darwin, precisely the ability to think relationally, the savage apprehending only the objects of Nature, the lexical items or words, as it were, while the scientist possesses the syntactic knowledge to order them into a language. "He who is not content to look, like a savage, at the phenomena of nature as disconnected, cannot any longer believe that man is the work of a separate act of creation" (*DM*, 607). The savage does not, of course, apprehend Nature in this way, as Lévi-Strauss has shown us (*The Savage Mind*), and the metaphysician is no less mythopoeic in his thinking, as Derrida has pointed out.[25] But Darwin, who counted himself a "poor critic" (because he lacked "the great quickness of apprehension or wit" of a Huxley [*A*, 67]), was actually a great critic, according to our contemporary notions, because he discovered the modes of signification that make of Nature a text. If genetics is analogous to linguistics in its exploration of microevolutionary processes, then Darwin's macroevolutionary work functions as a kind of poetics of Nature.

The philosophical ramifications of Darwin's theories are so immense that they strike at the most fundamental oppositions at the heart of Western culture: the difference between human and animal, male and female, Nature and culture. He reverses a system of signification at least as old as the Greek *polis* with whose emergence the images of hybrid and intermediary forms (centaurs, Amazons, Cyclops) were banished to the realms of monstrosity and otherness.[26] With the disappearance of the Author from Darwin's universe, these oppositions, which had been elevated virtually to the status of logical categories or necessary ways of thinking about the world, collapsed into a kind of Derridean freeplay. In reading the traces of natural life, the interplay of presence and absence in the fossil record or in the vestigial or rudimentary organs in living creatures, Darwin discovered form as linked not to the eternal action of mind or the intelligence of a Creator, but to the absent action of force: force extinguished and obliterated, or deferred in its effects, by time. Natural form becomes the representation not of an anthropomorphic Divine thought but of the forces of nature, which exist only in the present moment, but which disperse their signatures of violence or desire among the past and future matter of the world. Michel Serres speaks of the "isomorphic relation between force and writing"[27] with respect to the politics of knowledge and to the reading and decoding of Nature, and, indeed, one could probably best represent the affective consequences of Darwin's discoveries with the metaphor of his own 1835 experience of the earthquake at Valdivia (Chile). "A bad earthquake at once destroys our oldest associations: the earth, the very emblem of solidity, has moved beneath our feet like a thin crust over a fluid;—one second of time has created in the mind a strange idea of insecurity, which hours of reflection would not have produced" (*JR*, 302).

By the time he wrote *The Origin of Species*, Darwin had abandoned the Baconian notion of treating the universe (and particularly the "geological record") as an encyclopedia and had begun to speak of it as a disorderly and incomplete sort of museum.[28] "The crust of the earth with its imbedded remains must not be looked at as a well-filled museum, but as a poor collection made at hazard and at rare intervals" (*O*, 448). The spatial metaphor of the museum, with its abolition of time (by exhibiting historical objects simultaneously) and force (by displaying them static and discrete) is inadequate to represent the historical drama of inscription that produced the palimpsest of the earth.

> Successive formations are in most cases separated from each other by blank intervals of time of great length; for fossiliferous formations thick enough to resist future degradations can as a general rule be accumulated only where much sediment is deposited on the subsiding bed of the sea. During the alternate periods of elevation and of stationary level the record will generally be blank. During these latter periods there will probably be more variability in the forms of life; during periods of subsidence, more extinction. (*O*, 431)

The earth's successive inscriptions and erasures, its imprinting and obliteration of organic forms upon its surface, is itself a writing born of trauma and produced by the active forces of nature, by upheavals of the land and the subsidence of the sea.

Darwin even speculates in the above passage that extinction and inscription are temporally linked, as common effects of the same forces. His lament, "The noble science of Geology loses glory from the extreme imperfection of the record" (O, 448), is prompted by the geological record's failure to provide him with the intermediary links he requires for the proof of his theory of gradual descent. Yet it is also disingenuous, for such "proof" would make of the earth a purely representational text, a museum, a genealogical table, an ancestral portrait gallery in which only types are represented while the traces of their warfares, their flourishings, their migrations and hardships, are elided. As a palimpsest, a surface of alternate inscriptions, erasures, traces, superimpositions, and blanks, the earth tells in the very nature of its inscription the historical drama of natural force behind the organic forms.

Darwin's journeys to the farthest reaches of the earth (Patagonia, Tierra del Fuego, Tahiti, Australia) eventually led him home in his scientific interests not only to the pouter pigeons and herbaceous borders of rural England, but, even more intimately, to the human body itself. The body, Darwin discovered, was as much a palimpsest as the earth, an irregular, haphazard, and incomplete inscription (and erasure) of its own evolutionary history—of changing conditions and their impact on its form, of habits acquired and abandoned, of necessities emergent and vanished, of instincts developed and repressed, and of shifting affinities and departures. In order to read the body in this way, certain metaphysical preconceptions about its unity and integrity had to be scuttled. No doubt the traditional purview of medicine over the study of the body, with its heuristic and normative orientation, perpetuated the Greek philosophical and aesthetic heritage of conceiving the body in Platonic and idealistic terms even when, as in modern times, the metaphor of its integration becomes the machine. But Darwin, like Freud in his approach to dreams, studied the human body *en detail* rather than *en masse*, not in its unity and internal coherence, but in its fragments (organs, structures, functions) and their correlation to those of other creatures. He found that, quite unlike an efficient machine, the human body exhibits many anachronisms, and *The Descent of Man* ends with the summary, "Man still bears in his bodily frame the indelible stamp of his lowly origin" (*DM*, 619).

Among the erasures of the human body Darwin counts the os coccyx at the base of the spine, the trace of the absent tail that "corresponds with the true tail in the lower animals" (*DM*, 23) and that suggests its own, somewhat comical, disappearance as man's ancestors became arboreal and erect and began to sit upon it: "the tail has disappeared in man and the anthropomorphous apes, owing to the terminal portion having been injured by friction during a long lapse of time" (*DM*, 60). The male breast and nipple, on the other hand, is very much present, and well enough developed to be potentially functional for lactation. "They often secrete a few drops of milk at birth and at puberty. . . . In man and some other male mammals these organs have been known occasionally to become so well developed during maturity as to yield a fair supply of milk" (*DM*, 163). The male breast speaks of an obsolete function, of a time when the ancestors of human females were multiparous, and their inadequacy to nurture their many young was supplemented by the lactating capability of the males. Amid the sentimental hoopla surrounding the birth of the Dionne quintuplets in 1934, scarcely anyone seemed to have reflected that the event was a biological retrogression, or "reversion," as Darwin would have called it: the production of a human litter. Human behavior is as marked by anachronistic residues as the body, as Darwin discovered in exploring emotional expressions. In anger, for example, the traces of animalistic aggression survive in the human grimace. "The lips, however, are much more commonly retracted, the grinning or clenched teeth being thus exposed. . . . The appearance is as if the teeth were uncovered, ready for seizing or tearing an enemy, though there may be no intention of acting in this manner" (*EE*, 241). To stress the role of cultural socialization in the repression and erasure of these instincts further, Darwin chooses a homely example. "Every one who has had much to do with young children must have seen how naturally they take to biting, when in a passion. It seems as instinctive in them as in young crocodiles, who snap their little jaws as soon as they emerge from the egg" (*EE*, 241). Read in this way, as a palimpsest, the human being is no longer the prototype of ideal form in its unity, its originality, its integrity, and its perfection. Hybrid and even teratoid, as it were, in both body and mind, it contains little bits and traces of other animals (the modified swim bladder of fish for its lungs, its hand homologous to "the foot of a dog, the wing of a bat, the flipper of a seal" [*V*, 1: 12]), aspects of male and female, and primitive instinctual glimmers suffused throughout its civilized behavior.

The palimpsest destroys the illusion of the purely representational nature of the text, and with it the validity of a positivistic approach to its interpretation. It is a performative text, written by force and desire, by the need to preserve some words and destroy others, by the wish to remember selectively and to forget, by the erosion of natural forces acting over time upon the material of inscription. Darwinian Nature signifies quite similarly, for it is also written by needs, deprivations, migrations, adaptations, sexual desires—by all of the absences that propel natural organisms in their relationship with their environment and each other, and that propel them through time. Because its language depends on differences, Nature speaks most loudly and eloquently through its least normative forms, through its excesses and anomalies. "According to Aristotle, neither accidental properties nor monsters allowed of explanation and hence were not the proper subject matter of science. . . . On the modern view of science, it is precisely the 'accidents' and 'monsters' which call for explanation. It was Darwin's attention to so-called accidental variations which led to his theory of evolution, and it in turn demolished the Aristotelian distinction between essential and accidental characteristics."[29] Darwin did indeed attend the spectrum of anomalies in Nature, such as "rogue" plants, black sheep and white rabbits; old hens that "assumed the plumage, voice, spurs, and warlike disposition of the cock" (V, 2: 26) and capons that brooded eggs and brought up chicks; human monstrosities like the hirsute Crawfurds or the even more unfortunate Lamberts with their "porcupine-like excrescences" (V, 2: 53). Without benefit of modern genetics and endocrinology[30] Darwin had to resort to a theory of atavism or reversion. But he accounted for his throwbacks without resort to the occult premises of his contemporaries ("Some naturalists look at all such abnormal structures as a return to the ideal state of the group to which the affected being belongs" [V, 2: 35]) and, without understanding recessive character in genes, he described its effect in metaphors the reverse of the erasures of the palimpsest: "written as it were in invisible ink, yet ready at any time to be evolved under certain conditions" (V, 2: 59).

Darwin's theory of the mutability of species struck at the normative thinking that made of monsters deviations from Platonic or ideal form. In a universe where the hybrid is perceived as a "living mosaic-work, in which the eye cannot distinguish the discordant elements" (V, 2: 23), the fabulous monsters of Greek mythology, for example, Pegasus and the Sphinx, centaurs and griffins, become conceivably no more than hybrids with their discordances exaggerated by selective reversions over vast periods of time. Modern women with supernumerary but symmetrical mammae ("Of this I myself have received information in several cases" [*DM,* 37]) are not so much living monsters to Darwin as creatures affected by a biological time warp, who would be perfectly normal had they lived eons ago among man's early progenitors, who were undoubtedly "provided with more than a single pair" (*DM,* 37), and who appear anomalous in modern times only because the ascendancy of the human species, with the resulting improvement in the conditions of its survival, made uniparity possible. Anomalies are thus symptoms of change, for the better, as in the case of humans who can successfully raise single offspring to maturity, or for the worse, as in the case of animals whose coloration marks the inevitability of their domestication. "Sheep have never become feral, and would be destroyed by almost every beast of prey" (*V,* 2: 5), and white rabbits, likewise, would not long survive in the wild, where their coloration would make them conspicuous to predators. Quite logically, then, Alice's white rabbit, with its watch and waistcoat pocket and white gloves, is depicted by Carroll as thoroughly domesticated. The whiteness of sheep and of rabbits speaks the desire of their masters for white wool, fur, angora, and the dyed woolens that may be produced from them.

Darwin's attention to monstrosity, excess, and incongruity makes his universe exceedingly strange and alienating to the modern as well as to the Victorian mind. Hyman repeatedly uses the term *surreal* to describe this brave new world: "The sexuality of the lower animals in the *Descent* is wildly surrealist. A cast-off cuttlefish tentacle goes off on its own and mates with the female."[31] Here, as with his Freudian reading of Darwin, Hyman engages in a circular metaphorics. Freud was made possible by Darwin, as was Surrealist art and thought. Darwin's Nature does not imitate Surrealism; Surrealism expresses the ruptures in conventional ways of thinking about the world inaugurated by Darwin's discoveries. Biological forms are infinitely plastic, and they conform to no a priori logical or conceptual categories. Consequently, notions of the fixity of living form, for example, of unity, uniformity, homogeneity, constitute fictions that correspond to an older metaphysics of Nature. Darwin discovered that no normative representations exist in Nature and that even parts of the human body are so infinitely variable from one individual to the next that in one particular study of human musculature "a single body presented the extraordinary number of twenty-five distinct abnormalities" when compared to "the standard descriptions of the 'muscular system given in anatomical text books'" (*DM*, 27). The human body is inevitably perceived and represented in tropes of a cultural nature ("the beau-ideal of the liver, lungs, kidneys, &c., as of the human face divine" [*DM*, 27]) that imply a spurious identity among individuals of the same species. These infinite variations among individual organs are elided in our own thinking because they no more signify than do the infinite phonetic variations of the sounds of a single phonemic pair. But Nietzsche finds it important to emphasize not only the fictive nature of form itself, and particularly biological form, but also that these figurations, these fiction-making processes, are themselves anthropomorphisms that serve human psychological needs.

> *Form* counts as something permanent and therefore more valuable; but form is merely something invented by us. . . . Form, species, law, idea, purpose—here the same error prevails in each case in that a false reality is slipped under a fiction. . . .One must not understand this need to form concepts, species, forms, purposes, laws ("a world of identical cases") as if we were thereby able to fix the *true* world; but rather as need to ready a world for ourselves that makes our existence possible—we create thereby a world that is calculable, simplified, intelligible, etc., for us. (4, *PW*, 17)

Darwin would quite have agreed as to the purely conventional and anthropomorphic nature of scientific categories: "I look at the term species as one arbitrarily given, for the sake of convenience, to a set of individuals closely resembling each other" (*O*, 67).

Darwin's famous analogy between natural and artificial selection (a controversial argument because of the disrepute of analogy as a logical tool)[32] could be easily misconstrued as a reintroduction of the Author, here the breeder in the guise of the artist, as the originator of natural form. Darwin cites Mr. Youatt's deific description of using selection as "the magician's wand, by means of which he may summon into life whatever form and mould he pleases" (*O*, 48). Lord Somerville reputedly endowed breeders with Platonic powers ("It would seem as if they had chalked out upon a wall a form perfect in itself, and then had given it existence" [*O*, 48]) as though the breeder were a kind of Pygmalion able to give both form and life to his desires. The implication of these deific artistic metaphors for the eugenicist is

Darwin's Reading of Nature

that it makes Nature once more representational, a reflection or realization of preexisting forms, like the sketch of an artist or the statue of the sculptor ("The sheep are placed on a table and are studied, like a picture by a connoisseur" [*O*, 48]). Indeed, these metaphors are inspired by the protean quality of natural forms being described as a kind of plasticity ("Breeders habitually speak of an animal's organisation as something plastic, which they can model almost as they please" [*O*, 48]). Organic reproduction, an unconscious process impelled by natural forces and animal instincts, is transformed by eugenics into representation, an intellectual, conscious, anthropocentric process governed by human desire in the form of the idea, or the fantasy of the ideal.

While in the beginning of *The Origin of Species* Darwin stressed the breeder's power to modify and alter domestic breeds of plants and animals radically, in *The Variation of Animals and Plants under Domestication,* published almost a decade later, he took pains to dismantle the eugenicist's role. He did so by pointing out that the natural process remains independent of the breeder, who can control its direction but not its workings, and whose intervention will therefore have the same effect whether it is conscious or unconscious, voluntary or involuntary. "It is an error to speak of man 'tampering with nature' and causing variability. If a man drops a piece of iron into sulphuric acid, it cannot be said strictly that he makes the sulphate of iron, he only allows their elective affinities to come into play. If organic beings had not possessed an inherent tendency to vary, man could have done nothing" (*V,* 1: 2). By implication, then, sulphate of iron would be produced whether the man were a scientist intent on producing the compound or a bystander walking past the vat of sulphur, who accidentally trips and drops his iron key into it. Darwin stresses that many of man's modifications of domestic breeds are quite unconscious and, strictly speaking, unintentional. "We may confidently infer that no man ever selected his water-dogs by the extent to which the skin was developed between their toes; but what he does, is to preserve and breed from those individuals which hunt best in the water, or best retrieve wounded game, and thus he unconsciously selects dogs with feet slightly better webbed. The effects of use from the frequent stretching apart of the toes will likewise aid in the result. Man thus closely imitates Natural Selection" (*V,* 1, 42). The breeder *imitates* natural selection. When he culls the inferior members of a herd and destroys the weaklings to prevent their reproduction, he *imitates,* consciously or unconsciously, the action of animal predators.

We might resort to a linguistic analogy to say that the process of natural selection, like linguistic competence, is beyond conscious control or interference. Human action influences the performance, as it were, and the eugenicist, like the rhetorician, exercises sufficient conscious control over the performance to achieve specific results. Of course, modern recombinant DNA research and biogenetic engineering do indeed allow man to control natural genetic processes that, like linguistic competence, were once beyond human influence or interference. Darwin, who worked without benefit of even Mendel's theories of heredity (which did not become known until the turn of the century) could scarcely have imagined a field like modern biotechnology, in which man indeed "tampers with nature" and performs virtually deific acts of creation. Darwin's difficulty in distinguishing the breeder's anthropocentric teleology ("domesticated breeds show adaptation to his wants and pleasures" [*V,* 1: 4]) from the faulty implication that artificial selection actually anthropomorphizes the natural process (permitting breeders to "create" new species) results largely from the anthropomorphic encrustations of scientific language. Much as he tries, Darwin cannot rid himself of them, and his only recourse is to protest the figurative nature of much of his discourse. "For brevity sake I sometimes speak of natural selection as an intelligent power;— in the same way as astronomers speak of the attraction of gravity as ruling the movements of the planets, or as agriculturists speak of man making domestic races by his power of selection" (*V,* 1: 6).

In place of an Author, or a governing intelligence, Darwin discovers force and desire (including human force and desire) as the power shaping natural forms. Adaptations in natural organisms speak of it, and whether or not the human desire behind domesticated forms can be articulated is ultimately irrelevant to its power. A breeder explains to Darwin the crass economic motive behind the "complete metamorphosis" (*V,* 2: 182) of the domestic pig: "The legs should be no longer than just to prevent the animal's belly from trailing on the ground. The leg is the least profitable portion of the hog, and we therefore require no more of it than is absolutely necessary for the support of the rest" (*V,* 2: 178). Indeed, the domestic pig has been appropriated entirely to human food production and the cost to itself in

Darwin's Reading of Nature

terms of its animal autonomy can be measured by comparison with the wild boar, which is equipped with tusks for defense, longer legs for mobility and flight, and a more compact musculature for powerful impact in battle. Yet beneath the layers of human cultural motives, the desire for economic profit and agricultural efficiency, competition with other breeders, and so on, lurks Darwin's blind survival instinct. From a wider evolutionary perspective, the farmer's "development" of the biologically monstrous domestic pig is an adaptation in the interest of human survival at least teleologically equivalent to the giraffe's development of a grotesquely elongated neck in order to reach the foliage of tall trees. In a parenthetical remark deleted from the published *Journal of Researches,* Darwin notes, "If an animal exerts its instinct to procure food, the law of Nature clearly points out that man should exert his reason & cultivate the ground" (Gruber, 433; from the *Beagle Diary*).

Darwin not only places biological man within Nature, giving him an animal genealogy and a mutable mammalian form, but he places reason, morality, culture, art, and language within Nature as well. In the most famous passage of the "N Notebook" he writes: "To study Metaphysics, as they have always been studied appears to me to be like puzzling at astronomy without mechanics. —Experience shows that the problem of the mind cannot be solved by attacking the citadel itself. —*the mind is function of body*" (Gruber, 331; my italics). The most anthropoid attributes are consequently *read* and explicated for traces of man's animal ancestry: reason is explained as a refinement of instinct, morality as a development of social and parental instincts, taste and art as elements of sexual desire and gratification, language as a sophistication of animal communication systems. Darwin's "consistent interest in the dethronement of reason and conscious will as the sole governors of human behavior" (Gruber, 369) prepared the way for Freudian psychology, as his correlation of morality with the social organization of the human species anticipated Nietzsche's *Genealogy of Morals.* Human cultural evolution is as much propelled by force and desire as the rest of organic creation, which is a nonidealist, non-Hegelian view of human history. Only in his attempt to grapple with those mysteries of human desire that require a more complex phenomenological grasp of intersubjectivity than he possessed—an ability, for example, to understand the relationships among human desires—did Darwin encounter a cul-de-sac that prompted him to cry out in the notebooks, "What is the Philosophy of Shame & Blushing?" (Gruber, 293).

In *The Descent of Man*, Darwin states flatly, "My object in this chapter is to shew that there is no fundamental difference between man and the higher mammals in their mental faculties" (*DM*, 66). Darwin collapsed perhaps the cardinal traditional difference between humans and animals by suggesting that the mind is not a fixed spiritual entity but a heuristic form as protean as the body. Not only did it evolve, diachronically, from animal instinct and even plant tropisms (for example, the movement of climbing plants: "It is hardly an exaggeration to say that the tip of the radicle . . . acts like the brain of one of the lower animals"[33]). But also, viewed synchronically, the mind consists of myriad conscious and unconscious, rational and irrational heuristic behaviors (emotions, curiosity, imagination, memory, reason, self-consciousness, among others) that take their forms not from ideal entities but from the forces, needs, and desires that propel the body also in its relation to the world. "Plato / Erasmus / says in Phaedo that our *'imaginary ideas'* arise from the preexistence of the soul, are not derivable from experience.—read monkeys for preexistence" (Gruber, 290).

Darwin's notebooks show two complementary arguments developing for breaking down the differences between animal and human intelligence, and they both depend upon his psychological approach to questions of mental function. Humans, he reasons, can think without (strictly speaking) "thinking" consciously, while animals can know without (strictly speaking) "knowing" consciously. His physician father's theories about the gradation between sanity and insanity, and the ambiguity of such twilight conditions as intoxication, delirium, somnambulism, and what he calls "double consciousness" (Gruber, 288), provide him with evidence of modes of intelligence disengaged from reason. But although such conditions might be extruded on grounds of their pathology, Darwin also monitored his own dreams and made proto-Freudian observations on them. "Characters of dreams no surprise, at the violation of all ⟨rules⟩ relations of time ⟨identity,⟩ place, & personal connections—ideas are strung together in manner quite different from when awake" (Gruber, 285). Without benefit of a theory of repression, he nonetheless detected the palimpsestic nature of the human psyche, whose topology Freud was to mark as a terrain of inscriptions, erasures, superimpositions, blanks, and traces. "Now if memory / of a tune & words / can thus lie dormant, during a whole life time, quite unconsciously of it, surely memory from one generation to another also without consciousness, as instincts are, is not so very wonderful" (Gruber, 267). Darwin adumbrated in this cybernetic analogy of human memory and organic replication a common grammatological principle, a notion of writing as the production of traces, underlying the continuity of life.

Concerning the higher mental processes, particularly the power to abstract and to form general concepts, Darwin questions whether animals (no less than savages) might not possess them *in effect,* that is, practically, intuitively, being able to demonstrate but not articulate them. Darwin points out, for example, that monkeys are as frightened of a stuffed or dead snake as a live one, and that their fear seems attached to a category of animal, perhaps the reptilian category, rather than to particular threatening signals, such as movement or a hiss. "It would almost appear as if monkeys had some notion of zoological affinities, for those kept by Brehm exhibited a strange, though mistaken, instinctive dread of innocent lizards and frogs" (*DM,* 72). He reports examples of animals that without benefit of Newton's laws behave in practical ways as though they understood the law of gravity, for example, Houzeau's parched dogs searching hollows and depressions on the desert surface for water. In his "M Notebook," Darwin writes, "It will be good to give Abercrombie's definition of 'reason' & 'reasoning' & take instance of Dray Horse going down hill . . . & then go on to show, that if Cart horse argued from this into a theory of friction & gravity, it would be discoverer [of] 'reasoning' or 'reasoning' [*sic*]—only rather more steps. —dispute about words" (Gruber, 293). Darwin reports a relatively complex reasoning process in some monkeys, who, accustomed to receiving lumps of sugar wrapped in paper, were stung when a live wasp was put in the paper instead: "after this had *once* happened, they always first held the packet to their ears to detect any movement within" (*DM,* 78). The monkeys apparently discriminated animate from inanimate on the basis of movement, and, consequently, sound. Another account tells of polar dogs that "instead of continuing to draw the sledges in a compact body, diverged and separated when they came to thin ice, so that their weight might be more evenly distributed" (*DM,* 75). They thereby exhibit what appears like a practical, intuitive knowledge of the relationship of mass, stress, and surface. "All Science is reason acting /

systematizing / on principles, which even animals practically know (art precedes science—art is experience & observation) in balancing a body & an ass knows one side of triangle shorter than two" (Gruber, 333). No doubt, many of these interesting examples of animal intelligence could be reduced to crude stimulus-response behavior by modern behaviorist psychology. But it is symptomatic of our prevailing anthropocentrism that animal psychology has been by and large relegated to behaviorism with its occlusion of the mind's inner life, while the human psyche reserves the complexities of psychoanalytic explanations for itself.

A crucial factor in Darwin's attribution of reason and moral sense to animals is the argument that possession of these faculties is not identical with consciousness of their possession. Referring to the intuitive search of savages and dogs for water in low places, Darwin notes, "The savage would certainly neither know nor care by what law the desired movements were effected; yet his act would be guided by a rude process of reasoning, as surely as would a philosopher in his longest chain of deductions" (DM, 77). An analogy with linguistic competence bears him out: the possession and use of language does not presuppose or require a conscious awareness of the laws of syntax.

Although careful not to oversimplify the question, and giving cultural factors their due (DM, 132), Darwin grounds morality in the social and familial instincts of animals and even gives conscience a biological etiology as the discomfort attending the frustration of the protomoral instincts in social creatures. Aware of the ramifications of such notions—that morality thereby becomes as subject to heredity as insanity and that the "above views would make a man a predestinarian of a new kind, because he would tend to be an atheist" (Gruber, 279)—Darwin nonetheless dismantles "free will" by arguing its determination by prior, ulterior, unconscious, and irrational motives.

When a man says I will improve my powers of imagination, & does so,—is not this free will,—he improves the faculty according to usual method, but what urges him,—absolute free will, motive may be anything ambition, avarice, etc., etc. An animal improves because its appetites urge it to certain actions, which are modified by circumstances, & thus the / appetites themselves become changed.—appetites urge the man, but indefinitely, he chooses (but what makes him fix!? frame of mind, though perhaps he chooses wrongly,—& what

Darwin's Reading of Nature

is frame of mind owing to—) I verily believe free will & chance are synonymous. (Gruber, 271)

Morality and virtue themselves become factors in the evolutionary scheme of things, and Darwin reads them not only for their biological origins, but also for their eugenic effects. And although Darwin finds particular virtues counterprogressive (for example, courage, which causes the boldest young men to fall in battle and leave fewer progeny; or chastity, which lessens the fecundity of individuals) he maintains that morality ultimately serves a positive genetic function in promoting the survival of larger social units. "A tribe including many members who, from possessing in a high degree the spirit of patriotism, fidelity, obedience, courage, and sympathy, were always ready to aid one another, and to sacrifice themselves for the common good, would be victorious over most other tribes; and this would be natural selection" (*DM,* 132).

Although aesthetic sensibility may arguably be considered the most distinctly anthropoid trait next to language, Darwin also displaces the concept of beauty from the realm of the ideal and the spirit and attaches it to the sexual and erotic instincts in humans, animals, and even plants.—"We can to a certain extent understand how it is that there is so much beauty throughout nature. . . . Flowers and fruit have been rendered conspicuous by brilliant colours in contrast with the green foliage, in order that the flowers may be readily seen, visited and fertilised by insects, and the seeds disseminated by birds" (*O,* 436). Interestingly enough, Darwin implicitly suggests that desire (for oral gratification, as in the case of the bee or the hummingbird, or for sexual gratification) requires a process of selection (since a bee may visit only a limited number of flowers, or since only a single mate may be accommodated at any one time) that operates precisely on the determination of *difference.* In other words, since the female can choose only one mate from among all of her possible options (for any given copulation), she will choose the most conspicuous, the one who is distinguished from the rest by a difference, perhaps a difference from herself or her own sex (an "other" that is still the same),[34] and in so doing she genetically institutionalizes and perpetuates that difference. One could ask, of course, why some species such as birds have highly distinguished sexes, while the sexes of dogs are virtually indistinguishable in terms of secondary sexual characteristics. The most plausible answer might be that birds, having keener vision because of their aerial habits, respond more readily to visual stimuli and therefore differentiate minute color variations, while dogs with their terrestrial habits might respond more readily to such nonvisual stimuli as odors. This state of affairs has interesting implications for the roles of the sexes, for it suggests that in many species it is the female whose erotic desire works through her "intellectual" activities (acute perception, attention to detail, powers of discrimination) ultimately to call into being the red of the male cardinal, the splendid fantail of the peacock, or the wonderfully complex horns of the stag. "Just as man can give beauty, according to his standard of taste, to his male poultry . . . so it appears that female birds in a state of nature, have by a long selection of the more attractive males, added to their beauty or other attractive qualities" (DM, 211).

Darwin discovers that sexual selection depends on animal subjectivity, on an awareness of the "other," although its status (whether as object, force, or subject) remains indeterminate. Unlike Hegel, who distinguishes animal subjectivity from human intersubjectivity, Darwin cannot finally solve the mystery of why humans blush and animals do not. "Blushing is the most peculiar and the most human of all expressions. Monkeys redden from passion, but it would require an overwhelming amount of evidence to make us believe that any animal could blush" (EE, 309). The mystery is significant for it would make blushing a rather singular phenomenon: physiological in nature, depending on the involuntary actions of the circulatory system, and yet seemingly purely cultural in origin. Darwin reports contemporary interpretations of the blush as a kind of automatic writing of the soul, a sign of the conscience, an internalized Scarlet Letter, as it were, "designed by the Creator in 'order that the soul might have sovereign power of displaying in the cheeks the various internal emotions of the moral feelings;' so as to serve as a check on ourselves, and as a sign to others, that we were violating rules which ought to be held sacred" (EE, 336). Darwin humanely points out that most blushing is caused by shyness and modesty and benefits neither the blusher nor the spectator. He further produces two significant insights: that blushing is the product of psychological phenomena ("When a blush is excited in solitude, the cause almost always relates to the thoughts of others about us" [EE, 335]) and that it is part of an intersubjective experience ("It is not the simple act of reflecting on our own appearance, but the thinking what others think of us, which excites a blush" [EE, 325]).

Darwin's Reading of Nature

These same insights might have served to explore other intersubjective emotions that baffled Darwin ("Is [sic] shame, jealousy, envy all primitive feelings, no more to be analyzed than fear or anger?" [Gruber, 294]) and to produce more rigor in ascribing them (along with emulation and deception) to animals. Without benefit of a psychology of object relations and without a consideration of the ontological status of mediated objects, Darwin could not explore what is, perhaps, the cardinal difference between human and animal: the perception of the desire of the other and the alienation that comes with perceiving the self as a mere object in the other's consciousness. Darwin did not consider that competition for pure prestige might indeed be of a different ontological order from competition for survival.

But Darwin's research leads him to the abolition of differences rather than their definition. As Hyman writes of *The Expression of the Emotions in Man and Animals,* "the final sense we get is of a community of feeling and reaction in infant and adult, elephant and keeper, degraded woman and galvanized man, Darwin and small American monkey sharing his snuff. It is a world as teeming with emotion as the natural world teems with life."[35] Hyman sees, I believe, a natural connection between Darwin's humanistic tendencies (his humanizing of beasts and anthropomorphizing of Nature) and the peculiarly literary qualities of his scientific writing with its heavy dependence on the imaginative use of metaphor and anecdote. But Darwin's writings express an even more complex activity of the literary and critical imagination: an awareness of the constraints placed upon scientific thought by a language whose very syntax permeates Nature with the metaphysics of the subject ("It rains," "*Es regnet,*" "*Il pleut*") and whose words for natural processes (*selection, creation, affinity*) must be continually purged of their anthropocentric residue. Conversely, the animal, qua animal, comes ontologically into its own, as an autotelic product of natural forces, living for itself. It is no longer a mere metaphor standing for the repressed and censored aspects of human nature nor, strictly speaking, even a "creature," product and object of a designing mind. "Origin of man now proved," Darwin writes in his notebook. "Metaphysics must flourish.—He who understand [sic] baboon would do more toward metaphysics than Locke" (Gruber, 281).

3

Darwin, Nietzsche, Kafka, and the Problem of Mimesis

Darwin's evolutionary theory crossed disciplinary boundaries from the moment of its publication, to exert a revolutionary impact on political theory, economics, and particularly the social histories of Marx and of the Social Darwinists. Less well known is the genealogy of Darwin's influence in the realms of philosophy and art, where we may trace him as the author of a theory of imitation that reverses the Aristotelian aesthetic by showing life itself to be mimetic under certain conditions. Furthermore, the theory of imitation derived by Nietzsche, and subsequently Kafka, from Darwin preserves its political teleology, and therefore functions as a secular and vitalistic complement, if not alternative, to René Girard's religious and psychological neo-Hegelian theory of imitation (see chapter 1, note 2).

If Aristotle writes in the *Poetics,* "Imitation is natural to mankind from childhood on: Man is differentiated from other animals because he is the most imitative of them,"[1] Darwin discovered that in the world of Nature both plants and animals "practice" mimicry or imitation in the interest of protective adaptation to ensure the survival of their species.

> Insects often resemble for the sake of protection various objects, such as green or decayed leaves, dead twigs, bits of lichen, flowers, spines, excrement of birds, and living insects; but to this latter point I shall hereafter recur. The resemblance is often wonderfully close, and is not confined to colour, but extends to form, and even to the manner in which the insects hold themselves. The caterpillars which project motionless like dead twigs from the bushes on which they feed, offer an excellent instance of a resemblance of this kind. (*O,* 205)

The implications of this discovery are enormous: that imitation belongs to the realm of Nature rather than culture, to the inhuman as well as the human, that its practice might be organic, unconscious, and involuntary, that its teleology might be political rather than aesthetic, and that it may serve as a pivot of

53

historical change. These implications inform a radical revaluation of mimesis and theater in the works of Friedrich Nietzsche and Franz Kafka.

Working without benefit of psychology, Darwin draws analogies between natural and artificial selection that result in ascribing "creativity," if not an actual motive, to natural selection.[2] Animal mimicry is therefore provided with a heuristic explanation as a mediated process serving, in protracted and statistically significant form, the ends of protection and defense. "Assuming that an insect originally happened to resemble in some degree a dead twig or a decayed leaf, and that it varied slightly in many ways, then all the variations which rendered the insect at all more like any such object, and thus favoured its escape, would be preserved, whilst other variations would be neglected and ultimately lost; or, if they rendered the insect at all less like the imitated object, they would be eliminated" (O, 205). Nietzsche, taking the analogy between natural and artificial selection literally enough to toy with eugenics in his later writings (4: PW, 113), gives Darwin's protective adaptation a psychological interpretation from which he draws certain political inferences. He concludes that imitation is a strategy, unconscious or conscious, organic or intellectual, serving the weak in their struggle against the strong, and that it is consequently a sufficient threat to life, passion, and power to justify a lifelong antipathy to imitation that culminated in his conflict with Wagner over the Bayreuth enterprise, but whose beginnings may be found in the attack on New Attic comedy in *The Birth of Tragedy*.

Kafka comes to evolutionary theory through Darwin, Haeckel, and Nietzsche, a complex and impure pedigree in which Nietzsche's psychological, antiprogressive and antianthropocentric interpretation of Darwin wins out. Kafka likewise exposes the devious political ends of imitation, reenactment, and performance in several of his fictions, and in "A Report to an Academy" he directly links animal mimicry and theatrical performance as evolutionary strategies in the struggle for survival. Kafka appears to subscribe to the idiosyncratic Nietzschean elaboration of Darwinian theory by which certain organic processes (protective imitation, camouflage, adaptive behavior, morphological resemblance) and intellectual acts (deception, lying, rationalization, self-delusion) are treated as homologous and analogous. His aversion to imitation, like Nietzsche's, seems to derive from insight into the ontological implications of instinctual and rational doubling.

Darwinism, "the last great scientific movement" (2, *GS,* 500), played a complicated part in a series of major shifts in Nietzsche's thought following *The Birth of Tragedy* that are difficult to localize but that together comprise what might be called Nietzsche's "scientism": the shift from the dualistic metaphysical principles of Dionysus and Apollo to the monistic will to power, from problems of aesthetics to problems of psychology, from the methodologies of philology to those of the natural sciences, and from dialectical logic to a model of mind in which rationality and consciousness are explained as forms of compensatory behavior. Nietzsche, who in *Untimely Meditations* deplores David Strauss's misuse of Darwin, goes on to demonstrate a better appropriation. Much preoccupied with the problem of history, he apparently returned to animal history for the same reasons Darwin turned to geology: in the hopes of finding a hermeneutical theory of development and change that would be free from the kind of historical prejudices and perspectival distortions of human self-interest he criticized in Strauss. It would seem that Nietzsche also sought in Darwinism a psychology of primitive life, of the organism's behavior prior to corruption by culture and philosophy, but exempt from the moralistic distortions of such eighteenth-century Romantic notions as Rousseau's noble savage.

The ways in which Darwinism fails to fulfill Nietzsche's need for a developmental psychology are as important as the ways in which it serves it. For example, Nietzsche accepts Darwin's description of primary instincts in economic terms at the same time that he rejects, and indeed reverses, the specific economic assumptions underlying Darwin's theory of the struggle for survival. "What concerns the famous 'struggle for survival' seems to me, for the time being, more asserted than proven. It occurs, but as an exception; the total condition of life is not the emergency, the state of hunger, but rather wealth, opulence, and even absurd waste—where one fights, one fights for *power*" (3, *TI,* 444). Nietzsche defines his own primary instinct, the will to power, as an economic opposite of the survival instinct, as a physiological will to growth, prodigality, excess (2, *GS,* 489; 3, *BGE,* 24), a will not only to life, but to *more* life in the sense that the organism requires not only adequate conditions for the maintenance of life but an excess of resources to enable profuse growth, reproduction, and a reckless expenditure of energy. He further orders these two instincts, the prodigal will to power and the conservative survival instinct, into a relationship of priority: the will to power is primary, the survival instinct secondary and derivative, in keeping with its exceptional, occasional, and contingent nature as an instinct activated only in times of want and danger and stimulated by the emotion of fear. The relationship might also be formulated by saying that the will to power and the survival instinct are offensive and defensive versions of one another, or that the survival instinct is the defensive expression of the will to power in the weak.

By placing the survival instinct in a derivative relationship to the will to power, Nietzsche is able to formulate their instinctual operation not only quantitatively, in terms of excess or dearth of power, but also directionally, a concept crucial to understanding the function of doubling in Nietzsche's psychology. The difference between the will to power and the will to survival is not only that the former expends (an outward movement) and the latter conserves (an inward movement), but actually something far more complex, a matter of directness (appropriation) and indirectness (strategic surrender) that creates a doubling of motives (ostensible and ulterior) in the weak organism. For example, in adapting to arctic conditions, the bear no longer simply appropriates his enemies in a fight but practices a form of strategic surrender of its power that resembles a kind of deception. Instead of risking its life in battle, it survives by eluding its enemy, by appearing to be invisible, by masking itself as snow when its fur turns white. Its adaptation is organic cunning.

By retaining the defensive and reactive function of the survival instinct, Nietzsche also incorporates Darwin's psychology of compensatory supplements into his critical model. The most important consequence of this maneuver is that it allows him to demonstrate the secondary and derivative nature of intellectual life. Nietzsche can now explain the history of consciousness as a defensive adaptation that requires a series of supplements to compensate for an original lack of power. Consciousness is a function of the herd instinct and follows human socialization. The increased dependency of individuals on the herd makes communication necessary, and Nietzsche postulates that consciousness, particularly self-consciousness, was originally required to enable communication. "That our actions, thoughts, feelings, and movements become conscious to us—or at least partially so—is the consequence of a terrible compulsion that has long governed the human being: as the most endangered animal, he *required* help and protection, he needed his own kind, he needed to express his distress and to know how to make himself understood. For this he first needed 'consciousness,' in order to 'know' what is wrong with him, to 'know' how he feels and what he thinks" (2, *GS*, 494). Because it is a form of Darwinian adaptation, this evolution of consciousness does not signify progress or improvement of the species to Nietzsche. Rather, it is a symptom of the decadence of the organism that accompanies the transition from feral existence to domestic society, for it functions as the epistemological *ersatz* for the repressed and atrophied animal instincts.

> What happened to these animalistic creatures, happily adapted to the wild, to warfare, to roving and adventure, is no different from the probable fate of aquatic animals when they were forced to become land animals or face extinction: all at once their instincts became devalued and "unhinged." . . . They felt too awkward for the simplest tasks, they lacked in this new, unknown world the guidance of their old unconscious, self-regulating, safety-oriented drives. They were reduced to thinking, drawing inferences, calculating, deducing from cause and effect—to depending on their "consciousness," their frailest and most fallible organ! (3, *GM*, 270)

Darwin's deconstruction of organic morphology—when, by inferring extinct and theoretically possible forms from traces (fossils) and differences (variations), he showed that existing organic forms are neither eternal nor inevitable—suggested to Nietzsche a way of challenging the privileged forms of intellectual life. For example, Western logic may owe its status as providing normative principles of reasoning to its heuristic value rather than to its intrinsic validity. "Countless creatures that made inferences in a way different from ours became extinct; still, their reasoning may have been truer" (2, *GS*, 392).

Nietzsche eventually elaborated Darwin's compensatory psychology into a hermeneutical tool that anticipates several of the salient features of Freudian psychoanalysis. Freudian interpretation, like the Darwinian, explores developmental histories in which defensive strategies determine new forms of the self that embody the traces of their weakness in the symptomatic form of their adaptation. Freud's description of the symptom as a substitution unspecified as to form allows for various manifestations including the somatic (the hysterically affected organ), the behavioral (the obsessive ritual), and the ideological (delusion).

Darwin, Nietzsche, and Kafka

The supplement in Nietzsche can likewise take all of these forms, and it is this play of substitutions that allows him to apply his critical model to the study of disparate historical phenomena: philosophical, political, social, intellectual, and even zoological.

Paul Ricoeur rightly lists Nietzsche with Freud and Marx as thinkers whose interpretation is an exercise in suspicion.[3] Nietzsche's suspicion is directed toward any evidence of mediated desire. Only the unmediated behavior of simple appropriation, for example, the predation of wild animals, the militarism of Caesar and Napoleon, the rapacity of the Borgias, is beyond suspicion and critique. Nietzsche's will to power therefore approximates Hegel's animal desire rather than the condition of the Master precisely because it lacks self-consciousness. Nietzsche's Masters require no recognition. The "great style" of the monumental architectures in their honor (presumably Roman, French Empire, and Italian Renaissance) represent "power that no longer requires proof, that disdains to ingratiate itself . . . that feels no witnesses around it and lives without consciousness of contradiction; that reposes within *itself,* fatalistically, a law among laws" (3, *TI,* 443). The French Romantics, in contrast, fired by the *ressentiment* ("Pöbel-Ambition") of the Slave, camouflage their iconoclastic aims to destroy the ruling class with a beautiful style that deliberately imitates their aristocratic betters in expression and sensibility (3, *TI,* 439).

Nietzsche's theory of development and change yields consistent results even when applied to objects as different from Freud's and Darwin's as biography, intellectual genealogies, and political histories. In every pathological development he finds the same structure: a power differential, an ulterior motive, the compensatory function of a supplement, and a mimetic adaptation. For example, Socratic reason is born when Socrates, an ugly, low-born Greek, acting from motives of *ressentiment,* is able to persuade his aristocratic betters to adopt mimetically his own exaltation of reason over instinct. Nietzsche critiques Greek rationalism by arguing that it was not a spontaneous, progressive development, but the result of a clever trick prompted by Socrates' personal ulterior motives: his desire to overcome the disadvantage of his lack of beauty (by exalting mind over body) and his plebeian status (dialectical inquiry levels the aristocrat's advantage by making the opponent prove he is not a fool). The Athenians succumb to the ploy because, suffering from a surcharge of strength, a dangerous anarchy of the instincts, they require the Socratic *pharmakos* to save them from self-destruction. Nietzsche recognizes the paradoxical therapeutic value of this supplement: it is a medicine of equivocal power, both cure and poison, cure *by* poison, saving the Greeks from their self-destructive strength by enervating and sickening them. In imitating the rationalism of Socrates, the Athenians practice the strategic surrender of their passions in the interest of a life-preserving, if costly, adaptation (3, *TI*, 397–402).

Using his Darwinian model, Nietzsche is able to encompass Christianity, democratic socialism, and French Romanticism in a continuous critique ("Continuation of Christianity in the French Revolution" [4, *PW*, 23]) that interprets their libertarian, fraternal, and egalitarian ideals as signs of the supplement in the service of political strategy: "justice" as the demand for concessions from the powerful, "freedom" as the desire for disengagement from the powerful, "equal rights" as the restriction of the acquisition of power among one's peers (4, *PW*, 116). Nietzsche even insists on the political teleology of Romantic emotionalism, regarding the cultivation of feeling and sympathy as polemical rather than aesthetic in purpose since it results in portrayals of suffering that stimulate pity for the weak: the misfit in Hugo, the woman in Rousseau, the slave in Harriet Beecher Stowe (4, *PW*, 23; 121; 166).

By treating their ideologies as purely supplemental functions, survival strategies in the form of compensatory substitutions, Nietzsche is able to evaluate cultural phenomena in terms of their evolutionary effects. He is therefore able to describe the result of Christian morality, which in his view historically destroyed the natural aristocracy of the noble Roman ruling class by leveling hierarchies with its fraternal and altruistic ideals, in genetic terms, as a kind of mongrelization or creation of "mishmash-people" (3, *TI*, 425–28; *BGE*, 132), as he calls them. His diagnosis of the modern spirit reveals a symptomatic set of moral vanities concealing the unfitness that is the heritage of centuries of bad breeding and hybridization: "tolerance" as the inability to say yes or no to an issue, "great sympathy" as a combination of indifference, curiosity, and excitability, "objectivity" as lack of character, personality, and the ability to love, "passion" as a screen for disorder and intemperance, and so forth (4, *PW*, 108). Nietzsche's most extreme remedy for this genetic chaos is to combat the detrimental effects of Christian *Zähmung* (domestication) with Darwinian *Zucht* (eugenics), since only artificial breeding can circumvent the deleterious effects of adaptation in natural evolution. "Not only a Master

Darwin, Nietzsche, and Kafka

Race whose duty is limited to ruling: but a race with a singular sphere of life, with a surplus of strength for beauty, bravery, culture, manners, to a most spiritual degree; a yea-saying race that may grant itself every great luxury; strong enough to dispense with the tyranny of the virtue-imperative, rich enough to dispense with thrift and pedantry, beyond good and evil; a hothouse of exotic and select plants" (4, *PW,* 113).

By exploring at such length the function of supplementarity in Nietzsche's thinking, I hoped to situate it as the mediating term between Nietzsche's primary (will to power) and secondary (will to survive) instincts, and to suggest thereby its ultimately Darwinian origin and political nature. My aim was to establish the supplementary nature of mimesis, to depict it as the repetition of an absence rather than a presence, which appears not spontaneously, prompted by pleasure, as Aristotle suggests, but in response to the danger of a lack, a need, or a threat. Mimesis has for Nietzsche a political function irrespective of context (history, philosophy, art, religion), a fact that allows him to conceptualize nonaesthetic phenomena in terms of dramatic structure.

He describes morality, for example, as "consequence, symptom, mask, tartufferie, disease, misunderstanding" (3, *GM,* 214). Because it is a supplement, a substitute for a deficiency, morality is overdetermined (as Freudian symptoms, the return of the repressed, are overdetermined). Nietzsche's *Genealogy of Morals* is a tracing back of morality to its repressed origins in health and power differentials and in somatic and affective conditions. Morality as *Tartüfferie,* however, catches up in a single word the entire drama of that particular religious hypocrisy in which prudery masks prurience and exerts its tyranny over the healthy and strong. Nietzsche likewise perceives in the doubling of sacred and erotic imagery in Thomas à Kempis's *Imitation of Christ* a kind of spiritual striptease that makes him sniff contemptuously, "This mystic has a manner of discoursing on love that could arouse the curiosity of the *parisiennes*" (3, *TI,* 438). Nietzsche is sensitive to the hypocrisies that mask the libidinization of thought, the ostensibly rational dialogue concealing the sublimated homosexual agon of the beautiful Greek youths under Socrates' tutelage, or the purity of French neoclassical art, infused with the erotic energy of heterosexual competition (3, *TI,* 400; 450).

Nietzsche's aversion to mimesis, his dislike and fear of masks, theater, mime, and particularly "the dangerous concept of the 'artiste'" (2, *GS,* 508), spring from the Darwinian form of their supplementarity. Nietzsche feared above all the effects of natural selection by which both a tendency to mimicry and the illusion or appearance, the mimetic trick expedient for survival, become genetically incorporated into the living organism as a "surplus of adaptive capacities of all kinds that is no longer satisfied in the service of the most immediate and specific utility." Nietzsche's passage describing the genesis of the mimetic "instinct" deserves to be quoted in full because its language betrays both the Darwinian process and the political teleology Nietzsche attributed to imitation.

> Such an instinct will easily have reached its greatest sophistication among families of the lower classes, who must survive under changing pressures and compulsions, in deep dependency, and who must, with suppleness, adapt to their blankets, continually adjusting to new circumstances, adopting new postures and expressions, until by degrees they become able to turn their coats with *every* wind and thereby virtually to become a coat, as masters of the incorporated and incarnated art of the eternal game of hide-and-seek that is called *mimicry* in animals—until ultimately this capacity, accumulated from generation to generation, becomes dominant, unreasonable, uncontrollable, an instinct learned to lord it over other instincts, and which generates the actor and "the artist." (2, *GS,* 508)

Interestingly, Nietzsche's first adverse response to mimicry is to the New Attic comedy of Euripides, which is also, in his view, the first mimetic drama. Although his excoriation is found in the early *Birth of Tragedy,* Nietzsche objects to New Attic comedy on much the same political and Darwinian grounds that preoccupy him in his late writings: Euripides caters to the audience, "a power whose strength is only in numbers" (1, *BT,* 67), and he teaches survival skills—Socratic survival skills, at that—to the common man, to any spectator who wishes to imitate his revolutionary dialectical discourse.

> This was not the only pleasure: one even learned to speak from Euripides, as he himself boasted in the competition with Aeschylus: how people learned from him now to observe artfully and with sly sophistication, to conduct transactions and draw inferences. . . . And so the Aristophanic Euripides justifies his prize by noting how he represented common, familiar, everyday life and activity, which everyone is capable of judging. If the masses now philosophize, govern their land and estates with amazing shrewdness, and conduct their own tri-

Darwin, Nietzsche, and Kafka

als, it is thanks to his service and the consequence of the wisdom he inculcated in the populace. (1, *BT,* 65)

Another symptom of supplementarity in New Attic comedy is found in its realism, its imitation of the actual life, which makes drama self-conscious: acted rather than lived in the body. Unlike the older, nonmimetic forms of Greek drama that were rooted in the living experience of the Dionysian *Rausch,* the festival, the dithyrambic music, the plays of Euripides reenact or counterfeit passion. If one believes Nietzsche's own urgent accounts, it was a similar substitution of living music by theatrical production that occasioned the rift in his friendship with Wagner.

The most pervasive theories of the Nietzsche / Wagner split assume that because their estrangement coincided with Wagner's rise to fame and power, Nietzsche succumbed to *ressentiment.* But Nietzsche's own repeated asseverations of the purely professional nature of his attack suggest different interpretations for the significance of the timing: for example, that Wagner's move from Tribschen to Bayreuth marked a shift both in his art (from music in the salon to opera on the stage) and in his politics (from "French" Wagner to "German" Wagner, from unconventional free spirit to paragon of Reich idealism).

Wagner becomes a case for Nietzsche's evolving theory of aesthetics that began as a "metaphysics of art" in *The Birth of Tragedy* and ended in the physiologism of *Nietzsche Contra Wagner* ("Aesthetics is, after all, nothing but applied physiology" [3, *NCW,* 487]) and whose constant aim is the deconstruction of aesthetic idealism. Beauty is to Nietzsche a fiction, an anthropomorphism—whether the "beautiful soul" or the "golden mean" of Greek aesthetics, or the concept of *Das Schöne an sich* (3, *TI,* 447)—that results from misunderstanding that the physiological nature of one's aesthetic response depends on the somatic and affective condition of the subject. To Nietzsche the perception of beauty is an instinctive response to health, vigor, and richness of life. The sense of ugliness is a response to physical degeneration and decay. This aesthetic formulation allows Nietzsche to appropriate art as a function of the will to power, an aphrodisiac, a stimulant to life, an excitation of the overall affect system akin to Freud's infantile polymorphously perverse sexuality.

To Nietzsche the transition from hearing Wagner's music to seeing Wagnerian opera performed at the *Festspielhaus* illustrated perfectly the logic of his antipathy to imitation: that in the theatrical spectacle an ideological supplement intervenes that politicizes the art. Onstage, Wagner's music loses its physiological effect, a kind of natural lubrication of the organism's animal functions, and becomes subjugated to the dramatic effect of manipulating the conscious audience response, namely, "to intoxicate the audience and impel it to a moment of powerful and lofty feeling" (2, *GS*, 360). Music is transformed from a private physiological experience into a political herd experience, and that life it once stimulated in the body is replaced by a factitious opinion or attitude of mind. "One becomes one's neighbor" (3, *NCW*, 488), Nietzsche remarks of the applauding Wagnerian spectator, in a comment that anticipates Heidegger's critique of otherness in *Sein und Zeit*. Nietzsche's own response to the first Bayreuth season was dramatically somatic: he became physically ill. "Doesn't my stomach also protest? My heart? My circulation? Aren't my bowels afflicted?" (3, *NCW*, 487).

Nietzsche claimed that he noticed no actual change in Wagner until he received the folio of *Parsifal;* but as early as the first season Wagner was rendered unrecognizable by the propoganda of his followers. The triumph of "attitude" and "heroic posture" onstage was imitated in life. Wagner fell victim to Darwinian camouflage: he became his own "coat," his own media image and reputation. Nietzsche had described this genetic transmutation earlier when he wrote, "The reputation, name, and appearance . . . thrown over things like a garment and entirely foreign to their nature and even to their skin, grows from generation to generation merely because people believe in it, until it gradually, so to speak, accretes and assimilates to a thing and turns into its very body" (2, *GS*, 352). Yet Nietzsche never made the most obvious charge consistent with this Darwinian formulation of Wagner's transformation: that Wagner sold out to secure the much needed patronage of the Bavarian king. But in light of Nietzsche's antipathy, Wagner's shift of loyalties certainly is ironic: from the music-loving Nietzsche to the idealistic, drama-loving, and mimetic Ludwig II, who elaborately reproduced Wagnerian motifs in the histrionic visual and architectonic forms of his castles (the Wagner rooms at Neuschwanstein, or the grotto at Linderhof, for example).

Nietzsche distinguishes the "French" from the "German" Wagner not only by the replacement of Cosima's influence with that of the Bayreuth idealists, but also by degree of pathology or decadence (3, *EH*, 592–97). He saw the earlier Wagner sharing with the French late Romantics (Delacroix, Berlioz, Baudelaire) the voluptuous overrefinement of the senses that manifests itself in a feel for nuance and a fanatical concern with virtuosity of expression. Even the sweet, seductive *Tristan* of this phase already betrayed the unwholesomeness of life attenuated by this self-conscious preoccupation with the conveyance of feeling. But if the "French" Wagnerian music is morbid, the "German" is macabre. The heroic operas use the unliving figments of the mental world (illusions, virtues, nationalism) to mimic life, and it is not surprising that Nietzsche applied to Wagner's Bayreuth disciples metaphors of pickling and taxidermy, describing them as stuffed trophies or specimens labelled *Geist,* a travesty of life (3, *EH,* 565). Nietzsche sees *Geist* (spirit, mind, intellect) in all forms of decadent behavior reflecting enervation of the instincts and deception: prudence, patience, cunning, dissemblance, self-control, and mimicry (3, *TI,* 445).

Before turning now to Kafka's "Report to an Academy," one more example of the Darwinian and political function of acting as adaptive, compensatory behavior, which illustrates the entire psychology, may be helpful. According to Nietzsche's formulation, the poor, Jews, and women are "natural" actors and role players (2, *GS,* 509), whose degeneration may be explained in this way. To Nietzsche the perfect woman (not to be confused with the "ideal" woman) is the maenad, the bacchante, whose will to power flows unrestrained until it culminates in the orgiastic moment of *sparagmos* in the Dionysian rite. Since for the woman the will to power as growth, prodigality, and fecundity takes the form of procreation, she must appropriate the male to achieve her fertilization. The result is the battle of the sexes, a deadly, instinctual power struggle waged maniacally and ruthlessly by the woman with the aim of using (and merely using) the man to produce the child that is her effusion of power (3, *EH,* 550–51). But the woman who is weak and who stands to be vanquished in the fight does not recklessly squander the last of her diminished powers in a brilliant and doomed last stand. Instead of submitting to the patriarchal marriage, which is founded not on superficial and transient feelings of romantic love but on the power instincts of the male (the sexual instinct, the property instinct, the mastery instinct), she resorts to political and ideological supplements for survival. Joining the herd, she calls for suffrage ("cattle voting rights"), and sublimates her sexual lack in the fictive ideals of the "'woman-in-herself,' 'higher woman,' 'idealist woman'" (3, *EH,* 551–52). She dissembles and pretends—cunning, treacherous, and dangerous—

and in fits of ghastly mimicry she even masquerades as a man by wearing trousers, like the notorious George Sand (3, *TI,* 440).

Whether Kafka intended his "Report to an Academy" to satirize Jewish adaptation by conversion, as William Rubinstein suggests,[4] or whether it was written as a reverse "Metamorphosis," the story exhibits the hallmark of Nietzsche's Darwinian antipathy to imitation. Kafka might, of course, have borrowed the story's central conceit, the ape's accelerated evolution by "aping" the human, directly from his own youthful study of Darwin.[5] Nietzsche's influence, however, is clearly stamped on the witty twist by which Kafka makes the ape's mimicry intellectual rather than biological. "The intellect, as a means for the preservation of the individual, develops its chief powers in dissimulation," writes Nietzsche (3, *Truth,* 1018).

If his friendship with Jizchak Löwy and the Yiddish theater troupe at the Savoy[6] stimulated Kafka's interest in drama, it did not turn him into a playwright. Instead, Kafka assimilates drama into the themes and structure of his fiction until the philosophical center of many of his stories is situated in the performance (although performance encompasses a variety of exhibitions and accomplishments) and in the narration, which becomes dramatic monologue and narration in his later stories.

Performance and narration often form a pair that is either self-contradictory or mimetic. "The Great Wall of China" and "The Burrow" both open with a sentence that displays a successful architectural achievement: "The Great Wall of China was finished off at its northernmost point" and "I have completed and furnished my burrow and it seems to be successful."[7] The narrator then introduces an incremental series of qualifications (the Great Wall has lacunae; the burrow is vulnerable) that amount to a contradiction by stories' end. Kafka's "Josefine, the Singer or the Mouse Folk" is both self-contradictory and mimetic. The story begins with the acclamation, "Our singer is named Josefine. Whoever has not heard her does not know the power of song" (172). The narration then proceeds to enact or imitate what it describes. It diminishes Josefine's reputation, by gradually stripping her of all distinction, as it describes the diminution of her song, which becomes shorter, weaker, less elaborate, and, finally, silent. The narration retracts itself like a rug that is being rolled out at one end while it is being rolled up at the other. By story's end the opening sentence has been negated, Josefine has disappeared, her song is a memory, and to obliterate her memory the story has to cancel or erase itself, which it does by narrat-

Darwin, Nietzsche, and Kafka

ing that the mice practice neither music nor history. The narration is only a trace.

The Kafkaesque performance always results in death or madness or effacement of some sort, a clue to its mediative position in a power conflict. The hunger artist and the officer in the penal colony both perform for their lives (both fast and execution are conducted as theatrical "shows") in an effort to convince those in power, the indifferent audience and the new regime, of their effectiveness. The narration of Josefine is a performance, a performance of historical narration in competition with Josefine's musical performance, a competition the narrator can win only by losing. Both "The Great Wall of China" and "The Burrow" are defensive narratives about defensive constructions. Narration and performance in Kafka's stories serve political functions in a setting of Darwinian competition. The stake is survival.

Kafka's "Report to an Academy" is his most pointed illustration of the Darwinian political teleology of the mimetic performance. The three types of performance given by the ape (the imitation of the sailors on shipboard, his variety show act, and the report to the academy, which is the narration itself) are arranged in successive stages of dissimulation. While they are all acts of mimicry, the first betrays its adaptive and defensive purpose most bluntly while the tour de force of the scientific performance conceals it most expertly. In extant fragments of early versions of the story the narrative frame is a provincial admirer's interview of Rotpeter, a device structurally reminiscent of the explorer's interview of the officer in "In the Penal Colony." Kafka clearly shifted the narration to Rotpeter and gave it the form of the dramatic monologue in order to make the narration a mimetic doubling of the earlier performances. By shifting the frame to the arena of science, the Darwinian role reversal, the ape as guest lecturer on evolution, also serves as evidence of the ultimate, if degrading, effectiveness of adaptive behavior.

In contrast to the *non sequitur* of Gregor Samsa's metamorphosis, Rotpeter's evolution emerges from the cultural consequences of Darwinism, which aroused European curiosity in exotic fauna, and particularly in marginal and transitional species, the "thinking" and "talking" animals and feral humans displayed in travelling circuses and menageries at the turn of the century. Hagenbeck, the company that captures Rotpeter, was, in historical fact, conducting extensive collecting expeditions from Hamburg at that time. However, the repressed element of this phenomenon (repressed because it becomes visible only from the animal's perspective) is that the ostensibly philosophical and scientific interest in exotic creatures not only justified the brutal techniques of capture and taming but also concealed a hidden competitiveness, an ontological insecurity that turned the intersubjective relationship of captor and captive, viewer and exhibit, scientist and specimen, into a covert power struggle.

Although the members of the academy never appear in Kafka's story except as implied listeners ("Exalted gentlemen of the academy!") their competitive presence may be inferred from the defensive maneuvers Rotpeter executes in his report. He achieves a number of significant role reversals when, at the outset, he shifts the topic of his report from the story of his ape life (requested by the academy) to that of his progressive evolution from ape to man. This allows him to shift from object to subject by identifying himself firmly with the members of the academy in opposition to the animal "other": "Your life as apes, gentlemen, insofar as you have something of this sort behind you, cannot be farther from you than it is from me" (RA, 148). Conversely, by focusing attention on the barbaric methods of his humanization and civilization, he makes human behavior the specimen, the inexplicable object of his study. His report thereby functions as a verbal imitation of the gesture deplored by the press as rude and uncivilized: he lets down his trousers. And although Rotpeter accuses the offended reporter of not being able to tell the difference between showing one's scar and showing one's ass, he manages to get away with doing both. In his report to the academy, the ape triumphs over violence by concealing his submission to its continued victimization, that is, he acts as the successfully adaptive Darwinian organism.

Rotpeter's defensive behavior serves also as a symptom of the tremendous risks incurred in making his report. His narrative reveals explicitly the power differential between humans and apes: apes are consigned to boxes and cages unless they can convince their captors that they are human. Rotpeter's report to the academy therefore differs neither in form nor in purpose from his earlier performances before the sailors or on the variety stage. When he tells his listeners in a shocking parenthesis that he has since drunk many a bottle of good wine with the leaders of the Hagenbeck expedition who shot and captured him, we may infer that this gesture is less a symptom of his new "human" equanimity than a chilling repetition of an earlier mimetic act, when he was forced to drink the hated schnapps with the sailors in order to survive. Rotpeter is still imitating

Darwin, Nietzsche, and Kafka

humans for his life. He admits his vulnerability in the guise of a boast when he tells his listeners, "Even so I could certainly hardly tell you even these trivial things, were I not perfectly sure of myself, and had I not unshakeably secured my position on all the great variety stages of the civilized world" (*RA,* 148). The imperious postures he strikes in his dealings with his underlings (his subjugated chimpanzee mate and his servile manager) are less symptomatic of his human ascendancy than of his continued need to camouflage himself as a master.

Because Rotpeter's adaptation functions as a paradigm for human evolution, Kafka carefully introduces a convincing transitional etiology for camouflage and mimicry into the story. He rejects Aristotle's autotelic motive (imitation as intrinsically pleasurable) on the one hand, and such anthropomorphic motives as idolatry and *ressentiment,* on the other. "I repeat: there was no allure in imitating humans; I imitated them to find a way out, and for no other reason" (*RA,* 153). In Nietzsche's protoexistential ethic, the ape's other alternatives to finding "a way out," either submitting to captivity and domestication or attempting suicidal flight, would have been more acceptable "weak" and "strong" responses, respectively. But Kafka had the ape choose adaptation precisely to demonstrate Nietzsche's pessimistic Darwinism: that the genesis of reason in human evolution signifies not progress but decadence. Becoming human, the *sapiens* acquired by the ape takes the form of wily intelligence, an originally "doubled" rationality, a linguistic and rhetorical (rather than integumentary) camouflage.

In a mimetic gesture learned from his masters ("The first thing I learned was the handshake" [*RA,* 148]), the ape perjures himself at the outset by pledging openness and candor to the academy. Indeed, he will deliver to them what passes for honesty or "truth" among humans: imitable gestures like the handshake itself. But for the ape, as for Kafka, truth appears to be defined precisely as that which is inimitable, namely, physical pain. "Seen from a primitive point of view, the only real, incontestable truth, undistorted by external factors (martyrdom, sacrifice for another human being) is corporal pain."[8] Only traces of this truth (the ape's pain) remain in the form of the scars on cheek and thigh, and their exhibition in the face of modesty ("Everything lies open and above board; nothing is to be concealed; when it comes to truth, every highminded person discards even the finest manners" [*RA,* 149]) costs the ape the censorship of the fastidious reporter. According to Nietzsche, pain inaugurates memory, reason, and defensive duplicity in the human animal. The ape's animal past may therefore be engulfed in amnesia precisely because it was happy, while the painful experiences of his capture are simultaneously remembered and cleverly dissembled to avoid further pain. "Without question, the actual *effect* of punishment must be sought in the sharpening of wits, in the improvement of memory, in a desire to proceed henceforth more carefully, suspiciously, and secretly, in the recognition that one is ultimately too weak for many things, in a kind of improved self-judgment" (3, *GM,* 270).

The ape's narration exhibits these effects in the use of an impressive repertoire of rhetorical strategies designed to serve a series of overdetermined functions. The ape will have his cake and eat it too. From his masters he has learned how to use "doubled" language to reveal and conceal, affirm and deny, flatter and denigrate, all at once. For example, he can deny, yet affirm, the violence done to him by describing it in purely mechanical terms with all reference to sensation, emotion, or intention deleted: "the site of entry of that shot" (*RA,* 149), "pressed my thumb into the bowl of the pipe" (*RA,* 152), "held the burning pipe to my fur, until it began to smolder" (*RA,* 153). Referring to his scar, he turns the focus from the act of aggression to the act of reportage, emphasizing his own punctilio and sang-froid in describing the infliction of the wound: "the scar caused by—let us choose a specific word for a specific purpose, to avoid being misunderstood—the scar caused by a wanton shot" (*RA,* 149).

This device is part of a larger strategy of shifting indignation from the attack on his body to attacks on his pride, a form of indignation more acceptable in an artiste with "the average education of a European" (*RA,* 154). Rotpeter therefore forgives or exonerates the tormenting sailors, whose brutishness he softens ("They are good people, in spite of everything. . . . Their jests were coarse, but hearty. . . . Their laughter was always mixed with a menacing, but ultimately harmless, cough" [*RA,* 150–51]), and whose cruelties he overlooks (they clearly give him the lit pipe in hopes that he will burn himself), neutralizes (he points out that the sailor both ignites and extinguishes the fire on his fur) or inflates with philosophical motives ("He wanted to solve the enigma of my being" [152]). His rage is vented instead on the journalist who wounds his vanity *as a human* (by imputing a residual bestiality to the ape) and toward whom he adopts a punitive posture that mimics his own oppressors. "That fellow

Darwin, Nietzsche, and Kafka

should have every little finger of his writing hand blasted away, one by one" (*RA*, 149). Using a similar series of displacements, he shifts his outrage from the pain and disfigurement of the wound that scars his face to the name it earned him, Rotpeter, Red Peter. The shift preserves a certain logic insofar as the name signifies him as a victim of both physical and psychological imperialism (scarred *and* named by the human), a logic he nonetheless undercuts by deploring the name as a blow to his "human" vanity in insufficiently distinguishing him from another performing ape. Identifying himself with the human, he prefers to publicize an injured sensibility over an injured body, a name in bad taste over a shot in the face.

As part of Rotpeter's devious strategy of narrating his victimization as a triumph, he resorts to a technique of appropriating violence to art and science, that is, to culture and reason. The technique depends on covertly inflating and deflating the same event. For example, he begins by describing his evolution as the successful advancement of an artistic protégé by dedicated impresarios, "part-ways accompanied by superb people, advice, applause, and orchestral music" (*RA*, 147). His later shipboard narrative retains the shape of the artistic experience: the "training" in schnapps drinking with theory and praxis, the festive debut before officer and men to the tune of the gramophone "orchestral music," the triumphant gesture of flinging away the empty bottle "no longer as one in despair, but as an artist" (*RA*, 153). At the same time, it decodes the "superb people" as the brutish sailors—slow, dumb, spitting, grunting, smoking, guzzling, guffawing—their good advice as their teasing and goading, and their applause as their sadistic approval of his fear, confusion, and pain. Rotpeter manipulates the audience by means of an ambiguity inherent in the artistic performance: apes imitating humans (Rotpeter's act) and humans imitating apes (the arboreal swinging of the trapeze artists) represent both trained artists and disciplined animals. If he chooses to tell his story of the taming of the beast as a portrait of the artist, it is to achieve a complex set of aims. He can indict humans for cruelty without offending them by supplying them with the cultural and rational motives consistent with the self-congratulatory vanity that allowed post-Darwinian man to consider himself the pinnacle of creation. At the same time he transforms himself from mistreated animal to disciplined artist merely by bartering pity for applause.

The ape's initial artistic achievement finally consists of imitating humans as animalistic and passional creatures, that is, their spitting, smoking, drinking, and rubbing their bellies with gratification, a set of behavioral gestures only arbitrarily distinguished from the ape's own scratching, flea hunting, coconut licking, or head banging. Clearly, then, the ape's performance before the scientific academy requires a performance different in kind, not just in degree. Specifically, in order to qualify as a scientific report, Rotpeter's narration must imitate the human as a rational, objective, analytical creature capable of suppressing passion, emotion, desire, and self-interest. He consequently analyzes his civilizing process in terms of its effectiveness, even concluding his description of his cruel confinement in the crushing box by explaining, "One considers such confinement of wild animals in the beginning to have advantages, and today, after my experience, I cannot deny that from the human point of view this is actually the case" (RA, 149). He assumes here the ultimately sadistic posture of the scientist who rationalizes a deliberate apathy toward the pain and suffering of his experimental animals by subordinating it to a higher purpose. The ape further aggrandizes himself by attributing his progress to the development of scientific and rational powers of mind, rather than to a survival instinct, that is, the powers of objectivity (the inward calm he learns from the sailors), his powers of observation, and his skill at inductive modes of reasoning.

The report to the academy is the most brilliant of the ape's mimetic performances, for it is theater in which the violence is rational, and it consists in its own negation of violence. The ape's suave, eloquent disavowal of his own pain and suffering is the mimetic posture of the trained animal subjected to portraying both the sadist and the masochist according to Deleuze's characterization of those postures (see chapter 5). The ape mimics the rational violence of the sadist when he negates his victim's pain with the language of objectivity, apathy, and with the patently fraudulent rhetoric of the scientific demonstration. He mimics the aesthetic violence of the masochist when he situates his pain in the context of art, and he disavows his own role in the theatrical performance of the scientist. "Furthermore, I desire no one's judgment; I wish only to disperse knowledge; I only report, to you too, exalted gentlemen of the academy; I have only reported" (RA, 155).

This scholarly pose is merely another version (with rational and rhetorical rather than behavioral and gestural tricks) of Rotpeter's variety stage act. But how does its theatrical nature manifest itself

Darwin, Nietzsche, and Kafka

in the narration? By a lapsus, a wince, an almost involuntary betrayal. "By day I do not want to see her," he says of his chimpanzee mate, "for she has the madness of the bewildered tamed animal in her eye; only I recognize it, and I cannot bear it" (*RA,* 154). This admission attests to an identification that gives us a glimpse at a mask behind the mask: Rotpeter is to the academy as the chimpanzee is to him. Does he flinch because he identifies with her as victim or because he recognizes himself as her victimizer? Either way, his reaction contains an important lesson: to wince is to look away. If his audience flinches, they will not see him and he will fail as a performer and lose his *Ausweg,* his way out. He must therefore not only camouflage himself as a nonvictim (by concealing his own insane, bewildered look in the aforementioned ways) but he must also camouflage his audience as nonvictimizers in his imitation of them.

Ultimately, the ape's report to the academy is classical theater insofar as it is a performance that pretends not to be a performance, that "forgets" the stage and, to use Derrida's formulation, functions as "a mark of cancellation that lets what it covers be read."[9] Kafka further creates a "reversion of texts"[10] by manipulating his readers' response to the narration, to imitate the academy's putative response to the report. Like the academy, we interpret the narration as opaque rather than transparent (we fail to "see through" it) and we practice suspension of disbelief toward the performance. Allegorical readings of Kafka ("Kafka, like Swift, implies that man is a beast"[11]) interpret the ape as representing man, as symbolizing man, but not as imitating man. The distinction is crucial because, by attributing a textual strategy to the author but not to the ape, we fall into the anthropocentric trap prepared for us.

Kafka's philosophical aim is to devalue and deprivilege reason, an enterprise that places him in the critical tradition of Darwin, Nietzsche, and Freud. He shares with them the conviction that historical change, in nations, individuals, ideas, or species, is propelled by neither intellect nor imagination, but by physiological and psychological necessity. Reason and art play brilliant but mediated roles in this process by virtue of their instrumentality, their tendency to be used in the production of signification, and, particularly, of multiple signification, of "doubled" talk, of lies, and illusions. Kafka engages the reader's interpretive abilities to make the acute point that the human reader can claim to be truly *sapiens* only when he recognizes that he has been outwitted by an ape using his own most cherished attributes.

Beasts of the Modern Imagination

4
Nietzsche's *Ecce Homo*:
Behold the Beast

Nietzsche's *Ecce Homo* is not only an "act" (as Michael Ryan has ably discussed),[1] but, I will argue, an animal act, a bestial gesture, intentionally subversive of its anthropocentric title. As subject and object, speaker and audience of this ontological interrogation of himself, Nietzsche both vindicates and emulates Pilate in his attempts to demythify the Messiah and clear away the ambiguity of the false doubles: "Hear me! I am such and such. Above all, do not confuse me with another!" (3, *EH*, 511). But the man thus revealed is not the spectacle of suffering, the exhibit of mortal vulnerability offered to arouse the pity of the rabble. Nietzsche, as ever, scorns the spectacle in the interest of penetrating the body's mysterious processes, to throb to the pulse and warm to the currents of the blood coursing into the mysterious heart of organic *life*. On his forty-fourth birthday, then, at the peak of his intellectual maturity and notoriety, Nietzsche offers us his physiological autobiography, his portrait—no, demonstration—of the philosopher as *Naturwesen*. This bestial gesture informs the mysterious rhetorical play of the work that destroys the conventional relationship between author and reader. If the animal is truly autotelic, living from and by and for itself in an oblivion of the "other," beyond the reach of the consciousness, recognition, and judgment of the "other," then Nietzsche as a creatural writer and philosopher must negate his audience and rehabilitate his own polemical motives to serve purely self-reflexive ends. "And so I tell my life to myself" (3, *EH*, 515). Like Pilate, who denied Messianic authority when he foreclosed an answer by posing, What is truth? as a purely rhetorical question, Nietzsche enforces a distinction between authority and power in his aggressive polemic. Authority has reference both to truth and to the "other"; power has reference only to itself. *Ecce Homo* is Nietzsche's anti-Messianic exercise of animal vigor.

In this enterprise Nietzsche must counter and reverse all the normal psychological and literary strategies of autobiography.[2]

73

His animal "act" must have a spontaneity and unselfconsciousness that sets it apart from the self-dramatizations of confessional literature, as well as from their denial in sincere, "natural," and self-effacing postures. Nietzsche, who argues that repression and censorship inevitably mark the site of truth (3, *EH,* 512), uses an exaggerated boastfulness to restore explicitness to the brutal self-interest behind much modest autobiographical self-examination: "Why I am so wise," "Why I am so clever," "Why I write such good books," "Why I am a destiny." To mistake this braggadocio for vanity would erroneously impute to Nietzsche a laughable rhetorical naïveté that overlooks his transparently mischievous intention. He knows that his tone will repel his readers and abort any possibility of aggrandizing his philosophical reputation. But oblivious to the response of the "other," he discharges his high animal spirits in the very flamboyance of his expression, in the reckless transgression of good manners and modesty, in the exuberant childishness of the diction. Nietzsche calculates no return on his discourse; it is a deliberate throwing away of talent, a squandering of wit, like the style of *Zarathustra* itself ("Till then no one will grasp the artistry that was wasted here" [3, *EH,* 550]).

Whereas conventional biography treats the self as a cultural product, a nexus of genius and *Bildung,* Nietzsche's exploration of the natural etiology of his being reduces even his parents to purely genetic prototypes, to proleptic models of his own biological fate. "I have, to express it in riddle, already died as my father; as my mother I am still alive and will grow old" (3, *EH,* 516). His negation of cultural influence, both received and exerted, guarantees his originality and individualism, a claim beyond egotism since it lodges his creativity in the blind, animal genius of his organism. This, then, is the fiction upon which *Ecce Homo* is founded: the fiction of Nietzsche as a child of Nature, discovering his body, his instincts, his physiology experientially by creatively working through his illnesses and convalescences without benefit of book learning or scientific theorizing. That his physiological, vitalistic approach itself is inevitably derivative of Darwinian discoveries[3] is a truth appropriated by another animal gesture—a kind of "forgetting"—that, unlike repression, does not turn truth into a pathogen but allows it to exert its effects naturally, instinctively, unconsciously. Yet we can find in Nietzsche's early works the complex concatenation of influences (for example, idealistic appropriations of Darwinian

theory) that he had to "overcome" in a kind of Zarathustran
Überwindung.

Another version of his denial of cultural influence, and
related to it, is Nietzsche's fear of being mistaken for another or
confused with a false double. Unless its action of biological
"overcoming" is perceived, this fear of misunderstanding might
easily be misconstrued as an all too human concession to vanity
and regard for public opinion. But Nietzsche seeks neither to
protect the credulity of his disciples (as does Christ) nor to control the fidelity of his reputation. Rather, something ontological
is at stake for him: the danger of attenuated being that comes
with appropriation by an "other," akin to animal adaptation or
domestication, a danger that must be countered offensively
rather than defensively. His most dangerous "doubles" are controversial and notorious figures like himself, ostensible heretics
who are, paradoxically, no more than sheep in wolves' (or apes')
clothing: Charles Darwin, for example ("other academic oxen
[*Hornvieh*] have suspected me of Darwinism," [3, *EH,* 547]),
and even, implicitly, David Strauss, whose misappropriation of
Darwin ("With a certain coarse contentment he cloaks himself
in the hairy dress of our ape-genealogist and promotes Darwin as
one of the greatest benefactors of mankind" [1, *UM,* 167])
he excoriates in *Untimely Meditations.* Nietzsche's attack on
Strauss's disguised humanism obscures the genuinely iconoclastic impact of Strauss's mythopoeic New Testament criticism (*Das
Leben Jesu,* which cost him his theological chair at the University
of Zurich) as well as the proleptic relationship of Strauss's last
confession (*Der Alte und der Neue Glaube*[4]) to *Ecce Homo.* The
physiologism of Nietzsche's autobiography could well be mistaken for the scientific materialism of Strauss's book.

Nietzsche's physiologism (the referral of all of his actions,
attributes, and achievements to his living body) is perhaps *sui
generis,* if we allow for its circular origin in his psychological
appropriation of his own *Bildung.* He does conduct in *Ecce
Homo* (as in his earlier works) a radical Darwinian critique in
accordance with his own early exhortation of David Strauss ("His
task should rather have been to draw out and seriously explain
the phenomena of goodness, mercy, love, and self-abnegation,
actually at hand, from his Darwinistic premises" [1, *UM,* 168]).
But he does so in action, not in words, thereby correcting
another Straussian fault: "He cannot muster an aggressive
action, only aggressive words" (1, *UM,* 167). From his early

Nietzsche's Ecce Homo

admiration in his letter of 4 August 1877 to Malwida von Meysenbug, in which Darwin, as contributor to *Mind,* is counted among the "philosophical greats" and "authorities" of English intellectual life (4, *PW,* 732), to the later insults of Darwin's exactitude and diligence as marks of intellectual mediocrity (3, *BGE,* 165), Nietzsche's critique of Darwin is governed by a discernible logic: he consistently attacks the putative power of the environment in Darwin's theory. "The influence of 'external conditions' is ridiculously *overestimated* by Darwin: the essence of the life process is precisely the monstrously formative, from the inside creative power, that uses and exploits 'external circumstances'" (4, *PW,* 481). This explains such apparent contradictions as Nietzsche's argument for the deep effects of adaptation and the superficial effects of domestication, an argument that makes sense only if adaptation is granted a genetic and domestication an environmental origin. But even if, arguably, Nietzsche is here guilty of a *méconnaissance* of Darwin's quasi-vitalistic premises, it permits him the act of appropriating to himself the radical residue of Darwinian theory (the primacy of irrational, unconscious power as the source of the organism's life, behavior, and knowledge) while extruding the optimistic, progressive, humanistic, and utilitarian "Darwin." Nietzsche thereby acts out his own will to power: his organism knows and does what it is fated to know and do (with or without Darwinian theory), creating from the inside, while Darwin is exploited and discarded as a mere environmental factor.

Nietzsche's quarrel with Darwin is less over the "facts" of natural selection than over their interpretation, a hermeneutical dispute that, if cast into aesthetic categories as a conflict between a tragic and a comic view of nature, helps not only to identify the affective impetus behind Nietzsche's anti-Darwinism, but also "naturalizes" the cultural terms by exploring their biological resonances. "Fundamental errors of biologists to date: it is not a question of species, but of more strongly effective individuals. (The many are only a means.) Life is *not* the adaptation of internal needs to external ones, but a will to power, which from the inside increasingly subjects and appropriates [*einverleibt*] the 'external'" (4, *PW,* 490). Nietzsche critiques Darwinian Nature as imbued with a utilitarian bias, as a comic universe whose survival and perpetual reintegration is effected by the expulsion of the misfits and weaklings who dilute the strength and welfare of the racial and social group. To Nietzsche, then, the environment, the species, numbers, the "other," are all mediating factors ("die Vielen sind nur Mittel") in several senses of the term: they are inserted into the organism's natural play of power and instinct and require it to behave reactively or defensively, and by obliging the organism to compromise its power and desire vis-à-vis the exigencies of environment, group, or "other," they cause it to become average and mediocre. Nietzsche construes Darwin as interpreting this state of affairs optimistically, while he himself views it as the tragedy of the powerful individual, the hero, the passionate organism destroyed by its own greatest qualities (its aggressiveness, its libidinal excess, its wild courage, its lonesome pride) in order that the mediocre *niveau* might live. Like all hermeneutical disputes, this one hinges on a question of value, and Nietzsche leaves to Darwin the conservative values of comedy, with its preservation of the status quo, while arrogating to himself the dangerous profligacy of the tragic.

> "Useful" [*nützlich*] in the sense of Darwinian biology means: to prove itself advantageous in the fight with others. But I would consider the feeling of excess [*Mehrgefühl*], the feeling of becoming stronger, quite apart from its usefulness in battle, as the actual *progress*: the will to fight originates in these feelings. 'Useful' in relation to accelerating the tempo of development is different from "useful" in relation to the greatest security and permanence of the developed organism. (4, *PW*, 487)

Although Darwin does not reckon with the mediation of lacks, gaps, and deficiencies as a producer of culture, Darwin and Nietzsche both believe in the vitalistic continuity of Nature and culture, a belief with inevitable self-reflexive implications for the irrational basis of their own intellectual endeavors. For Nietzsche, his research into the natural genesis of all forms of cultural life (note his titles, "The *Birth* of Tragedy," "The *Genealogy* of Morals") required a methodological innovation he called "backward inference" ("jene schwierigste und verfänglichste Form des Rückschlusses") "from the work to its creator, from the deed to the doer, from the ideal to the one who *needs it,* from every way of thinking and valuing to the governing desideratum behind it" (2, *GS*, 519). In exploring the intellectual heritage of learned individuals, Nietzsche argues that occupational and environmental conditions became internalized in those unfit to overcome them ("the form of the paternal occupation became their content" [2, *GS*, 488]) and were genetically transmitted to their scholarly progeny. Clerks and secretaries therefore produced scholars limited to a barren schematizing. But the best medical doctors are the sons of medical doctors, like Nietzsche's personal physician, Dr. Eiser ("I have much regard for the *born* physicians" [Nietzsche to Malwida von Meysenbug, 4 August 1877, 4, *PW,* 732]). Along the same line, Nietzsche dismisses those aspects of Darwinian theory he most abjures— the Malthusian premise of scarce resources and the primacy of the ensuing struggle for survival—as the symptoms of an impoverished and plebeian ancestry. "All English Darwinism is enveloped in something like the suffocating air of overpopulation, like the smell of little people in need and tight straits" (2, *GS,* 489). Never mind that Charles Darwin, married to a Wedgwood pottery heiress from his own family, raised ten children on a spacious, airy estate in rural England. Nietzsche discounts present environmental factors in favor of genetic predisposition.

Ecce Homo is an application of Nietzsche's "backward inference" to himself and his philosophizing, and both his motives and his methods are biocentric, giving biological play to his organism while explaining its biological and psychological constitution. He thereby fulfills the function of the "philosophical physician" he had called for years before, in *The Gay Science,* who dares to say, "All philosophizing to date has been a matter not at all of 'truth,' but of something else entirely, let us say health, future, growth, power, life" (2, *GS,* 286). It is, therefore, not his authority as a philosopher that he aims to establish in *Ecce Homo* but his *fitness* to philosophize, an ultimately medical fitness in a broad sense of the term: a demonstration of organic and instinctual soundness, of aggressiveness and courage, of vitalistic excess and exuberance. "In this one it is his deficiencies that philosophize, in another his riches and strengths" (2, *GS,* 284). A valid comprehension of the body can be guaranteed only by a fine biological condition, a health organically and instinctually won: not by the theoretical and abstract knowledge of the scientific doctor, but by the inner, experiential knowing of the animal, the affective, intuitive gay science that might heal the nearly fatal errors of the old philosophy. "And often enough I have asked myself if, taken in a broad sense, philosophy to date has only been an interpretation of the body, and a *misunderstanding of the body*" (2, *GS,* 285).[5]

Ecce Homo is Nietzsche's assertion of the health and power behind his "wisdom," "cleverness," and "ability to write such good books," an assertion that in the aggressiveness of its impudence transcends mere posturing to function as a living demonstration of a strong constitution. But in order for the human to "become what one is," namely, a robust *Naturwesen*, it must be governed by a comprehensive physiological, psychological, and cultural hygiene that insures that the organism's every action is stimulated from the inside and flows from its will to power. Nietzsche's task is to make this hygiene explicit, not as a kindness or help to his readers and followers but as a Zarathustran gift, which is to say, a self-reflexive gift motivated only by the giver's need to discharge his excess riches, his superfluous good health, his opulent happiness. Neither does *Ecce Homo,* therefore, function as a hygiene manual, because its example and advice are inimitable, cannot be copied or learned, and, therefore, function in neither an exemplary nor advisory fashion. Nonetheless it is offered, albeit for Nietzsche's, not our benefit: a comprehensive grounding in the physiological basis of Nietzschean philosophy, from diet, climate, and manners, to discourse, rhetoric, and style.

In exploring the bestial gesture of *Ecce Homo,* I hope to demonstrate the grammatical collapse of its title, in which the putative object, the human or "man" on exhibit, is the same as the one commanding our attention, the "man" in the act of exhibiting or displaying. Nietzsche's imperative rhetoric therefore resonates with a recursive syntax: "Look at me telling you to look at me telling you to look at me telling you. . . ." Interpreted further, to focus its circular activity more precisely, it might read as, "I want you to look at me not because I want to see myself reflected in your eyes, but because I enjoy the power in the activity of telling you to look at me. . . ." In this action is demonstrated the *Übermensch,* whom I interpret as a recuperated animal, an animal "recovered" in both related senses of the word: as a human creature cured of its pathogenic culture and vitally reclaimed by its instinctual nature. But this human "becoming what one is" requires a series of animal acts, that, for the writer, include such literary (or perhaps antiliterary) strategies as "forgetting" the figurative meanings of metaphors, allegories, and parables, and restoring to them their repressed, literal, or bodily sense and their exuberant dithyrambic affect. Nietzsche had already performed these acts in *Thus Spake Zarathustra,* a work with a privileged place in *Ecce Homo* and in the Nietzschean *oeuvre* ("Within my writings, my *Zarathustra* stands for itself" [3, *EH,* 512]), and attention to the interplay between the mythopoeia and demythification, the poetic and

Nietzsche's Ecce Homo

critical practice of these works will shed further light on Nietzsche's biomorphic literary enterprise. "Have I been understood? I have finally uttered no word that I might not have already spoken five years ago through the mouth of Zarathustra" (3, *EH*, 604).

I will proceed to explore the five sections of *Ecce Homo* (Preface, "Why I Am So Wise," "Why I Am So Clever," "Why I Write Such Good Books," "Why I Am a Destiny") in order, albeit with occasional reference to *Zarathustra*, because they do represent an elaboration of Nietzschean physiology into increasingly complex forms of behavior, social relations, and cultural problems. I will take the content of the work seriously, and *literally*, while treating it as the production of the ontological and stylistic gestures that are my major interest. I hope to show in this exploration, as throughout this work, that the textual expressions of the animal and its physiology are as varied, interesting, and instructive as the literature of the spiritual life of cultural man. And, finally, I will remain mindful of my own negated position as a critic, confronting a text beyond interpretation, whose yield of "meaning" remains irrelevant to the "act" that constitutes it. Reading *Ecce Homo* is like listening to a lion roaring in the wilderness.

The preface of *Ecce Homo* mirrors the crisis shaping Nietzsche's soul in the three months preceding his complete collapse in the Piazza Carlo Alberto in Turin. I am not thereby taking sides in the fierce, expert debate over the etiology and timing of Nietzsche's illness[6] and its implication for the philosophical validity of the indisputably brilliant 1888 productions: *Der Fall Wagner, Der Anti-Christ, Dionysos-Dithyramben, Götzendämmerung, Nietzsche Contra Wagner,* and *Ecce Homo*. The preface (which actually consists of two prefaces or distinct sections, and which functions, synecdochically, as a preface to a preface, since *Ecce Homo* is itself treated as a prologue to a greater work) is of a divided and doubled nature, which I find symptomatic of Nietzsche's strategy for protecting the integrity of his enterprise by dealing physiologically with his increasingly complex role (real or imagined) as a cultural phenomenon. In the first preface he announces the misunderstandings threatened by his growing impact, influence, and fame; in the second he neutralizes these problems by treating his personal and literary success as a natural, organic ripening ("Not only the grape is turning brown" [3, *EH*, 515]), a physiological fulfillment ("I am now the most grateful man in the world—of an *autumnal* mind [*herbstlich* gesinnt] in every good sense of the word: it is my great *harvest time*" [Letter to Franz Overbeck, 18 October 1888, 4, *PW*, 915]).

The two prefaces reflect the most conspicuous emotional features of Nietzsche's correspondence during that fateful Turin autumn: his megalomania on the one hand ("In two years we shall have the whole earth in convulsions. . . . In two months I shall be the first name on earth. . . . I will from now on rule the world" [4, *PW*, 926–38]), and his exuberant health and happiness on the other. There are indisputable somatic links between them, regardless of the diagnosis, since both delusions of grandeur and a delirium of manic well-being could be symptomatic of all three major contenders: tertiary syphilis, schizophrenia, and cannabis addiction.[7] However, they function as perfectly plausible expressions of an illimitable will to power, provided that the egotism of the first does not betray Nietzsche to the social mediations that enthrall him to the power of the "other" and deliver him to the insidious hypocrisies of a Messianic role. Nietzsche's resistance to the blandishments of vanity was not perfect; stung by his sister's brutal insult that he was famous only among riffraff and Jews ("like Georg Brandes" [4, *PW*, 937]), he exaggerated Brandes's list of Nietzschean disciples into an admiring cortege of select aristocrats and geniuses. But even in this childishly boastful letter to his mother (written at Turin 21 December 1888, shortly before his collapse) he begins to neutralize his vain enthrallment by erasing all mediations of his success ("You see, that is the masterstroke: without name, without rank, without riches, I am here treated like a little prince" [4, *PW*, 935]) and by claiming the real or imagined homage he receives not for his philosophy, his books, or his ideas but for himself, as a person, as a distinctly noble creature. In his correspondence with Peter Gast, to whom Schlechta attributes responsibility for the markedly scientific bent of the late Nietzschean output (5, Appendix, 97), Nietzsche transforms the homage of underlings from recognition and respect into something almost like the spoils of the hunt and the battle offered to the ruling lion by his pride. "Without question, I receive in my *trattoria* the best-tasting bites [*die besten Bissen*][8] they have: they are always recommending the most successful dishes. Between us, I have never known until today what it means to eat with a hearty appetite, likewise what I need to maintain my powers" (Nietzsche to Peter Gast, 30 October 1888, 4, *PW*, 918). Where earlier he had playfully wondered if someone was

Nietzsche's Ecce Homo

bribing service personnel to treat him well, he now implicitly refuses to attribute the excellent service to his excessive tipping; conversely, he tips not for better service, but because his largesse flows from his bounteous nature. The economic reciprocities are repressed in favor of maintaining the fiction of a natural homage tendered to a natural aristocrat.

The prefatory function both of the *Vorwort* and of *Ecce Homo* as a whole is in no sense a mere formality or convention. As the word before his own word, the words that precede his utterance, the Nietzschean preface is deliberately tautological, superfluous, excessive, an excrescence or lagniappe, like the tips dispersed to the waiters and vendors of Turin. His preface fills no gap in his writing and augments no lack of explanation or defect of clarity. In relation to his own work, past and future, *Ecce Homo* represents a doubling, a kind of spontaneous repetition motivated more by the pleasure of the activity that by any hermeneutical necessity. Nietzsche will argue in "Why I Write Such Good Books" for the interchangeability of his works and concepts. "In every psychologically decisive place the text deals only with me: one may carelessly substitute my name, or the word *Zarathustra* there where the text gives the word *Wagner*" (3, *EH,* 558). But the Nietzschean preface functions as *Vorwort* also in a second sense, not only as word before Nietzsche's own word, but also as the word before the word of "others," for example, the readers of various sympathies and self-interest who will respond to his word. In this sense, the temporal component of the preface, its precedence or coming *before,* defines Nietzsche's gesture as appropriative, as he preempts or takes the critical ground as his own and thereby banishes the "other" (readers, critics, disciples) before they arrive on the scene and in advance of their utterance. Timing is crucial in Nietzschean conduct, in which the only genuine act is the preemptive act, the action "before the action of the other"; Nietzsche acts rather than *re*acts, fends rather than *de*fends, and moves spontaneously rather than mimetically.

Both prefaces of *Ecce Homo* function to banish the "other" as object, recipient, beneficiary, or target of the work, and of Nietzsche's philosophy as a whole. The first preface does so by stating its denial explicitly. "No 'prophet' speaks here. . . . No fanatic speaks here. . . . No one 'preaches' here, no 'faith' is demanded here" (3, 513); the "other" is evoked only in the context of its revocation. The second preface demonstrates its denial by simply omitting all reference to the "other." The terms of cultural relations and exchanges that emerge in both prefaces—obligation (*Pflicht*), gratitude ("How could I not be thankful to my entire life?" [3, 515]), the gift—are all emptied of their function in social reciprocity or symbolic exchange and are instead endowed with circular, self-reflexive, physiological functions. Nietzsche's *Pflicht* dramatizes, according to Michael Ryan, "the necessity of affirming, by submitting oneself to, the power of fate, instinct, physiology."[9] Nietzsche's gratitude to his life is merely an unmotivated discharge of excessive gladness, an emotional overflow without a recipient or a purpose beyond achieving affective relief. And the gift of Nietzsche's thought, particularly *Zarathustra* ("With it I made humankind the greatest gift that has ever been made to it") is a gift stripped of all reciprocal function, of all economic motive, of all mediative power and social utility. Nietzsche restores his word to Nature by transforming it, like Zarathustra's teaching, into a fated, inevitable, organic foison, a wild autumnal harvest shed indiscriminately upon the unembarrassed and ungrateful creatures of the wild.

> Figs fall from the trees, they are good and sweet: and as they fall, their red skin tears open. I am an arctic wind to ripe figs.
> So, like figs, these teachings fall to you, my friends: now drink their juice and eat their sweet flesh! It is autumn hereabouts and pure sky and afternoon. (3, *EH*, 513)

Nietzschean rhetoric, then, is also emptied of its social, instrumental, and strategic function. *Ecce Homo* is delivered in the rhetoric of bounty; it is a harvest celebration, a thanksgiving prayer, a blessing that, like Zarathustra's curse (with its violent eruption of thunder and lightning)[10] is nontriangular and nonreciprocal. It is not a Te Deum, a spiritual discourse with God or with a personified Nature, in which organic gifts and the speech of thanks function as symbolic gestures of mediation. "*How could I not be grateful to my entire life? And so I tell my life to myself*" (3, *EH*, 515). Here, as in *Zarathustra*, the soliloquy fulfills less a psychological than an ontological function, of defining the speaker as a self-generating organism. The genesis of discourse in Nietzschean thought is therefore grounded not only in the metaphor of the gift but also in specifically natural metaphors and analogies of self-generation, fertility, and overflowing. Zarathustra, in his aubadelike opening, squanders his blessing on a sun that is fated only to give, never to receive, and

Nietzsche's Ecce Homo

whose perpetual self-generation stands for him in ontological contrast to the reflective, mediated moon with its borrowed light (as it later does for D. H. Lawrence).

> For ten years you've come up here to my cave: you would have become glutted with your light and tired of your path but for me, my eagle, and my snake.
> But we awaited you every morning, relieved you of your excess and blessed you for it. See! I am glutted with my wisdom, like a bee that has gathered too much honey; I need hands stretched out to me. (2, Z, 551)

In *Ecce Homo* Nietzsche likewise presents himself as a producer of harvest (not a reaper), that is, as a Nature. The perpetual wellspring and the eternal waterfall serve as other Nietzschean metaphors of the self-generating discourse. "I have become mouth entirely and totally, and the rushing of a brook from tall cliffs: I want to crash my speech down into the valleys" (2, Z, 616). Elsewhere the need to discharge his excess is given the particularly physiological exigency of fertility ("But his wisdom grew and caused him pain with its fulness" [2, Z, 615]) although the implicit bovine metaphor of swollen udders is suppressed.[11]

Nietzsche, aware that metaphors themselves function as media of exchange in the cultural economy of meaning and communication, strips his metaphors as much as possible of their symbolic value. "Autumn," in *Ecce Homo,* is such a one, its layers of abstract significance peeled back to a primary reference, a literal residue, a "fact," a biological truth. The preface to *Ecce Homo* was written in autumn of 1888, and its "now" *was* the fall of the year. It was written on Nietzsche's birthday, 15 October, making the biological Nietzsche himself an autumnal product, brought forth at the time of organic ripening and fruition, harvested with the wheat. In refutation of the conservative significance of the birthday as a symbolic event—a celebration of survival, of longevity, of the quantitative accumulation of years—Nietzsche celebrates the vitality of his perpetual "now." "Not in vain did I today bury my forty-fourth year; I *could* bury it: what was life in it is saved, is immortal" (3, *EH,* 515). But that this indestructible residue of his life must not be construed as the immortality of fame is attested by Nietzsche's Dionysian dithyramb, "Ruhm und Ewigkeit," written in the same autumn as *Ecce Homo.*

This coin, with which
The whole world pays,
Fame;
I grasp this coin with gloves
And trample it in disgust.
(3, 707)

Nietzsche implicitly contrasts the reciprocal and triangular economy of prestige ("You invite a witness when you want to speak
well of yourselves; and when you have seduced him into thinking well of you, then you think well of yourselves" [2, *Z*, 598])
with the direct and unilinear economy of nonaltruistic giving,
the highest "virtue." For that, Nietzsche invokes a complex
metaphor of gold stripped of its symbolic, anthropomorphic,
endowed value to stand as an unappropriated natural object,
"rare, useless, with a shining and mild glow; it gives itself" (2,
Z, 610). The "value" of *Ecce Homo,* too, I believe, is meant to
be that of gold found in Nature, self-radiating whether read or
unread.

In his first investigation, "Why I Am So Wise," we see how
neatly Nietzsche's argumentative strategy outstrips his explanations to serve as demonstration or dramatization of his "wisdom." By rights, that is, by any conventional logic, Nietzsche's
chronic, debilitating ill health, which forced him on pension at
the age of thirty-five, should be an excruciating embarrassment
for someone who believes that wisdom is the organism's successful struggle for physiological and instinctual health. But it is
precisely Nietzsche's refusal to be embarrassed, along with his
refusal to deny, minimize, circumvent, or defend the problem,
that dramatizes his triumph, his appropriation and exploitation
of his illness. Nietzsche thereby *enacts* his complex and consistent theory of the automedical process and its epistemological
consequence, his *Kranken-Optik,* a short-lived tour de force that
succumbed to the impending ravages of his physical and mental
breakdown but nonetheless withstands the denigrating psychoanalysis of such clinicians as Max Kesselring, who patronizingly
puts Nietzsche, with his entire philosophy, in his psychotic place
in an anthropocentric, moralistic, rationalistic medical model.
"The mistrust against everything that he formerly revered in
himself and in others, this mixture of scorn, jaundice, disgust,
shame, wilfulness and relish in wilfulness, the aimless quest in a
desert and, simultaneously, the effort, amplified by a powerful
ambition, to reverse *all* values—are these 'drives' toward the

Nietzsche's Ecce Homo

'establishment' of a new philosophy not in themselves proof of a 'Diseased-Optic' at work, even if Nietzsche had not expressly confirmed this?''[12] Nietzsche's theory of health in *Ecce Homo* is consistent with the remaining *oeuvre* in positing, as wellspring of life, the will to power, that primal appropriative instinct that turns every biological factor and environmental event to its own advantage. Health is the animal's organic work. Rhetorically, Nietzsche begins by appropriating his own genetic history— combining and incarnating the contradictory constitutions of both his parents to *become* them both genetically, and to reca- pitulate in his own body their organic histories. He therefore relives his father's morbidity, reaching an acute medical crisis during his thirty-sixth year, the year of his father's death. "In the same year his life declined, mine declined too: in my thirty- sixth year I reached the lowest point of my vitality; I survived, but without being able to see three steps in front of me. At that time—it was 1879—I gave up my Basel professorship" (3, *EH*, 516). But Nietzsche's medical model, which reflects a precise, modern grasp of the physiological principles of inoculation, treats the mother's sturdy constitution as his legacy of a funda- mental soundness that exploits the father's debility like an immunological serum, becoming strengthened and enriched by it. "From 1882 on, things moved, very slowly, of course, upward once more: the crisis was overcome (my father died very young, exactly in the year in which I myself came closest to death)" (4, *PW*, 879). Strategically, also, Nietzsche has transformed the inauspicious paternal legacy into a triumph worthy of a boast rather than an apology.

Since Nietzschean wisdom is experiential and instinctual, it is a matter of ontology, a knowing equated with being. His double parental heritage therefore makes him doubly wise. "I have a keener nose [*eine feinere Witterung*] for the signs of ascent and descent than anyone else. . . . I know both, I am both" (3, *EH*, 516). Nietzsche's *Doppelgänger* role (3, *EH*, 519) is racial as well as genetic, although the racial and genetic advantages are com- plementary rather than analogous. He proudly claims Polish (*noble* Polish, even, in his *Vita* sent to Georg Brandes [Nietzsche to Brandes, 10 April 1888, 4, *PW*, 877]) ancestry on his father's side and German on his mother's (albeit only as *angesprenkel- ter*, that is, spotted, or polka-dotted, German): another anti- thetical legacy that leaves him wiser as a quasi-foreign critic of German culture who knows, racially, of what he speaks. But Nietzsche is only too sensitive to the paradoxical danger of this doubling: his multiplicity of experience, the reversals of perspective created by his *Kranken-Optik,* his decadent epistemology, all share the drawbacks (as well as the advantages) of the dialectical imagination. In addition to repressing the instinctual in favor of the intellectual, and resulting in conciliatory rather than aggressive argument, Nietzsche fears in dialectic the debilitating effect of yielding advantage in the interest of ethical fairness and some notions of Socratic truth. He himself escapes these dangers by exploiting his morbid insights and experiences in the intuitive pursuit of his physiological advantage. In praxis, this meant a growing retreat from physicians and conventional medicine, from letting himself be doctored (*beärzteln*): "I act like a sick animal in the wild and *hide myself* in my 'cave'" (4, *PW,* 828). Medicine becomes for him a wholly intuitive and internal "science," a matter of instinctively choosing the correct means, of guessing the right remedies, of developing accurate, intuitive principles of selecting a healthy environment, including a healthy cultural environment, society, books, landscape, etc. Strategically, Nietzsche once again claims success: "I took myself in hand, I made myself well again" (3, *EH,* 518).

The action of taking charge of his health, of taking a kind of physiological responsibility for both the causes and cures of his illness, solves Nietzsche's crucial rhetorical problem of devising a way of speaking of his ill health without making an appeal for sympathy and pity. This task is made the more difficult by his determination not to deny or evade the problem of his infirmity, which obliges him to produce graphic, clinical descriptions. "An extremely painful and stubborn headache emerged, which exhausted all my powers. It accelerated over long years to a peak of habitual painfulness, so that that particular year contained for me 200 days of pain. . . . My specialty was to endure extreme pain *cru,vert* [presumably without narcotics] with total clarity, for two or three days in a row, under conditions of prolonged vomica" (Letter to Georg Brandes, 10 April 1888, 4, *PW,* 878). Nietzsche's antidote to self-pity and the pity of others is his animal fatalism about his body, which serves several important functions: it gives him an active, rather than a passive, invalid role and thereby certifies the continued efficacy of his powers, and it denies the lack or weakness that invites the appropriation of the "other" (doctors, relatives, friends). His autotherapy therefore repulses the well-meaning meddling of the "other," thereby not only giving his own remedial instincts a chance to work but actually conserving his strength by preventing its surrender to the "other." He exhibits this strategy in practice by imploring Overbeck (Nietzsche to Overbeck, 22 February 1883) not to betray the address of his lair in Genoa, presumably to escape the solicitous clutches of his sister. "I will seek for my health in the greatest reclusiveness, on the previously tried paths. My mistake, last year, was to *give up* my solitude" (4, *PW,* 794).

The ontological wisdom governing his medical hygiene extends to other potentially embarrassing spheres of Nietzsche's life, particularly his social and professional relationship to others. After years as a controversial figure, during which, if he was recognized at all, it was at best as *enfant terrible,* at worst as madman, Nietzsche was a ripe candidate for *ressentiment,* the debilitating, rancorous enthrallment to an ill-disposed "other" that would not only distort and invalidate his judgments but, more seriously, also undermine his own physiological and temperamental health. Once again he acts out his therapy in his rhetorical strategy. He instinctively produces a social innocence that virtually preempts the effect of the "other" altogether by recognizing little ill will toward himself ("One can turn my life this way and that; one will seldom find, and then only traces, that anyone has ever had 'ill will' [*bösen Willen*] toward me" (3, *EH,* 520), and he thereby pulls out from under himself the ground of a defensive posture. This strategy is so successful that it inadvertently lays a trap for the reader: the tone of mellow equanimity that animates these passages has, to the untrained ear, strong resonances of Christian (which he denies) and Buddhist (which he admits) philosophy. To disentangle these false doubles of Nietzschean fatalism and Christian self-abnegation, one must follow the clew of the motive: when Nietzsche sends good after bad, "a pot of marmalade to get rid of a *sour* business," (3, *EH,* 522), as he puts it, it is neither altruism nor forgiveness but an act of sheer self-serving appropriation.

Nietzsche relates to other people as organism to organism, thereby negating them as the "other," that is, as another consciousness that relates to oneself intersubjectively, as subject with the power to bestow or withhold recognition. He does this with a physiologically appropriate metaphor, by smelling and pawing the other organism to determine whether it is clean enough, wholesome enough, healthy enough, to remain in his company. "I possess a perfectly uncanny irritability of the cleanliness instinct so that I perceive physiologically—*smell*—the proximity—what am I saying?—the innermost parts, the

Beasts of the Modern Imagination

'entrails' of every soul" (3, *EH,* 526). These acutely sensitive instincts preserve him from the pathological contamination of unclean humans, riffraff, *Gesindel.* In the event that he is touched or attacked ("in cases where a little or a *very great* nonsense is started with me"), Nietzsche forecloses all conventional reciprocities, allowing himself neither retaliation, protection, defense, nor justification, all actions that would proceed from a position of disadvantage. Instead, he eschews reaction altogether, if possible, not only in order to retain the initiative, to maintain his freedom of original action, but in order physiologically to preserve the strength of the organism from fruitless erosion by the vexations of revenge. Above all, he avoids a mimetic response, a tit-for-tat reprisal, which would signal a surrender of his activity to the "other's" determination of its form and its nature. This is the rationale of Nietzsche's unconventional satisfactions: the "thanks" or the "request" in response to a mischief, for example.

Nietzsche's most extreme remedy against the disease of *ressentiment,* whose affects "burn" one out, is *"Russian fatalism,* that fatalism without revolt, with which the Russian soldier, for whom the forced march has become unbearable, finally lies down in the snow. . . . The great logic of this fatalism, which is not always the courage to die, as life-preserving under the most life-endangering circumstances, is the reduction of metabolism, its deceleration, a kind of will to hibernation" (3, *EH,* 523). Its oriental counterparts, the catatonia of the eastern fakir and the Buddhist's great inner tranquility ("This is *not* morality speaking; here speaks physiology") are merely variations of the same hygiene: to avoid the ravages of the self-consuming responsive emotions (anger, hypersensitivity) that cause the rapid depletion of nervous energy, the accelerated secretions of excessive bile, and other bodily damage. Nietzsche is careful to distinguish this particular kind of genuine, inner passivity in the face of attack from its false double, the "silent treatment," a mere strategy of feigned indifference and equanimity whose cost to the individual is a painful introjection of rage that upsets the stomach and causes dyspepsia.

Finally, Nietzsche advocates as a healthy and normal mode of human relationship the condition of warfare, but a curious metaphorical warfare reduced to an almost pure animal aggression with all cultural and social content cancelled. Nietzsche's warfare is effectively unmotivated, and with neither ideological nor personal agenda: no cause to promote, no imperiled honor to

Nietzsche's Ecce Homo

defend, no grudge to settle, no personal animus to express. It is without hostility, a sort of joyful exercise of creatural power. To that end his *Kriegs-Praxis* reflects a set of conditions that appear deceptively like rules of fair play, until one notes their perfect self-reflexivity. Since Nietzsche's object is not victory but the exercise of power, he spurns cohorts and consensus in favor of the solo match. Since a true test of strength requires strong, equally matched fighters, he disdains the inferior opponent, who would provide an insufficient challenge; the despised opponent, for fear of *ressentiment*; and the *ad hominem* attack or insult, which is aimed at the "other" and therefore retrieves the "other" from its ontological exile beyond Nietzsche's arena. His opponents are inevitably somewhat abstracted, since it is strength and power that he attacks: the success of David Strauss's book, for example, or the hypocrisies of Wagner as Bayreuth idol rather than as erstwhile Tribschen friend. "On the contrary, attack by me is proof of good will, and, in certain cases, gratitude. I honor, I distinguish by associating my name with a matter or a person: pro or contra makes no difference to me" (3, *EH*, 525).

In the next section, "Why I Am So Clever," Nietzsche reveals "how one becomes what one is" only at the end, in a brilliant tour de force of paradoxical wit that serves as praxis at the very moment it claims to offer theory. His answer requires shifting the ground of *Klugheit* (cleverness, acumen) into the realm of the unconscious and the irrational, thereby transforming it into its antonym while preserving its connotations of obliquity and doubling. This move is both anti-Socratic and proto-Freudian, as one becomes what one is through error and ignorance, by not "knowing" oneself at all, thereby casting one's cleverness into the form of its own negation as "self-forgetfulness, self-*misunderstanding*, self-diminution, -narrowing, -levelling" (3, *EH*, 541). The logic of this argument is that only by erasing the consciousness, wiping it clean not only of "ideas," like a tabula rasa, but also of desire ("One must keep the entire surface of consciousness—consciousness *is* a surface—clean of any great imperative" [3, 541]) can all of the manifold and contradictory drives and instincts of the organism flourish in uninhibited oblivion. Human desire, in the Hegelian sense, is the great enemy of fatality, of "becoming what one is." Instead of letting oneself be, instead of waiting to see what kind of "self" will emerge from one's gestating and proliferating instincts, human desire propels the individual to conform to phantasms of the self modeled upon the alien image of the desire of some "other." It is as combatants to human desire that Nietzsche paradoxically embraces selflessness and altruism in this section. But one must not lose sight of his "greater cleverness" here, his appropriative gesture of exploiting those Christian virtues as useful diversions from the specular images of desire while the subterranean consolidation of the beast progresses. Nietzsche claims just such an organic and chthonic etiology even for his cultural self, endowing his talents and capabilities with the spontaneous generation of biological excrescences that, presumably like Athena from the brain of Zeus, sprang forth one day without benefit of education, training, cultivation, or discipline. In another gesture of cultural innocence that transforms all of his achievements into spontaneous fulfillments of destiny ("So, for example, I found myself one day as University professor, having never remotely considered anything like it, since I was barely 24 years old" [3, *EH*, 542]), he divests himself of all desire, exonerates himself of all ambition, and denies all straining after achievement. "I lack any recollection of ever having exerted myself; there is no trace of struggle [*Ringen*] in evidence in my life; I am the antithesis of a heroic nature. To 'want' something, to 'strive' for something, to have a 'purpose' or 'wish' in sight—I don't know any of this from experience" (3, *EH*, 542). Through these gestures, this act, Nietzsche embraces himself as a destiny, appropriates himself as an animal, a plenum, a creature driven by no lacks or gaps or unfulfilled chasms in its being. "I don't in the least wish that anything should be different from what it is; I myself don't want to become different. . . . But I have always lived like this" (3, *EH*, 542). "My formula for greatness in human beings is *amor fati:* that one wants nothing different, not ahead, not behind, not in all eternity" (3, *EH*, 544).

Because of its wily, shrewd, self-preserving connotations (cf. Odysseus as classical prototype of the clever man), Nietzschean *Klugheit* is difficult to reconcile with his disdain for defensive measures unless one makes a crucial distinction between self-preservation as the protection and conservation of meager and diminished resources, and self-preservation as the protection of great strength from erosion by undermining influences. It is in this second sense that Nietzschean cleverness is effective. But as the instinct that governs external influences upon the organism, the first "cleverness of cleverness" is to protect itself, by functioning as little as possible, only when necessary, and then only by concerning itself with influences that matter, that are real, elemental, "literal," the things that "flow into" the body or impinge upon it such as nutrition, place, climate, and such cultural elements as books that contribute to the body's recreation. Nietzsche preempts the accusation that he demeans his philosophical enterprise with such trivial questions as the proper choice of beverage by arguing that it is the traditional figments of the imagination ("'God', 'soul,' 'virtue,' 'sin,' 'beyond,' 'truth,' 'eternal life'" [3, *EH,* 543]), not the so called little things that determine the fundamental conditions of biological organisms, that are beneath his notice. His analysis culminates in sets of racial profiles (for example, German "heaviness": starchy cuisine, beery muzziness, overcast skies, ponderous realism) whose playfulness is lodged in the delicate tilt between the physiological and the metaphorical nuances of the description. "The bad habit of an ever so slight intestinal sluggishness suffices to transform a genius into something mediocre, something 'German'; the German climate alone is enough to discourage strong, even heroic bowels" (3, *EH,* 531).

Nietzschean cleverness is the instinctive selection of influences beneficial to the organism. Since the process of refusal and rejection, like that of self-defense, is itself debilitating ("Warding things off, not letting them come near, is an expenditure—one should not be deceived on this point—a squandering of power to negative purpose" [3, *EH,* 539]), the individual requires a kind of automatic or instinctual filter against the environment. He calls this instinct "taste" (*Geschmack*), and he restores it to its literal sense of intuitively "knowing" through one's perceptual organs, one's palate, one's gorge, what the organism may safely ingest and tolerate. Nietzsche, particularly sensitive to the ideological and semiological functions of food since his early brush with Schopenhauerian and Wagnerian vegetarianism (4, *PW,* 606) is a militant carnivore in the interest of both physical and mental health: "spiritually productive and emotionally intensive natures *must* have meat" (Letter to Carl von Gersdorff, 28 September 1869, 4, *PW,* 606). In *Zarathustra,* he likewise invokes the literal residue in the eucharistic notion of spiritual nourishment, by transforming the symbolic and sacrificial lamb (the Passover lamb, the Lamb of God) into a delicious Middle Eastern dish (in a parody of Jesus' words whose humor springs from substituting more food for spirit): "But man does not live by bread alone, but also from the meat of good lambs of which I have two. These should be quickly slaughtered and prepared, spiced with sage: that's how I like them" (2, *Z,* 795).

Nietzsche's nutritional advice often preserves this metaphoric interplay of the spiritual and the comestible, for example, his tongue-in-cheek, yet practical, antiidealistic rejection of alcohol or "spirits" ("gegen jedweges 'geistige' Getränk"), but with an instinct, even a kind of etymological insistence, for the priority and primacy of the food and drink of the body.

Geography is for Nietzsche identical with atmospheric conditions, and the "influence" of place is therefore a matter of its most sensuous aspects (such as brightness, humidity, and temperature) not as they gratify the senses but as they modify the metabolism, the *Stoffwechsel*, the tempo, range, and thoroughness of the internal chemical appropriations of the body. Since his own body eventually becomes as sensitive as a living barometer, the question of where to live is an obsessional matter fraught with fatality for the itinerant Nietzsche. "I still need to be extremely cautious even today," he writes in the Brandes *Vita*. "A few climatic and meteorological conditions are indispensible. It is not by choice, but by necessity, that I spend the summer in the Upper Engadine, the winter on the Riviera" (4, *PW,* 879). He strips all European cities to their elemental components, sweeping aside the very cultural and historical conditions of artistic Meccas with his own inverted argument. "If one collects all the places that have or have had brilliant people, where wit, sophistication, malice happily belonged, where genius made itself indigenous almost of necessity: they all have an exceptional dry air. Paris, Provence, Florence, Jerusalem, Athens: these names prove that genius is *conditioned* by dry air and a clear sky—that is, through rapid metabolism, through the possibility of continually furnishing an enormous, even monstrous, amount of power" (3, *EH,* 531). In antithesis to the Romantics, Nietzsche also strips landscape of its aesthetic features in favor of a purely prophylactic assessment. He is utterly blind to the ravishing beauty of the Engadine but persuaded of the therapeutic powers that reside in the pure mountain air and the elevation above pestilential cities. His favorite demonstration is his friend Heinrich von Stein's magical, if temporary, transformation from Wagnerian enthusiast to free spirit during a three-day visit to Sils Maria. "I have always told him that this is the effect of the good air up here; everyone experiences the same thing; one is not for nothing 6,000 feet above Bayreuth" (3, *EH,* 521). Nietzsche's prevalent Alpine metaphors, especially in and in relation to *Zarathustra*—"This book, with its voice beyond the millennia, is not only the highest book there is, the genuine mountain air

Nietzsche's Ecce Homo

[*Höhenluft*] book" (3, *EH*, 513)—are rooted in his faith in the atmospheric etiology of spiritual health.

The final influence subject to Nietzschean cleverness is reading, which is lumped, under the rubric of recreation, with the other physiological influences of nutrition, place, and climate. This deliberate blurring together of nature and culture in the realm of "influences" creates a playful and complicated reversion of values. If it seems a trivialization of literature and music to give them the function of a good cut of meat, then we are reminded that in Nietzschean hygiene a good cut of meat is no trivial matter. If Nietzsche insists that he does only recreational reading, then, logically, the great range of literature he cites, from Pascal to Heinrich Heine, all become "light" reading, reading not to be taken seriously: "Reading gives me release precisely from *my* seriousness" (3, *EH*, 533). And so it does, because, following the same precautions established for diet and locale, he refuses to read defensively, as a critic, or to treat literature as an "other" in the sense of granting it authority or meaning, yielding to its demands, or honoring it with imitation. These measures have the salutary effect of totally separating Nietzsche's reading from his writing, a necessity if his originality, his spirit *sui generis* is to be preserved. Reading, finally, robs the scholar of the ability to think for himself and transforms him into a friction-match "that must be rubbed in order to give sparks—'thoughts'" (3, *EH*, 540).

By denying literature the status of "other" as authoritative or superior consciousness, Nietzsche preempts both models and rivals and saves himself utterly from any "anxiety of influence." But by preserving literature's "otherness," its strangeness and unfamiliarity, he preserves the recreational value of reading as a form of spiritual travel "that allows me to promenade [*spazierengehen*] in foreign sciences and souls" (3, *EH*, 533). Nietzsche uses the metaphor of the "foreign" with care, to preserve his sense of reading as an appropriative activity. He therefore maintains some xenophobia toward books, especially new, untried ones, fearing if not invasion then infiltration. This is why he bans books and sequesters himself during periods of writing: "Would I permit a foreign thought to climb secretly over the wall?" (3, *EH*, 533). But inviting himself to stroll in foreign parts of knowledge leaves Nietzsche free to appropriate them: to *love* Pascal, to appreciate de Maupassant, even to envy (playfully) Stendhal. As usual, Nietzsche's metaphor of the "foreign" with respect to books has a literal residue: his favorite books *are* foreign ones, predominantly French, some English (Byron's *Manfred,* Shakespeare's *Julius Caesar*). He admires few Germans, and then it is for their foreignness, as he admired Wagner, for example, for his alienation from the German, for Cosima's French influence upon him. "I perceived, I honored him as foreign territory [*Ausland*], as antithesis, as incarnate protest against all 'German virtues'" (3, *EH,* 536).

Nietzsche opens his next section, "Why I Write Such Good Books," with a statement that requires the ambiguity and play of Derridean *différance* to prevent it from cancelling the entire performance of *Ecce Homo*: "I am one thing, my writings are another" (3, *EH,* 545). This distinction might appear capriciously contradictory to the interpreter of *Ecce Homo* as Nietzsche's act, his ontological gesture, to which he himself points the way ("I am, namely, myself this *homo,* reckoning in the *ecce*" [Nietzsche to Meta von Salis, 14 November 1888, 4, *PW,* 924]), unless one remembers to test ever for the literal residue of his language. Nietzsche, the body, the living organism, the animal, is not (of course) our "Nietzsche," the books, the *oeuvre,* the philosophy. But it is with the implications of this obvious state of affairs, particularly for the future, when this cleavage will have become absolute (and when the Derridean deferral of difference, *différance,* will have taken effect) that Nietzsche is concerned. "I myself am not yet in my time; some are born posthumously" (3, *EH,* 545), he writes, against a time when he will cease to be premature and untimely, and when his works will be read and understood only because people have learned to read and understand themselves. But at that future time, when his works speak without him, posthumously, when his disembodied voice comes into fulfillment, Nietzsche's creatural existence, his living body, his animal life, will have become mere excess, a useless superfluity, a ridiculous excrescence. "I am one thing, my writings are another." Here, in *Ecce Homo,* he resists his proleptic ontological extrusion by restoring, at least literally, the excess of himself to his writing.

In this section Nietzsche confronts a problem seemingly even more embarrassing than his illness. Looked at naïvely, this chapter begins with a confession of professional failure: a history of popular neglect and critical abuse of his literary output, of the coldly polite encouragement of his acquaintances, and of the candid incomprehension of his friends ("Doktor Heinrich von Stein honestly deplored not understanding one word of my *Zarathustra*" [3, *EH,* 545]), that mocks the bravado of his title.

But once again, in a rhetorical master stroke whose ontological inversions constitute a "bestial gesture," Nietzsche trumpets his lack of cultural success as a personal triumph, by stripping it of all traces of *ressentiment*, rendering it free of pathos, rancor, defensiveness, appeal or even challenge. His animal gesture, as he crows the greatness of his books with no more desire to impress or persuade than a cock crowing at daybreak, is the foreclosure of the "other." He withdraws his works from cultural circulation, as it were, making them independent of public reception, frustrating hermeneutical attempts upon them by making them inaccessible to interpretation, and restoring them to Nature by restoring himself to them, in the fatality of his sickness and health, his travelogues and weather reports, his moods and affects—the whole living, creatural, experiential excess that he knows will die with him yet is responsible for the greatness of his books. This is the tautological answer dispersed throughout each of his critical commentaries on his works: he writes such good books because he is what he is.

Because the reading and understanding of his works is ontologically determined, Nietzsche depends upon readers who are healthy and rich in themselves, and who already have everything that he has to give them so that his writings will be to them a gift, a superfluity. The fitness to understand Nietzsche is therefore a natural endowment, a matter of physiology ("Any spiritual brittleness disqualifies one, once and for all, even dyspepsia: one requires steady nerves and a merry lower anatomy [*fröhlichen Unterleib*]" [3, *EH*, 549]) that bars him from deploying the rhetorical arsenal with which writers normally overcome the difficulties or resistance of their readers. Because he cannot control their physiologies, Nietzsche cannot control his readers. That is why he must be fatalistic about them, why he defers them to the future and speaks of them proleptically. He can do nothing else. Nature alone can provide him with readers. In the meantime, he counts himself fortunate in his *non*readers and his *un*comprehending readers, who serve as guarantors of his radicality, originality, and "prematurity." They prove that he has made no concessions to a deficient public and that he has not contrived an inauthentic readership by wooing and manipulating weak spirits. Nietzsche is therefore vastly amused by the "innocence" of a Berlin University professor, who in wellmeaning helpfulness "gave me to understand I should use a different form: no one reads anything like this" (3, *EH*, 546). The advice that he should pander to the consumerism of the intellectual marketplace, and that he adapt his incomparable, multiplicitous style to the vulgarity of philistine palates, is no less wonderful in the absurdity of its professional "common sense" than in its demonstration of the success of Nietzsche's *Umwertung*. Nietzsche is no more offended than if his critic had been a flea.

Although Nietzsche playfully fantasizes about future university chairs for the interpretation of *Zarathustra*, he recognizes that, strictly speaking, his works cannot be taught. "In the end, no one can hear more in things, including books, than one already knows. For that which is inaccessible through experience, one lacks an ear" (3, *EH*, 546). This distinction between knowledge and recognition brings to light the crucial excess that experience, or the living of knowledge, brings to the understanding of Nietzsche's work. He provides us, as a marvelous illustration, the criticism of a Swiss commentator who "expressed his respect for the courage with which I work for the abolition of all decent feelings" (3, *EH*, 546). Nietzsche remarks that, by a curious quirk of the sarcastic and mocking rhetoric, everything this Dr. Widmann says is true about him if you turn it on its head, if you shift the values around, if you take his words literally without their sarcastic distortion of meaning. "One would basically need only to 'revalue all values' in order, in a truly remarkable way, to hit the nail on the head about me—instead of hitting my head with the nail" (3, *EH*, 546). But his naysaying critics pose no threat to Nietzsche, as his admirers do: "Whoever thinks he has understood me has manufactured something for himself out of me, according to his image, not infrequently my antithesis: for example, an 'idealist'" (3, *EH*, 546). If he were weak or foolish enough to be gratified by their flattering construction (as he believed Wagner to have been) he would incur the risk of deluding himself ("I don't want to be confused with another; that includes not confusing myself" (3, *EH*, 545). For this reason, the ideal critical stance toward himself, the one that he urges even upon his friends, is "a dose of curiosity, as though before a strange plant, with an ironical resistance" (Letter to Carl Fuchs, 29 July 1888, 4, *PW,* 900).

As Nietzsche goes on to review each of his books in turn, the superfluity of his gesture affirms the fatality of his works. He retracts nothing, he changes nothing, he revises nothing, he does not reinterpret, because his books could have been only what they are, no more, no less, no different. He demonstrates by the very redundancy of his performance ("I have finally

Nietzsche's Ecce Homo

uttered no word that I might not have already spoken five years ago through the mouth of Zarathustra" [3, *EH*, 604]) that it is essentially unmotivated, propelled by no lack. But if *Zarathustra* was inspired, if the entire first part "came to" him ("fiel mir . . . ein") on his wanderings in Rapallo, if he was one day "overcome" or ambushed by the type of Zarathustra ("er überfiel mich"), then the "ways" this happened ("Auf diesen beiden Wegen") are here retrieved from the metaphorical land of visiting spirits and restored to the fatality of the local geography, to roads, streets, and pathways: the morning walks on the splendid road to Zoagli overlooking an immense expanse of sea, and the afternoon strolls along the coastal promontory from Santa Margherita to Portofino. To this extent, Nietzsche offers a demythification in *Ecce Homo*: that if, in *Zarathustra*, metaphors, images, and parables came to him involuntarily, crowding around and offering their services, he now restores himself as their source. Perhaps the dance was a metaphor, but it was also the experience of climbing the walled cliffs above Nice, feeling his muscles made flexible by the creative effusion. "The *body* is enraptured: let's leave the 'soul' out of it. . . . One could often see me dance; in those days I could be underway for seven or eight hours in the mountains without any concept of fatigue. I slept well, I laughed a lot" (3, *EH*, 579).

Nature was never entirely alienated in Nietzsche's tropes, as it prevailed in the literal residues of his topographies, personifications, and calendars. But now, in *Ecce Homo*, the masks (stylized masks never intended to fool anyone) are removed from the mythical figures, and Nietzsche reveals himself behind them all. He was Wagner, as early as *The Birth of Tragedy* ("Even psychologically all the distinctive features of my nature were inscribed in Wagner's"); used Wagner and Schopenhauer both as semiotic devices for himself in *Untimely Meditations*; circumvented in *Human, All Too Human*, "the little word 'I' although this time not with Schopenhauer or Wagner but with one of my friends, the excellent Dr. Paul Ree" (3, *EH*, 568); and in *Dawn*, even emerges from the metaphoric hide of a sea creature sunning itself on the rocks ("Finally it was myself, this marine animal" [3, *EH*, 570]). Nietzsche everywhere reveals himself as a "tragic actor" behind these figures, one who "acts" spontaneously, like a participant in a festival, rather than mimetically. And he restores to his *mise en scène* the fugitive light, wind, and temperature that eluded even the Impressionists. His restoration of Nature to symbolic time is perhaps the most satisfying of his demythifications. He quotes, in *Ecce Homo*, the little verse that introduces into the fourth book of *The Gay Science* (entitled *Sanctus Januarius*) the theme of the great thaw symbolized by the miracle of the saint's liquifying blood: "You who with your spear and flame / fragment my soul's ice" (2, *GS*, 435; 3, *EH*, 573). In *Ecce Homo* he reduces the complicated tropological exfoliation of this figure (St. Januarius, the liquifying blood, Janus, the god of beginnings, of portals and entries, of the new year, and so forth) to its blessed, natural occasion: "a verse, that expresses my gratitude for the most wonderful month of January that I have ever experienced" (3, *EH*, 573).

The last section of *Ecce Homo*, Nietzsche's great prophetic finale, is as tautological, paradoxical, and excessive in its rhetoric as in the rhetoric of his title, "Warum ich ein Schicksal bin." Nietzsche invests himself with both the frightful enormity and the perfect naturalness implicit in *Schicksal*: he is necessity, ungovernable fate, unholy providence, driving force, because he is Nature, creature, organic life, living being. He prophesies, with his revaluation of all values, a repeal of culture as we know it and a reaffirmation of Nature, a message of catastrophe from an anthropocentric perspective but good news, *frohe Botschaft*, gospel, from a biocentric perspective. This parallax view creates the apparent contradictions in his rhetoric: the apocalyptic foreboding neutralized by the abiding fatality, the warnings of ultimate rupture cancelled by the promise of eternal recurrence, the glee of destruction founded upon the affirmation of yea-saying. The end of the world he trumpets is merely the *Götzendämmerung* that will free humans from the enthrallment of the "other" (to ideals and idealism, and to the mediations of morality) and therefore release a new play of natural power, "the great politics" ("Only after me is a *great politics* possible on earth" [3, *EH*, 599]) to replace the petty local politics of human striving for prestige.

Nietzsche closes *Ecce Homo* with a burst of apocalyptic rhetoric that delivers no threat, extorts no repentance, urges no conversion, and, consistent with his animalistic comportment throughout the work, demands nothing from the "other." He escapes a Messianic role in other ways as well, by probing, like Pilate or Zarathustra, into the origins of good and evil, premises of truth and falsehood, and by "smelling" the difference between them ("My genius is in my nostrils" [3, *EH*, 598]). He explicitly rejects sainthood with its orientation toward the "other" as model and object of imitation ("I don't want to be a

Nietzsche's Ecce Homo

holy man, even a clown would be better. . . . Maybe I am a clown'' [3, 598]) in order to appropriate the irrepressible animalism of the buffoon, the *Hanswurst*, whose feats are physical, spontaneous, libidinal, playful, self-generated, acted to repel and insult rather than inspire and enthrall the "other." *Ecce Homo* ends in the rhetoric of the Zarathustran curse like that expressed in his dithyrambs.

> Now thunder rolls over the vaults,
> What is frame and wall, now trembles
> Now lightning and sulphurous truths dart about
> Zarathustra curses. . . .
> (3, 706)

His curse is like his gift, his malediction like his blessing, a vigorous discharge of excessive aggression emptied of all cultural motives (punishment, revenge, hatred), which is harmless to life itself ("O Zarathustra! Don't clap your whip about so fearsomely! You know perfectly well that noise murders thought" [2, Z, 745]) while it is explosively destructive to ideals, morality, and all abstractions that denigrate and debilitate life ("The concept 'soul', 'spirit,' finally even 'eternal soul,' discovered to ridicule the body, to make it sick—'holy'—in order to bring an appalling fecklessness to all things, that deserve seriousness in life: the question of nutrition, dwelling, spiritual diet, medicine, hygiene, weather" [3, *EH,* 605]). We, too, as readers of *Ecce Homo* are rebuffed as disciples, as believers, and negated as critics, judges, and witnesses. But we are restored and affirmed as living creatures, as reading organisms, who apprehend Nietzsche intuitively and respond in our entrails, who will never believe him ("I *want* no believers, I think I am too malicious to believe in myself" [3, *EH,* 598]) or imitate him, who will negate him and thereby escape his domestication and appropriation to become, ourselves, wild beasts of the modern imagination.

5
The Fate of the Human Animal in Kafka's Fiction

Although Kafka's mature literary output includes four fully developed animal narrations ("A Report to an Academy," "Researches of a Dog," "The Burrow," "Josefine, the Singer or the Mouse Folk") that explore increasingly feral ontologies and attempt to produce a virtually "species-specific" fiction, it is two nonanimal stories, "In the Penal Colony" and "A Hunger Artist," that develop most fully the philosophical (or, perhaps, antiphilosophical) implications of cultural violence. In spite of their human victims, these too are animal stories, demonstrations of the oppression and suppression of all that is creatural in the human—the body, feeling, pain, libido—in the ostensible interest of the twin demigods of human culture, rationalism and idealism. Kafka's critical tool in unmasking the hypocrisies and absurdities of cultural violence is pornology, because pornology functions as a parody, a travesty, a *reductio ad absurdum* of cherished intellectual and spiritual habits, and celebrates, in the libidinization of thought, the ultimate anthropocentric triumph over the vanquished beast. I will present Kafka as a pornologist implicated in obsessional fantasies of cultural cruelty, yet shrewd enough to unmask their affinities to traditional cultural virtues (for example, scientific procedure, political order, spiritual ambition) and to unmask our enthrallment to them as libidinal perversion. I will therefore break my thematic sequence slightly at this point to explore the victimization of the human animal, in its body, its feelings, and its instincts, in the interest of cultural values.

Because of their puzzling nature, and because they fall into chronological clusters, Kafka's fictions are usually read in thematic or allegorical groups. According to this method, "In the Penal Colony" belongs with the law and punishment works of Kafka's earlier period ("The Judgment," *The Trial*, "The Stoker"[1]), while "A Hunger Artist" belongs with the art and asceticism theme of his later works ("Investigations of a Dog,"

"Josefine, the Singer or the Mouse Folk"). Whatever the merits of this method, it obscures the striking structural symmetry of these two stories: in each, a fanatical believer in meaningful suffering reenacts a spectacle that in an earlier age drew huge, festive crowds but now results only in sordid death and burial. Allegorical readings mask this symmetry by giving the stories different ideational contexts derived from the idea that governs the suffering in the work: the Law in "In the Penal Colony," and the Ideal in "A Hunger Artist." Reading the stories as companion pieces, however, suggests a new way of assessing the pain, one that renders the ideational contexts of the works wholly ironic. If suffering is seen as a means whose end is not the Law or the Ideal but pleasure, then Law and Ideal become mere pretexts, fraudulent rationales in a pornological fantasy.

On the status of pain in his writings, its transcendence or lack of it, hinges the question of whether Kafka is a religious or a pornological writer. He never depicted himself as spiritually as Max Brod depicts him. Not only did Brod's own religious zeal color his perceptions of Kafka's imagination, but his evident discomfort with *"das Peinliche"* (the pornological elements in Kafka's work, both painful and embarrassing) led him to find in religion a handy means of cloaking them. "This humor, an essential ingredient in Kafka's poetics (and his life style), indicates a higher essence beyond the weave of reality,"[2] Brod writes of "the most gruesome episodes" in "In the Penal Colony" and "The Whipper" chapter in *The Trial*. In his later years, Kafka became decreasingly abashed about his knowledge of pornological writing and his appreciation of its importance. "The Marquis de Sade, whose biography you lent me, is the actual patron of our time,"[3] he reportedly told Gustav Janouch. To Milena Jesenská he admitted, "Yes, torture is extremely important to me, I'm preoccupied with nothing but being tortured and torturing."[4] As evidence of his obsession he sent her sketches of hideous execution devices invented in his imagination. As Klaus Wagenbach demonstrates, Kafka need scarcely have resorted to his imagination, since gruesome material for his stories abounded: New Caledonia and Devil's Island, penal colonies for the Paris Communards and Dreyfus respectively; the "Rotatory Machine" of J.M. Cox, using torture to cure insanity; the documents of industrial mutilation Kafka himself compiled for the Workers Accident Insurance Company; and Octave Mirbeau's translated *Garten der Foltern*.[5]

Viewing Kafka as writing in a modern void of faith, most

commentators eschew Brod's frankly religious interpretation of Kafka's works: "Since the biblical Book of Job, God has not been so wildly quarreled with as in Kafka's *Trial,* and *Castle,* or in his *In the Penal Colony.*"[6] Walter Sokel, for example, finds in Kafka the "negative transcendence" of unpleasure that Lionel Trilling describes in *Beyond Culture:*[7] pain as an antidote to bourgeois torpor, a willingness (in "Penal Colony") to suffer "*Schrecken und Grauen*" rather than "*seelisch zu versumpfen*" in frivolity and utilitarianism.[8] J.M.S. Pasley finds in "In the Penal Colony" a nostalgia for "what Nietzsche called 'the ascetic ideals': deprivation and abstinence, punishment and suffering, discipline and self-discipline, as paths to purity and salvation.'"[9] Yet if Kafka derived his philosophy of punishment and asceticism from Nietzsche's *Genealogy of Morals,* as Bridgwater demonstrates,[10] then he derived it with Nietzsche's irony intact and, like Nietzsche, exposes the fraudulent modern teleologies of suffering. Nietzsche writes, "It is today impossible to say with certainty why there is punishment" (3, *GM,* 266) and goes on to give a list of "uncertain," "secondary," and "accidental" "meanings" of punishment. "What then do ascetic ideals mean?" he asks. "In the case of the artist, we now realize, nothing at all" (3, *GM,* 289).

Kafka's process in his stories, like Nietzsche's in *The Genealogy of Morals,* entails not only a historical reconstruction but also its simultaneous critique. Critics too often see in Kafka's evocation of a golden age of penal severity and hunger art a nostalgia for apotheosized pain. Rather, his "history," like Nietzsche's ironic genealogy, exposes the falsehoods and deceptions that constitute the civilizing process. Officer and hunger artist are robbed of a transcendence that was always fraudulent, and their carcasses are therefore disposed of with the unceremonious dispatch of animal burial, tossed into a ditch with dirty rags and batting, buried in a hole with the filthy straw of the cage. Nietzsche also uses the "education" of the animal as a mocking illustration of the civilizing process with its spurious "ascetic" rationalization of pain. "'I suffer: someone must be to blame for that'; thus thinks every sickly sheep. But its shepherd, the ascetic priest, says to it, 'Quite right, my sheep! Someone must be to blame: but this someone is you yourself. . . .' That's quite daring, and quite false" (3, *GM,* 315). Bridgwater attributes to both Kafka and Nietzsche an asceticism rooted in the desire to destroy the animal in man, since "obviously man has no particular significance as an animal, unless it be as the most vicious and

The Human Animal in Kafka's Fiction

unprincipled predator of all."[11] But Kafka's tortured *Tier-menschen* are often already domesticated, like the "submissive dog" of a condemned man in the penal colony, so docile "it seemed as though one could let him run free on the neighboring slopes and then only whistle, to make him return for the beginning of the execution" (*PC,* 100). Kafka wishes to recover pain—untranscended, mute, "animal" pain, stripped of *alatheia* and *telos* —from its cultural falsifications. "Seen from a primitive point of view, the only real, incontestable truth, undistorted by external factors (martyrdom, sacrifice for another human being), is corporal pain."[12] This is also Nietzsche's enterprise. "Apart from the ascetic ideal," he begins the last section of the *Genealogy,* "man, the animal *man,* had until now no meaning." It is Nietzsche's task to de-moralize suffering as an ascetic ideal, to explain its function, but without acceding to its pretensions. "But any meaning being better than no meaning, the ascetic ideal was in every sense the best 'lesser evil' that ever existed" (3, *GM,* 345).

What makes Kafka's two "histories" pornological while Nietzsche's "genealogy" is not, is a narrative and dramatic form that manifests the particular structural and expressive elements found in other pornological writings. The researches of Gilles Deleuze demonstrate that the symptoms of the psychological conditions known as sadism and masochism are literary rather than behavioral, and that their study requires a textual analysis. As Deleuze proceeds to discover in the works of Sade and Masoch a new language, invented to give expression to inarticulate drives and needs, the works of Kafka provided him with a modern perspective elaborated in his collaborative study with Felix Guattari.[13]

According to Deleuze, sadism and masochism always have a conscious and an unconscious component, philosophical and psychoanalytical, an understanding and manipulation of the effects and an ignorance of the causes of that compulsion to construct certain fantasies and write pornological texts. He is able, thereby, to shed new light on the ideational contexts in Kafka's works, to show, for instance, that tyranny is not merely a symbolic expression of the paternal role, the superego function, in sadism but that the sadist uses tyranny subversively to expose the absurdity of the Law, by enacting an extreme application of "the letter of the law," for example, as in "In the Penal Colony."

Deleuze argues that sadism and masochism are not subject to

transformations into the Freudian complex, and that there is therefore no such thing as sadomasochism. He then distinguishes the two perversions according to a system of philosophical and formal oppositions that include their philosophical antecedents (respectively, Spinoza / Kant), political structures (institutions / contracts), intellectual operations (demonstrative / dialectical), expressive modes (mathematical / aesthetic), temporal structure (cumulative repetition / suspense) and formal models (perpetual motion machine / frozen tableau). These distinctions help to elucidate the symmetry of Kafka's two stories "In the Penal Colony" and "The Hunger Artist." Besides de-moralizing pain and suffering, like Nietzsche's *Genealogy,* Deleuze's symptomatological model also provides a philosophical rationale for the "doubled" language in the stories, the language of hypocrisy and delusion, ulterior motives and deceptions. The irony in Kafka's stories emerges from the discrepancy between the "rational" and obsessional aspects of the discourse and is aimed like a blow at reason itself, specifically, the "rationalization" of suffering. By examining the ideational contexts of the two stories, "punishment" and "asceticism" as deceptive valorizations of pain consistent with the enterprise of sadism and masochism, their true subversive thrust can be salvaged from the critical tendency to make of Kafka one of the great religious writers of the century.

In both "In the Penal Colony" and "The Hunger Artist," execution and fast are doubled so that they occur twice, in past and present time, history and act, idealized and vulgarized form. But this "doubling" is not mere repetition, but repetition with a turn or a twist like a Moebius strip, to reverse our normal response to torture and thereby subvert the pretensions of justice and art that govern the event. Deleuze describes the "perversion" implicit in our attitude toward "perversion."

Nietzsche stated the essentially religious problem of the meaning of pain and gave it the only fitting answer: if pain and suffering have any meaning, it must be that they are enjoyable to someone. From this viewpoint there are only three possibilities: the first, which is the "normal" one, is of a moral and sublime character; it states that pain is pleasing to the gods who contemplate and watch over man; the other two are perverse and state that pain is enjoyable either to the one who inflicts it or to the one who suffers it. It should be clear that the normal answer is the most fantastic, the most psychotic of the three. (Deleuze, 103)

The Human Animal in Kafka's Fiction

The theatricality of the public spectacle in older times guarantees the community's assent to a Law and an Ideal that require public torture as proof ("Now Justice is being done"[*PC,* 111], the crowd thinks, as the execution begins.). The society colludes with enthusiasm, filling the valley of the penal colony a day early to secure good seats, subscribing to season tickets at performances of hunger art, and offering (in both stories) front-row seats to the children, in the penal colony by order of the old Commandant himself. The children's participation stamps public torture as an edifying, educational experience and enshrines the Law and the Ideal that require it. In fact, in both stories, unpleasant scenes of torture are narrated as though through the eyes of children, clasped in the officer's arms at the execution (*PC,* 111), or standing, "open-mouthed," before the cage of the hunger artist, "holding each other's hands for greater security" (*HA,* 164). The officer, who has a passion for theater (like the Marquis de Sade),[14] runs the execution like a one-man theater company, tending the props, giving stage directions, badgering a prospective patron to support a failing show, and eventually serving as an understudy for the lead.

Theater translates the abstraction into an action (justice = execution), and it is the incommensurate relationship between the two that reveals the irrationality of the proceeding. This discrepancy is not one of degree but one of specificity, as Deleuze points out (Deleuze, 75). For a Law or an Ideal that is never named and appears to have no content, a suffering is extracted that is obsessively specified as to duration (twelve hours for the execution, forty days for the fast), equipment (machine, cage), setting (hollow, dais) and quantity (the suffering of the criminal measured by precise observation of its physiological effects, the policing of the hunger artist to ensure his freedom from "cheating"). The Ideal of the hunger artist is as indeterminate as "justifiably to amaze the world" (*HA,* 169). The Law in the penal colony is also indeterminate, replaced by flimsy pretexts contrived to create an almost certain occasion for punishment (saluting a door every hour during the night).

The machine and the fast are not arbitrary means of inflicting or enduring pain. Because the actual nature of the violence in sadism and masochism is not physical but intellectual ("What happens in a novel by Sade is strictly fabulous," writes Roland Barthes[15]), the forms of the perverse fantasies are designed to serve subversive ends: specifically, to disavow the violence, make it impersonal and abstract, subordinated to a higher purpose, as though the sadist and the masochist had no hand in it.

The apparatus in "In the Penal Colony" is therefore metaphorically related to another machine designed by the old Commandant's mathematical diagrams. The apparatus, he tells the explorer, "works by itself even if it stands alone in this valley" (*PC,* 112), and he describes the old Commandant's political organization as so perfect "that his successor, even with a thousand new plans in his head, cannot change anything of the old way, at least for many years" (*PC,* 101). The use of machines and mathematical diagrams in torture serves to render the violence completely impersonal and thereby signifies a commitment to the "Idea of pure reason" (Deleuze, 19). Both Deleuze and Barthes stress that the subordination of personal lusts and passions to a sham rational system, the phenomenon of "reasoned crime"[16] is the violence behind the violence in sadism.

The forms of masochism (art, suspense, contract), like those of sadism (machine, perpetual motion, institutions), serve to have suffering executed in the interest of an Idea (Law or Ideal), as though without the intervention of human desire and will. Fasting becomes hunger art when the point of view shifts from sufferer to spectator (since spectators can only see pain, not feel it) and thereby assumes an aesthetic form whose essence is stasis, like painting or sculpture. In other words, the torture of the hunger artist takes the form of waiting and suspense (how long can he fast?) until he becomes a frozen *tableau vivant,* a human being who never eats and therefore virtually never moves. His aesthetic effect is heightened by means of theatrical lighting, such as the illumination of torches at night. Appropriately, the impresario displays photographs (still shots) of the hunger artist to the crowd. The masochist disavows his own need and will to suffer by turning the execution of his suffering over to someone else by means of a contract. "The masochist appears to be held by real chains," writes Deleuze, "but in fact he is bound by his word alone" (Deleuze, 66). Since the contract still implies his consent, the masochist attempts to undermine the volitional element by signing a "blank paper"[17] (Deleuze, 23), like the hunger artist, who, upon joining the circus, avoided looking at the conditions of his contract (*HA,* 168).

The idealized historical accounts of executions and fasting in the two Kafka stories are the product of a rhetorical intention to persuade or educate someone about the desirability of such spec-

The Human Animal in Kafka's Fiction

tacles. The tacit assumption behind this rhetorical effort is that torture in its meaningless (unvalorized) state is unacceptable to the rational mind unless it is justified by an Idea. Consequently, persuasion and education become exercises in hypocrisy, discourses fraught with ulterior motives and devious intentions that constitute a form of intellectual violence—the use of "reason" to assault reason.

Instead of convincing the explorer that Law requires punishment in the form of torture, the officer's discourse betrays the hidden "rationale," namely, that torture requires Law to "justify" it (make it just) as punishment. The most concrete of human experiences, physical pain, is put in the service of the most abstract of principles, mathematical precision and engineering efficiency. This tribute paid to "mind," the mathematical and mechanical mind, fails to convince the explorer or the reader. Deleuze writes of the "demonstration" in sadism, "But the intention to convince is merely apparent, for nothing is in fact more alien to the sadist than the wish to convince, to persuade, in short to educate. He is interested in something quite different, namely to demonstrate that reasoning itself is a form of violence, and that he is on the side of violence, however calm and logical he may be"(Deleuze, 18).

The officer's demonstration of the machine is itself a deliberate act of apathy toward the condemned man. The officer explains the prisoner's crime only at the insistence of the explorer, and then only as an irritable and reluctant digression from his demonstration of the machine. "But time is passing; the execution should be started and I am not yet finished explaining the apparatus" (PC, 105). The prisoner's status in the demonstration is mere machine fodder. He is rendered depersonalized, arbitrary, interchangeable (as we see when the officer takes his place) and his pain is of less interest than the workings of the machine (during the officer's execution the explorer's interest is captured entirely by the self-destructing mechanism). Apathy is part of the intellectual violence of sadism because it totally negates the pain extracted from the victim.

Apathy in "In the Penal Colony" also takes the form of a rigid complementary distribution of language whose function is to render the officer as total subject and the prisoner as total object. Barthes writes, "The master is he who speaks, who disposes of the entirety of language; the object is he who is silent, who remains separate, by a mutilation more absolute than any erotic torture, from any access to discourse, because he does not

Beasts of the Modern Imagination

even have any right to receive the master's word."[18] The prisoner's crime, the verbal threat that appropriates language, and thereby dominance, from his superior, is scheduled to be redressed by a total linguistic exclusion, from the discourse of his judicial process (charge, defense, sentence), the demonstration of the apparatus (conducted in French), and the message that will transform him into a human text, until the moment of his transcendence, when he will decipher the script on his body, and, presumably, reenter the universe of discourse. The officer, on the other hand, uses language demonstratively and speculatively, to construct entire scenes complete with imaginary dialogue, which he projects as models for the explorer's meeting with the new Commandant.

The officer's verbal demonstration of the apparatus is related to the actual execution that is supposed to follow as mimesis to praxis, to borrow the terms Barthes applies to the procedure at the Château de Silling: "The story being told [by the enthroned storyteller] becomes the program for an action [by the libertines]." In the same vein, the officer tells the explorer, "I will first describe the apparatus and then demonstrate the procedure itself. This way you will follow it much better" (PC, 102). The officer's own execution is itself only a narration for the reader, however, and we find in Kafka's story the same "reversion of texts" that Barthes finds in the writings of Sade: "The image appears to originate a program, the program a text, and the text a practice; however, this practice is itself written, it returns (for the reader) to program, to text, to fantasy."[19] The sequence of program, text, and practice obtains in the penal colony, where the old Commandant's program is literally committed to the mathematical text of his drawings ("I am still using the sketches of the former Commandant" [PC, 107]), which in turn is translated onto the (precomputer) program of the apparatus, to be translated once more into the living text on the condemned man's body. In this way, "the reasoned crime" of the penal colony emerges from the reversion of texts, the final version being Kafka's story itself.

As the Law is fraudulently invoked in the penal officer's "persuasion" (which is ultimately autotelic and functions as a form of intellectual violence) so the hunger artist uses "education," ostensibly in the service of the Ideal, but in fact in order to usurp the impresario's role and become the architect of his own suffering. Deleuze writes, "The masochistic contract implies not only the necessity of the victim's consent, but his ability to persuade,

and his pedagogical and judicial efforts to train his torturer"
(Deleuze, 66). The hunger artist strains mightily, but with little
success, to "train" his torturers in their role of policing his fast,
ostensibly to render the achievement of the ascetic Ideal perfect.
He sings when they refuse to watch him, tells them jokes and
anecdotes to keep them awake during their vigil, feeds them at
his own expense and before his eyes, and himself dictates a toast
("ostensibly whispered by the hunger artist to the impresario"
[*HA*, 167]) drunk to the public, not to himself. The stasis of his
art dooms the control of the fast to failure. "Of course, no one
was capable of passing every day and night uninterruptedly
guarding the hunger artist; therefore no one could know from
personal witness whether this was really continuous, flawless
fasting; only the hunger artist himself could be sure, only he
could therefore simultaneously function as the sole convinced
spectator to his own fast" (*HA*, 165).

Deleuze writes, "While Sade is spinozistic and employs
demonstrative reason, Masoch is platonic and proceeds by dialectical imagination" (Deleuze, 21). The hunger artist's ostensible
ideal is asceticism, the triumph of spirit over flesh, of human
over an animal nature ruled by Freud's "pleasure principle,"
and therefore organized to avoid pain. But the hunger artist's
asceticism is beset by a masochistic paradox that reveals its fraudulence: the hunger artist, like the masochist, desires pain and
finds the fast easy to endure: "It was the easiest thing in the
world" (*HA*, 165). The unnatural is natural to him, and the
hunger artist, troubled by his hypocrisy, launches a two-pronged
strategy to maintain the validity of his ideal: he confesses that his
fast costs him no effort of will (*HA*, 165), and he transforms his
ideal from a qualitative to a quantitative goal, the achievement
of a world record that can be measured in temporal form, with
clocks ("the only piece of furniture in the cage" [*HA*, 164]),
calendars ("the little board with the numbers of the completed
fast days, which in earlier times were conscientiously changed
every day" [*HA*, 170]), and vigils. By abolishing the forty-day
fast limit (which had only catered to the public's short attention
span rather than to his welfare anyway), his ideal can be rendered absolute by an achievement of *never* eating again. The
hunger artist's dying confession is therefore not a punch line, a
surprise ending, but merely the fulfillment of his lifelong ambition, the completion of an absolute fast and its simultaneous
disavowal: "You really shouldn't admire it. . . . Because I must
fast, I can do nothing else" (*HA*, 171).

Beasts of the Modern Imagination

The hunger artist's ideal, like the masochist's, is frustrated by his dependence on the collusion of others. In accordance with his strategy, this collusion takes dual forms: he needs the public to measure his fast in order to believe its authenticity and simultaneously to believe his disavowal of effort. In other words, he requires recognition of both his physical and his moral achievement, a recognition that his public withholds. They police him carelessly, then accuse him of charlatanism. They disbelieve such desperate proofs of his rigor as his singing ("They then only wondered at his cleverness in being able to eat even while singing" [*HA*, 164]), and reject his confession, holding him "for a publicity seeker or perhaps even a swindler, for whom fasting was, in fact, easy because he knew how to make it easy for himself, and then even had the gall to half-admit it" (*HA*, 165). These conflicts result in a series of dialectical reversals that continually shift the hunger artist's suffering from site to site, from physical endurance to mental anguish, from positive asceticism to negative frustration. The public functions like an analogue to Kafka's own personal spiritual "Negative," a power that neutralizes every achievement, "Then, as soon as I have climbed even the smallest step. . . I lie down and wait for the Negative, not to overtake me but to pull me off the little step."[20]

Both penal officer and hunger artist fail to convince the public of the value and meaning of suffering. The significance of their common failure is obscured by allegorical interpretations that deride the penal officer as a tyrant and exalt the hunger artist as a saint, that congratulate the explorer on his enlightenment and condemn the hunger artist's public for its secularism and philistinism. Such readings prejudge the issue by invoking accepted teleologies of suffering that generate a whole vocabulary to express mediated pain, pain subordinated to a higher (abstract) value: punishment, atonement, sacrifice, martyrdom, discipline, immolation, and so on. The failure of Kafka's protagonists in "In the Penal Colony" and "The Hunger Artist" to win adherents to Law and Ideal reflects a philosophical dismantling rather than nostalgia—a reversal of the processes of valorization (giving values), rationalization (making rational), justification (making just) and mythification (creating a system of belief)—that make pain acceptable to the human mind. Kafka restores physical, "animal" pain to its real and incontestable "truth"[21] by de-moralizing, demythifying, and de-signifying it.

Kafka's two stories, like sadism and masochism, have a conscious and an unconscious level, philosophical and psychoanalytic purposes. In other words, sadists and masochists know that they construct mythologies to justify their enjoyment of pain, although they may not know why they do so. Although the causes ascribed to Kafka are most often religious and moral, Kafka himself, it seems, delved into the psychological realm for an explanation of mastering pain that rather approximates Freud's explanation of the repetition-compulsion of children in *Beyond the Pleasure Principle*.[22] "Don't you feel the desire to exaggerate painful things as much as possible?" Kafka wrote to Grete Bloch. "It often seems to me the only way people with weak instincts can exorcise pain; one cauterizes the wound, as medicine, otherwise bereft of all good instincts, does. Of course, nothing final is accomplished in this, but the moment itself . . . is almost experienced pleasurably."[23]

Deleuze, however, offers a psychoanalytic explanation that would account for the erotic element in "In the Penal Colony," and would allow us at least to speculate about the hidden fears and tensions that control "The Hunger Artist." According to Deleuze, the erotic pleasure in sadism and masochism depends on a dialectical process of desexualization and resexualization that begins with the fusion of ego functions and the role of the parents. "Sadism is in every sense an active negation of the mother and an exaltation of the father who is beyond all laws" (Deleuze, 52). The old Commandant's inflation as an autocrat, as well as his overdetermination ("Did he combine everything in himself, then? Was he soldier, judge, builder, chemist, draughtsman?" [*PC*, 103]), are manifestations of his superego function. This superego serves to desexualize the subject by suppressing all feeling. However, once desexualization is complete, the libidinal energy that is unbound from feeling is cathected onto reason and the mind. "At the culmination of desexualization a total resexualization takes place, which now bears on the neutral energy or pure thought" (Deleuze, 109). In other words, although one is tempted to suppose that the torture itself (naked man, "bed", harrow as symbolic rape) is the eroticized element, the contrary is true: it is the intellectual processes, the "rational" discourse, the officer's demonstration of the machine and his defense of the autocratic system that are eroticized. "The essential operation of sadism is the sexualization of thought and of the speculative process as such, in so far as these are the product of the superego" (Deleuze, 109).

The problem that remains is finding an explanation for the ending of the stories. In each of the two Kafka stories, the lament for a lost golden age of apotheosized suffering is followed by a tarnished reenactment of the torture (machine befouled and broken, cage uncleaned, signs unpainted, calendar unmarked), robbed of its glory. This transition, which was earlier described as a movement from story to action, from demonstration to praxis, is also a movement from theorizing or fantasy to "reality," a disillusionment that Deleuze calls "disphantasization" in describing the ending of Masoch's novels (Deleuze, 56–57). In other words, the idea or fantasy is never entirely convincing to the sadist or masochist, who, in any event, "knows" their fraudulence: the disavowals, disguises, and displacements that constitute them. The discrepancy between fantasy and "reality" becomes in Kafka's fiction a temporal gap, the unhappy transition from a glorious, severe past to a squalid and lax present.

In "In the Penal Colony," the disillusionment of the officer results from the universal rejection of the superego function as new Commandant and explorer refuse to support the old regime, and the officer takes upon himself an overdetermined role as executioner and victim. If old and new Commandant here represent a "symbolic" and "real" father, particularly a "real" father who refuses to assume symbolic superego functions, then their relationship provides a bridge to the biographical situation of Herrmann and Franz Kafka. In Kafka's *Letter to His Father,* we find both processes in evidence: Kafka inflating his father to global and autocratic proportions, then (imaginatively) letting his father decline the honor by insisting, in his defense, that Franz has hypocritically foisted the superego function onto him. "For example: when you recently wanted to marry, you wanted . . . simultaneously not to marry, but wanted, in order not to have to exert yourself, that I help you with this not-marrying, by forbidding this marriage."[24] Kafka here recognizes the difference between the "symbolic" father in his fiction, the man who shies apples at his son or condemns his son to death by drowning, and the "real" father, the baffled Prague merchant who never understood the superego functions he was made to bear by his writer-son: "You asked me once, not long ago, why I maintain that I fear you."[25]

The disillusionment in "In the Penal Colony" expresses this recognition, and the officer's autoexecution is an appropriate ending, as the explorer himself notes. But Kafka discovered this solution only after much experimentation. In unused versions of the story in Kafka's diary, the characters shift in their principal

The Human Animal in Kafka's Fiction

roles as executioner, condemned man, and witness, roles first occupied by the officer, prisoner, and explorer respectively. The shift occurs when the explorer discovers that the executed man is not the prisoner but the officer himself, who (spike through forehead) accuses the explorer of murder: "I am executed, as you command."[26] This shifting of executioner, victim, and witness resembles the "modification of the utterance" that brings to light "the grammar of the fantasy" in Freud's 1919 essay, "A Child is Being Beaten."[27] In other words, Kafka's indecision and experimentation with the subject / object category ([SOME-ONE] executes [SOMEONE]) may betray similar repressions, projections, and evasions with respect to the sadistic fantasy.

Perhaps the most intriguing clue to "the grammar of the fantasy" is the snake, "the great Madame" who appears to enter the penal colony as a potentate of sorts, according to a fragment in the diary.

> "Move!" called our ever cheerful Commandant, "Move, you snake-bait!" Thereupon we lifted our hammers and for miles about commenced the most industrious pounding. . . . The arrival of our snake was already announced for this evening, by then everything must be pounded to dust, for our snake cannot tolerate even the tiniest pebble. Where else could one find such a sensitive snake? There is simply only this single snake, who is incomparably pampered by our labor, and thereby also incomparably denatured.[28]

"The great Madame" is clearly a figure from a different fantasy, the severe, cruel woman of the masochistic fantasy, Masoch's Wanda or Kafka's pampered, tyrannical Brunelda in *Amerika,* and her appearance in the sadistic fantasy is anomalous. One complicated explanation might account for her, namely Jacques Lacan's principle that something abolished on the "symbolic plane resurges in 'the real' in a hallucinatory form" (Deleuze, 56–57).[29] In other words, the mother, banished in the sadistic fantasy of the penal colony (the only women, the new Commandant's ladies, subvert and threaten the autocratic order of the inflated father) here reappears (literally, since the fragment tells only of her expected approach down the road) in the hallucinatory form of the snake.

"The great Madame" was omitted from the final version of "In the Penal Colony," and, according to Deleuze's formulation of the psychoanalytic configuration in masochism (a model based on Masoch's work), the oral mother is missing in "A Hunger Artist'' as well, if that work is to be considered a masochistic fantasy. Yet at the risk of raising phantoms or filling gaps that don't exist, I would like to speculate that the oral mother lurks invisibly behind the starving artist and that a hidden dialectic of oral fantasies (Who eats whom?) governs "The Hunger Artist" as surely as the superego fantasy (Who executes whom?) governs "In the Penal Colony."

If we return for a moment to the patterns of misunderstanding in "The Hunger Artist," we find that the Christian elements in the work belong among them. Deleuze explains Christology as providing a mystical justification for the masochist: man is "reborn" through pain inflicted by the oral mother, for example, the crucifixions in Masoch's work (Deleuze, 84–85). In "The Hunger Artist", Kafka alludes to Christ's asceticism, his forty days of fasting in the wilderness, an asceticism plagued by temptations including, presumably, the temptation to turn stones into loaves of bread and eat them. The hunger artist's tempters are the ladies, "seemingly so friendly but in reality so cruel" (*HA,* 166), who lead him to the unwelcome food out of misplaced sympathy and concern. The threat that women pose to a necessary and desired asceticism has numerous analogues in Kafka's own life, with the same result: an everpresent torment intensified by misunderstanding. In the running dispute with her son over his vegetarian diet, Kafka's mother once tried to enlist Felice Bauer's aid in bringing Franz to more robust fare. "Franz's mother loves him very much, but she hasn't the faintest inkling who her son is and *what he needs,"* Max Brod subsequently advised Felice. "Frau Kafka and I have had several confrontations over this. All the love in the world is inadequate if one has so little understanding. . . . After years of experimentation, Franz finally discovered the only effective diet for himself—the vegetarian. For years he suffered from stomach complaints; now he is as fit and healthy as he has ever been since I've known him. So, of course, his parents come along with their banal love and try to force him to return to meat and to his malady."[30] If Kafka intended Christ's fasting and temptation to serve as an analogue to his own dietary abstentions and ensuing family squabbles, then he clearly seems to aim at a humorous deflation of the saintly pretensions of his own "magnificent, inborn ascetic capacities."[31] At the same time, his parents' confusion about the sources of his suffering, blaming Kafka's vegetarianism and "literature" rather than his frustration at being unable to eat and write as he wished, to structure and control his

The Human Animal in Kafka's Fiction

own deprivations and sufferings, conforms to the same dialectical conflicts depicted in "The Hunger Artist." "This perversion of the truth, however familiar to the artist, always unnerved him anew and was too much for him. The consequence of the premature ending of his fast was represented as the cause of it!" (*HA*, 168).

If Kafka's mother is a nurturing, oral mother, urging unwanted food on her son, then we find in a small detail in "The Hunger Artist" an allusion to her monstrous opposite, the cannibalistic mother. The hunger artist "stretching an arm through the bars of the cage to let people feel his emaciation" (*HA*, 164) unmistakably recalls Hänsel in the Grimms' fairy tale (also caged, but to be fattened rather than to hunger), extending a chicken bone through the bars of his cage to convince the wicked witch that he is too thin to be eaten. If "The Hunger Artist" is in any sense an "anti-Märchen"[32] of "Hänsel and Gretel," then the meaning of the fasting becomes clear: fasting is a defense against being eaten.[33] If this seems far-fetched, one should remember the frightful fantasies of forced feeding and butchering that dot Kafka's personal writings. For Milena he conjures up a sanitarium that won't allow a vegetarian diet. "What shall I do there? Have the head doctor put me between his knees, and gag on the meat clumps he stuffs into my mouth with his carbolic fingers and then presses along my gullet?"[34] In his diary he writes, "Always the fantasy of a broad butcher knife that rapidly and with mechanical regularity drives into me from the side and cuts very thin diagonal slices that fly off in curled strips because of the rapid action."[35] Images of monstrous devouring occur throughout Kafka's fiction as well, in "An Old Manuscript" and "Jackals and Arabs," to name only two. Nor is the guise of the oral mother as a devouring monster incompatible with the masochistic fantasy, since in Masoch's works the women hunt the animals and the men,[36] thereby posing a similar danger.

Kafka's two stories, "In the Penal Colony" and "The Hunger Artist" are complements, then, pornologically and philosophically (sadism and masochism, Law and Ideal) as well as psychoanalytically (the son's relationship to the father and the mother respectively). Reading them in this way reveals in Kafka a subversive tendency that little supports pious notions of his own atonement and asceticism. Rather, he offers us a bestial gesture in the form of anatomizing an antibestial gesture: he unmasks the twin demigods of culture, rationalism and idealism, by exposing to us their double cruelty (simultaneous sanction and apathy toward the infliction of pain), their double violence (the simultaneous practice and denial of cruelty), and their double perversity (libidinous pleasure derived from the abolition of libido).

The Human Animal in Kafka's Fiction

6

Kafka's "Josefine":
The Animal as the Negative
Site of Narration

"Josefine, the Singer or the Mouse Folk," the last piece Kafka wrote, is not a story about art, or the repudiation of art, but a gesture of retraction not unlike his own last will and testament. In his several instructions to Max Brod, he requested the burning of his entire *Nachlass,* unread, and forbade the reprinting of published works ("Should they disappear altogether that would please me best"[1]) a request Brod not only refused to honor, but *told* Kafka he would refuse to honor. Brod, therefore, exonerates himself for defying his friend's wishes by interpreting Kafka's will in a more complex way, as a testament embodying the double gestures of Kafka's destruction and Brod's redemption of the works. "Convinced as he was that I meant what I said, Franz should have appointed another executor if he had been absolutely and finally determined that his instructions should stand."[2] Kafka was forced to leave us his works, albeit damned and with the mark of death upon them. But in "Josefine," his last work, he outwits his defiant readership by writing a narrative that consumes itself in the telling.

Kafka's last story marks the culmination of a generic revolution from representational to virtually self-referential prose. If "Josefine" had a literary antecedent it would have been Franz Grillparzer's *Der arme Spielmann*, a story Kafka loved[3] and whose major motif is dispersed throughout the Kafka biography as well as the works: the artist, self-deluded, obsessed, misunderstood, subject to the hard father, yoked to irksome work. Yet in "Josefine" these themes are drained of their significance except as negative indices of the character's dissolution. Josefine's unmusicality refers not to Josefine but to the narrator's other statements about her singing.

Kafka's last works have some of the self-referentiality of abstract painting, but for philosophical rather than formal ends that have to do with the ontology of the beast. The animal narrator enables the virtual voiding of representation from the

118

work, the deletion of all human features and cultural references except those the narration itself will prove spurious. But the result is not merely a simulacrum of animal consciousness with its necessarily anthropomorphic configuration. Instead, the narration constitutes a bestial gesture that marks the trajectory from signification to its obliteration, from remembering to forgetting. Becoming the beast is remembering to forget, as being the beast is forgetting to remember, a moment represented by Nietzsche in a hypothetical interlocution. "The human may well ask the animal one day, 'Why do you not talk to me of your bliss and only look at me?' The animal really wants to answer and say: 'It comes of always forgetting right away what I wanted to say.' But it forgot even this answer and was mute: so that the human could only wonder."[4]

The ontology of the beast must be situated not in a form of consciousness but in that border region on the edge of consciousness where every perception is erased at the moment of its inscription. This condition is the prehistory of the child, a condition articulated by Freud in "From the History of an Infantile Neurosis," in which he links the Wolf Man's prehistoric knowledge phylogenetically to the site of animal being.

> When one considers the behavior of the four-year-old child toward the reactivated primal scene, or even when one thinks of the far simpler reactions of the one-and-a-half-year-old child during the actual experience of the scene, one finds it hard to dismiss the view that a kind of hard to define knowledge, like the preparation to understanding, is at work in the child at the time. What this may consist of eludes every attempt to imagine it; we have only the single excellent analogy of the far-reaching *instinctive* knowledge of animals at our disposal.[5]

Freud's metaphor for the psychic process is the mystic writing pad, the child's toy whose prehistoric trace structure becomes more compellingly apparent if it is imagined as being operated by two hands: one writing, the other simultaneously erasing what is in the process of being written.[6] Kafka's narrative will constitute an analogous metaphor, a rhetorically and logically self-consuming fiction.

The narrator of "Josefine" is a mouse, as we infer from his identification with the pack and his representation of its collective point of view. The question raised by having an animal narrator is not, in the first instance, What sort of story would a mouse tell? or, How would an animal story differ from a human story? Kafka uses the narrative deviation of "Josefine" to raise questions about the very enabling of narration itself: Can a mouse tell a story at all? and, How can a story be told at all? The mouse narrator, it turns out, cannot tell a story after all, because of the peculiarity of his membership in the pack. Narrative depends on the ability to sustain differences, and, as Josefine's experience illustrates, it is impossible to maintain difference among the mouse folk. The narrator, like Josefine, fails, and instead of being told, Josefine's story becomes negatively inscribed in the failure of the narration.

"Our singer is named Josefine." The peculiarity of this opening statement is that insofar as it establishes a code, it has no consequence for the story. It doesn't finally matter what the singer is called, and there is never any question that she might actually be called something else. The actual function of the statement in the narration is antonomastic, as though it read, "Josefine is our singer," or "Josefine is called our singer." Josefine's identity depends entirely upon her function as the community's singer; singing constitutes the sole difference that makes her possible as a character in a story. Without this distinctive feature, only her name would remain, a difference, to be sure, but without narrative consequence. If Josefine is not a singer, she loses her function as a character and ceases to exist as a fictional figure; and, indeed, "Josefine, the Singer or the Mouse Folk" constitutes more than one kind of disappearing act. Indeed, the punctuation of the title ("Josefine, die Sängerin oder Das Volk der Mäuse") makes it clear that the opposition is not between Josefine and the mouse folk but between Josefine's identity as a singer and her membership in the pack. The story poses the conundrum, Is Josefine singular or is she plural?—a riddle that insists on the ungrammaticalness (and unintelligibility or logical extinction) Josefine incurs if she is a mouse folk.

The dismantling of Josefine, *the singer,* begins immediately, although without our quite realizing it. "Whoever has not heard her doesn't know the power of song. There is no one who is not carried away by her singing" (172). The litotic structure of these statements turns them into understatements, into intensified praises of the singer. Only much later, when we have begun to doubt that Josefine *is* a singer, that she has ever sung, or ever been heard, do we hear the literal residue behind the trope in these words.[7] The double negative, the denial of the contrary, suggests the possibility that there may have been nothing there in the first place—no song, no singer—and that the statements refer only to a void or a trace.

The narrator altogether eschews an idealistic or Platonic argument, that Josefine's song must inscribe some musical essence, in favor of a semiological analysis, that in order to constitute singing, Josefine's sounds must exhibit some distinctive features that allow them to be contrasted with ordinary mouse speech or piping. Josefine fails by this criterion, and to clinch any lingering doubt, the narrator evokes a cunning demonstration in the form of the innocent piping up of a silly little mouse during one of Josefine's performances: "Now, it was exactly the same as that which we also heard from Josefine . . . to describe the difference would have been impossible" (174).

Although Josefine's singing is reduced, as it were, to quotations as so-called singing, the effect of her performance, identical to that of an artistic performance, remains to be explained. The narrator attempts to do this with the modern argument (his nut-cracking analogy resonates with Dada and conceptual art theory) that art is whatever is perceived as such by artist and audience. The tautological nature of this reasoning is unassailable, but Josefine's audience refuses to validate her piping as singing. The narrator's theory shatters on the imperfect reciprocity between performer and audience that attends other strange conceptual performances in Kafka's works: the fasting in "A Hunger Artist", and the execution in "In the Penal Colony." The narrator submits the audience's devotion to Josefine to a series of rationalizations: the mice listen not to her piping but to the stillness surrounding it; they hear themselves, not Josefine, in her piping; they attend not a concert but an assembly of the folk; they cater to Josefine's temperamental whims not as to an artist but as to an indulged child, and so on. Ultimately, his argument achieves a wonderful sophistic circularity: "May Josefine be protected from the recognition that the fact that we listen to her is evidence against her song"(178).

Josefine is invalidated as a singer, the mouse folk are invalidated as her audience, and their difference is expunged, and with it one of the major anthropomorphic features of mouse culture. We are prepared for this by the earlier description of the mice's unmusicalness as a pure trace structure: they have only an intimation (*eine Ahnung*) of the songs that exist but cannot be sung. Yet the relationship between Josefine and the mouse folk

Kafka's "Josefine"

is expressed in another cultural metaphor, that of parent and child, which must also be emptied of its anthropomorphic overtones and restored to its purely biological significance.

The parental metaphor initially serves a political function. If we interpret her influence as a secondary effect resulting from the pack's indulgence, the power struggle between Josefine and the mouse folk appears to be resolved in their favor. "The actual riddle of her enormous influence" is solved by suggesting that her power is as illusory as that of the insistent child whose parent good-naturedly gives her her way. However, the anthropomorphic residue of the metaphor, which defines the child in terms of an ego development resisting socialization (selfish, irresponsible, foolish) suggests that in this struggle, power, like signification, is a function of difference. If Josefine can be distinguished from the mouse folk, even as an infantile brat ("Then inevitably she becomes enraged, then she stamps her feet, swears most ungirlishly, and she even bites" [175]), she becomes anthropomorphized, individualized, significant, and her story can be told. If not, she becomes appropriated by the mouse folk, animalized, obliterated, her story prevented.

The narrator consequently redefines the child metaphor in a way that empties it of its anthropomorphic ego-defining characteristics and obliterates its difference from the parent. The child's temperamental symptoms of ego immaturity are replaced by kinds of physical immaturity such as difficulty in running, piping, and seeing. The human cultural reference to schools is retracted ("We have no schools" [179]) and with it the notion of childhood as a temporal plenum. The young in the swarm are discontinuous within their momentum ("always, always more new children, without end, without interruption" [179]) but indistinguishable from one another. Childhood itself is a trace structure that disappears while it emerges ("A child barely appears and already it is no longer a child" [179]). The difference between child and adult is oxymoronically collapsed by making the mouse folk "eternally, inextinguishably childish" and "prematurely old" at the same time.

The parental metaphor also defines the controversy governing the relationship between Josefine and the pack with respect to dependency and protection. The predominant question, Who protects whom? is not in itself an anthropomorphic formulation. But corresponding similes, such as Josefine craning her neck above the crowd like a shepherd surveying his flock before a thunderstorm, generate cultural and literary resonances that resound in Kafka's other works. Among these, the demonic version of the Orpheus motif, the Pied Piper of Hamlin, would seem best to fit the ambiguously saving and dooming effect of Josefine's song. Josefine claims that her music saves, or at least sustains, the folk at times of political or economic emergency; they claim that her singing increases their jeopardy by attracting predators.

Kafka himself confounds the critical tendency to endow his fictional music with spiritual essence and transcendental effects ("For Kafka music was, after all, always a means of drawing man beyond all earthly borders"[8]) by satirically describing his childhood music lessons as exercises in mechanical Pavlovian conditioning. "In despair, my violin teacher had rather let me spend my music hour jumping over sticks that he himself held for me, and my musical progress consisted in his holding the sticks higher and higher from lesson to lesson."[9] Cacophonous circus music and blaring hunting horns reduce the canine narrator of "Researches of a Dog" to a writhing bundle of agony. If the animal's susceptibility to music is indeed physiological and compulsive, then an ironic, affirmative residue becomes audible in Gregor Samsa's famous erotesis, "Was he an animal, since music affected him so?"

Like Grete Samsa in "The Metamorphosis," or the Pied Piper of Hamlin, Josefine seems to serve as a musical *pharmakos* effecting good and ill, offering salvation and perdition. Either version of her character might confirm Josefine's influence, the negative version especially so, since it obliges the narrator to explain the mice's willingness to risk casualty in order to attend her performances. After a futile set of reciprocal denials—Josefine's rude "I pipe [fart] on your protection" (176) is interpreted as embarrassed, childish gratitude—the narrator redefines the parental function in a way that essentially extrudes Josefine from her own performances. The human sense of parenting as specific nurturant activity is translated in mouse culture into the generalized security conferred on individuals by membership in the pack. "The power differential between the folk and the individual is so enormous that it suffices to draw the weakling into its warmth, and he is protected enough" (176). The mice assemble not to hear Josefine sing but for the sake of an assembly that itself is emptied of all but zooaffective significance: "We submerge into the feeling of the mass, warmly pressed, body against body" (175).

Reduced to a producer of incidental music at her own performances, Josefine is effaced both as a singer and as a savior, not by having her influence denied but by having the concept of influence itself reduced to a meaningless anthropomorphism in mouse culture. The issue is not whether Josefine saves or betrays the pack but whether the concept of salvation has any significance at all for a fatalistic folk who survive not because they change the course of events but because their exceptional fertility neutralizes their exceptional mortality. The term *savior* itself becomes an acyron, as the narrator describes the mouse as a folk who somehow always manage to save themselves even at the cost of horrifying casualties. The statement makes no sense, the casualties contradict the saving (avoidance of loss or waste), and yet one more anthropomorphic feature in Josefine's differentiation from the pack has been deleted.

The final labor dispute between Josefine and the pack reveals the actual object of their struggle to be something other than either labor or art: "Clearly, Josefine does not actually aspire to what she literally demands" (182). The ulterior motive is differentiation; Josefine wants to be regarded as a goddess, that is, to have her difference acknowledged. The narrator confirms this when he concedes that the labor exemption would have no de facto significance in Josefine's life: she would work no less and her singing would grow no better. What she would achieve by being exempted from ordinary labor is "public, unequivocal, enduring, superlative recognition of her art" (182): not only differentiation, but recognition of difference.

The final conflict between Josefine and the mouse folk emerges as a phantom campaign in which the trace structure of difference becomes apparent. If Josefine possesses difference (and the narrator cites and rejects the argument that her very ability to conceive of demanding an exemption from work proves this), that difference, like a zero suffix, lacks the materiality to make itself perceivable or verifiable. It is simultaneously present and absent, as Josefine's strategies demonstrate. She offers not positive incentives (differences) but negative penalties (lack of difference) to further her cause: she will not sing at the limits of her talent if her petition is denied. Since her difference is immaterial, her threat to cut the grace notes from her song cannot be verified: "Reputedly she has carried out her threat, although I have noticed no difference from her earlier performances" (184). Her foot injury, likewise, is unverifiable, and the mouse folk believe her disability feigned. She has no means of effecting recognition of her difference.

Beasts of the Modern Imagination

The mouse folk's response to Josefine's stratagems is carefully emptied of its anthropomorphic residue to constitute a pure, abstract impermeability to difference. The narrator repeatedly describes the mouse folk in terms of the emotional equivalent to this ontological condition: cold, judicial, impenetrable—in short, profoundly indifferent. Their refusal of Josefine's petition lacks all human motives or rational basis. The narrator deliberately raises, and dismisses, the specter of a folk exasperated beyond endurance by Josefine's demands and actively resisting her dominance. He likewise presents no arguments for their refusal: "They also do not bother very much to refute the basis of her petition" (181). The mice simply do not change in their comportment toward Josefine; they admit no difference into their own behavior. "The folk listens to her song as gratefully and enchanted as ever, but makes very little fuss over its curtailment" (184). Their indifference does not represent an emotional or rational counterstrategy on the part of the mouse folk. It constitutes instead their radical animality.

Josefine's last stratagem is intrinsically ironic. Unsuccessful in modifying her song in a way that would create a noticeable difference (not singing as well as she could; cutting, restoring, or deleting her grace notes; singing in ostensible pain or weakness) she stops singing altogether. Josefine therefore disappears, not literally but logically, by obliterating her "difference" from the pack. Her technique achieves a singular circularity as she combats indifference (lack of recognition) by becoming indifferent (undistinguished). Only her anthropomorphic motive, her resort to a stratagem, distinguishes her disappearance from the "disappearance" indigenous to the animality of the mouse folk. Yet the narrator cancels even this last little anthropomorphism by suggesting that her ploy may have been no ploy, that her disappearance was not a stratagem at all but a destined instinctual act of her mouse nature. "Strange, how she miscalculates, the clever one, so wrongly, that one could think she doesn't calculate at all, but is merely driven on by her destiny, which in our world can only be a very sad one" (185).

Josefine's disappearance fully reveals the trace structure of mouse culture. Her silence is as indistinguishable from other silences as her piping was indistinguishable from other piping. Paradoxically, piping and silence (which should be mutually exclusive) become interchangeable and indistinguishable from each other. "How will it be possible to hold the assemblies in perfect silence? Of course, weren't they also mute with Josefine

Kafka's "Josefine"

there?'' (185). Accordingly, the mouse folk react no differently
to Josefine absent than to Josefine present. "She hides and does
not sing, but the folk quietly, without visible disappointment,
self-possessed, a self-contained mass . . . moves on its way"
(185).

The interplay of singing and silence, and its connection to a
hierarchy of cunning, is deployed so brilliantly in Kafka's very
short work, "The Silence of the Sirens,"[10] that it merits a brief
digression here. The piece shares the rhetorical structure of other
Kafka works, including "Josefine," that construct a dilemma
through a series of assertions and retractions.

> The song of the sirens is dangerous.
> Ulysses stops his ears with wax and chains himself to a mast.
> The song of the sirens pierces through wax and undoes chains.
> Ulysses trusts to his stratagem.
> The silence of the sirens is more dangerous than their song.
>
> (my paraphrase of the argument)

Ulysses appears doomed either way, since silence and singing,
which logically should be mutually exclusive, become interchangeable and undifferentiated in their effects.

The solution to the dilemma depends not on a stratagem per
se but on a failure to perceive the failure of a stratagem. By
thinking the wax and chains are successful, Ulysses mistakes the
sirens' silence for escape from their song. Not his cunning, but
the failure of his cunning, manages to drive a wedge of difference (or *différance,* if you will) between the silence and the
unheard song. But Kafka cannot resist the final convolution of
the conundrum, and he adds the following possibility in a codi-
cil to the story: wily Ulysses hears the silence of the sirens with
impunity by pretending not to hear their song. He appropriates
the trace structure of silence as both a presence and an absence
and neutralizes the danger of both the sirens' song and the
sirens' silence by collapsing them as positive and negative versions of one another. His ruse, the pretended failure to hear their
song, is interposed like a "shield" between himself and the
sirens' double danger.

Some of the features of this Ulyssean cunning pertain also to
the mouse folk of "Josefine," notably its complementary relationship to musicality. "With the smile of this cunning, we tend
to console ourselves for everything, even if once in a while—
although this never happens—we were to yearn for the happiness that music perhaps brings" (172). With its rational implica-

tions, this *Schlauheit* seems a peculiar distinctive feature to characterize the mouse folk until we note how it is modified to empty it of anthropomorphic significance. As a "perfectly harmless cunning" this prized attribute is stripped of the malice, the ulterior motive, the defensive emotional residue that colors its human manifestation. Furthermore, Josefine's "unworthy tactics," her attempts to manipulate and threaten the mouse folk into compliance, appear to be different from that uncalculated, fatalistic cunning that causes her, in the end, to outwit herself and unconsciously, inadvertently, rejoin the mouse folk. She does this through her failure, like Ulysses, to understand the failure of her stratagem. This zoomorphic cunning of the mice is irrational rather than suprarational, unconscious and instinctive, a matter of "inadequate and even childish" means.[11]

The cunning and slyness of the mouse folk operate on a double register of human and animal desire that is patterned on the historical models of Hegel and Nietzsche respectively. Josefine wants nothing less than "public, unequivocal, lasting, superlative recognition of her art" (182), that is, "pure prestige"[12] of the kind that animates the Hegelian Master in the evolution of human self-consciousness. The mouse folk not only deny Josefine her recognition ("She sings, in her own opinion, to deaf ears . . . she has long ago learned to forego real understanding, in her sense of her word" [174]) but they also refuse to enter into the antithetical relationship of the Master / Servant conflict by refusing to claim recognition for themselves. Instead of a dialectical conflict that engenders a human and spiritual evolution, the historical movement of the mouse folk is counterevolutionary, a surrender to the instinctual, the fated, the animal, the "becoming what one is," that marks the counterprogressive history of Nietzsche's eternal recurrence. Josefine herself loses her struggle for recognition to a Nietzschean *amor fati* when she submits to her animal fate in the very act and at the very moment she thought to triumph over it.

Mediating the relationship between Josefine and the mouse folk is the narrator of the story. This narrator must, in some respects, be seen as Josefine's double, since their respective enterprises—Josefine's music and his history (storytelling, criticism, philosophy)—form an anthropomorphic pair. Amid an acultural, ahistorical species that ostensibly practices neither music nor history, the singer and the narrator stand as diacritically marked ciphers. Both constitute difference ("Josefine is the sole exception; she loves music" [172]) and create difference (the narrator's creation of character, event, conflict). But as a member of the mouse folk the narrator can no more maintain difference than can Josefine. His story collapses as Josefine is retracted as a singer, her performances become indistinguishable from one another and from other piping and silence, and her conflict with the mouse folk dissolves in the convolutions of her double self-betrayal. The narrator's career is fated to follow the ontological trajectory of Josefine's career as a singer.

Josefine and the narrator function as creators of difference because they have subjectivity, a consciousness of the self as different from the other, from the mass, and as possessing an individualistic point of view. Josefine's subjectivity results in psychological and political centricity: she creates centers of opinion and performance amid the random dispersal of the mouse folk. Her centricity is literal and spatial as Josefine determines the site of her concerts not by the needs of her audience but purely by her presence. "She can do this wherever she likes; it need not be a widely visible place: any sheltered corner selected according to the accidental whim of the moment is just as useful" (175). Her performance is, in some sense, no more than an assembly of the mouse folk of which she is the center. The narrator, conversely, conducts his critique of Josefine from his own point of vantage, orienting himself initially to a centered Josefine. "And when you sit before her, you understand her; opposition works only from a distance; when you sit before her you know: what she pipes here is no piping" (174). Later the narrator revises his critique by shifting his point of view. Josefine becomes displaced as a producer of incidental music, and her performance becomes decentered, as mouse relates to neighboring mouse, pressed body to warm body.

The narration is sustained by the conventional literary difference of conflict between Josefine and the mouse folk. But if Josefine is positively marked among the mice with respect to music, the mouse folk are not defined as simply unmusical by contrast, like the other half of a phonemic opposition. The narrator clearly intends to confound their identity altogether, making them neither musical nor exactly unmusical, but rather catching them in a slippery rhetorical web of negatives, conditionals, and hypotheticals that simply dissolves their desire for music altogether into the undifferentiated fatalism of their animal cunning.

Quiet peace is our favorite music; our life is difficult, and, even when we have attempted to shake off our daily worries,

Beasts of the Modern Imagination

we can *no* longer elevate ourselves to such things as remote from our ordinary life as music. Still, we do *not* bemoan this very much; we do *not* get *even* so far; a certain practical cunning, which, of course, we need most urgently, we consider our greatest advantage, and with the smile of this cunning, we tend to console ourselves for everything, even *if* once in a while—*although* this never happens—we *were* to yearn for the happiness that music *perhaps* brings. (172; italics mine)

The musical difference between Josefine and the mouse folk is confounded by the literal residue of the metaphor that equates music with silence ("Quiet peace is our favorite music").

The dramatic center of the work is the political conflict between two groups, Josefine's sycophantic retinue and her opposition, a conflict whose anthropomorphic configuration makes it accessible to the allegorical interpretation that "Josefine" is a parable of the conflict between the artist and a philistine society.[13] But the narrator confounds this conflict too, first by qualifying his own position with respect to the opposition group ("to which I too *half*-belong" [174, my italics]), then by qualifying the opposition as "we *ostensible* opponents" (175, my italics), and finally by dismissing her opponents altogether as Josefine's paranoid delusion ("If she really had enemies, as she claims. . . . But she has no enemies" [182]). The conflict between Josefine's supporters and opponents is logically neutralized from the first, when their difference is expunged. They act exactly the same, as we are told that "the opposition, to which I too half-belong, surely admires her no less than the masses do" (174).

If Josefine's friends and enemies (or putative friends and enemies) behave in identical fashion by equally cheering and applauding her performances, and if both misunderstand her, as Josefine claims, albeit in different ways, then the significance of their difference is obliterated. Kafka indicates a reason for this when he tells us why it is impossible for the mouse folk to laugh at Josefine. "One does not laugh at something entrusted to you; to laugh at that would be a violation of duty" (176). Laughter is possible only when there is separation, alienation, distance, that is, difference. The inability to laugh at Josefine is a symptom of her oneness with the species, her interchangeability with every member of it, a symptom underscored later when we learn that Josefine's "enemies" do not laugh at her because they recognize that the folk would treat them in an identical way, were they to

Kafka's "Josefine"

try to establish their own difference. "For this reason alone, because the folk here presents itself in its cold, judicial posture, as one only seldom sees it among us. But even if you were to approve of this posture in this case, the mere consideration that the folk might one day treat you in a similar way, precludes any pleasure" (182). Josefine's "enemies" have imaginatively identified with her and exchanged places with her. The difference of their hostility (or the hostility of their difference) is collapsed.

There remains the reciprocal *méconnaissance* between Josefine and the mouse folk. But if Josefine believes this to be a mere confusion of signifieds, if she believes her song to be one thing while the mice believe it to be another, the narrator, who believes her song to be nothing, makes the misunderstanding more radical still. Yet the narrator, in treating her song as signifying nothing, treats it like the Lacanian *parole vide*,[14] the empty Word that retains social value while saying nothing, that stands for the possibility of communication even while communicating nothing, that functions, ultimately, as a tessera. "Josefine asserts herself; this Nothing in voice, this Nothing in accomplishment asserts itself and makes its way to us; it is comforting to think about" (178). Josefine's song is the trace, the presence of an absence, and serves, in this respect, as an analogue to Jakob's music in Grillparzer's *Der arme Spielmann*.

This *méconnaissance* becomes, in a sense, the irreducible difference of the work because it makes its trace structure possible. The narrator recognizes that it is equally important for Josefine to sing *and* to sing nothing. But if Josefine knew she were singing nothing, she would not sing at all. This clarifies the narrator's enigmatic reference to the public service rendered by Josefine's sycophants: by keeping her blind to the insignificance of her song, these flatterers keep her singing (177). Conversely, the folk, or at least the narrator, must understand the significance of the insignificance of Josefine's singing, a state of affairs that Josefine senses and that causes her dissatisfaction with her public adulation. "She surely has an inkling of this—why else would she deny so passionately that we listen to her?—but she continues ever to sing, piping this suspicion away" (178).

The also seemingly irreducible difference of sex or gender in the work cannot be dismissed as a merely grammatical attribution, a feminization because Josefine is *die Maus*. The narration displays cultural sexual attitudes toward Josefine anthropomorphic enough for Michael Feingold to speak of "her virtually feminist bitterness when mouse-males treat her as a mere love

winning play, *Josefine: The Mouse Singer*.[15] But like the parental
metaphor, these sexual allusions are also emptied of their cultural content in various ways and reduced to their biological and
insignificant difference.

Josefine's behavior contradicts the sexual stereotypes the narrator imposes on her. "She, who on the outside actually represents perfect delicacy, conspicuously delicate even among our
folk so rich in such feminine types, seemed at that moment
downright vulgar" (173). Elsewhere, Josefine flies into a terrible
rage, stamps her feet, "swears most ungirlishly" (175), and
bites, behavior still anthropomorphic but with its animal residue
violently erupting. Josefine's femininity is always introduced at
the moment it is denied, and her behavior signals not its cultural
opposite, masculinity, but its natural opposite, animality. If Josefine's gender distinction seems preserved to the very end, when
at her apotheosis she joins her brothers ("alle ihre Brüder"
[185]), it is preserved at the moment of dissolution and obliteration when Josefine is lost among them and forgotten like them.

The movement of the story of Josefine, such as it is, is
inscribed in its entirety in the first paragraph of the work: Josefine moves from music to nonmusic, from life to death, from
difference from the folk to identity with the folk. The narrative
"events" at the end of the story, when we learn that Josefine
refuses to sing, that she has vanished, that she will die, are
merely a mimetic enactment or repetition of the logical movement of the narration in the first paragraph. This interplay of
narrative and logic in "Josefine" reveals the awful secret of storytelling, which Kafka was by no means the first to discover:
Sterne's *Tristram Shandy* illustrates as well as any work that
storytelling requires the repression of its own logical processes
and that narration and narrative, logic and tale spinning, are
inevitably at war with one another.

In "Josefine" this problem is best explored as one of logical
direction. The narrator never gets on with a tale because instead
of the logical processes that propel a story forward (belief in
causality, the development of consequences, the drawing of
inferences and conclusions) his determination to analyze premises and assumptions and to explore the ground of Josefine's
ontological status preempts the narrative. With the pivotal statement, "I have often wondered how it actually is with this
music" (172), the narrator returns the story to its origin; the
story becomes the reverse of born, not its negation or opposite,

nor a stillbirth or abortion, but its directional reversal, which, for lack of a word or concept, can be illustrated only with comedienne Joan Rivers's visual joke when she suggested to her parenting class that for a lark they run their childbirth film in reverse and watch the infant disappear into the womb. Freud's mystic writing pad has a similar structure.

"Josefine is the sole exception; she loves music and knows also how to communicate it; she is the only one; with her passing, music—who knows for how long—will disappear from our lives" (172). As the narrator proceeds to explore the ontological question of "how it actually is with this music," and Josefine is revealed to pipe just like other mice, the logical erasure of Josefine's difference becomes identical with the death predicted for her. Implicit in all the ambiguous meanings of *Hingang,* that euphemism for death (passing, departure), is the notion that ontologically death is precisely an erasure of difference, a transition from difference to lack of difference, for is it not the case that in life we are all different while in death we are all the same? Or, to put it another way, is death not precisely the inability of the living to sustain their difference from the dead?

The narrator's sophistic logic, which might be paraphrased into the following syllogistic forms, makes just such a conclusion inevitable:

1. Josefine is different from the mouse folk because she has music while they are unmusical.
2. When Josefine is dead, she will be unmusical like the mouse folk.
3. The mouse folk, being unmusical, are dead.
4. If Josefine lacks music, like the mouse folk, then she is dead before she dies.

Just as music and silence, instead of being logically mutually exclusive, become identical elsewhere in the story, so life and death, which should also be logically mutually exclusive, become identical as their difference collapses. Josefine's *Hingang* is therefore ironic, for it is not a passage or a transition at all. This explains why the mouse folk will not miss her, either when she disappears or when she dies, why their comportment and sentiment are identical toward Josefine alive and Josefine dead, and why Josefine, like her song, is *unverlierbar,* impossible to lose. "Was her actual piping noticeably louder or livelier than its memory will be? Was it even in her lifetime ever more than a mere memory? Did not the folk, in its wisdom, value

Josefine's singing so highly precisely because it was, in this sense, beyond losing?'' (185).

Kafka turned to the animal in his late fiction because the radicalness of his ontological vision required a negative site of narration: the site of animal being. Kafka dismantles logic as Joyce dismantles language. He systematically deanthropomorphizes language by emptying the conceptual universe of its cultural residue and by emptying rhetoric of its metaphorical residue. This latter process is the Lacanian version of dream work, a reminder, like Freud's in the Wolf Man case, that the analogy of the unconscious and the infantile must also be extended to the animal.

Kafka's technique, finally antiphilosophical insofar as it depends on the dissolution of rational thought, appropriates the negative or deconstructed metaphysics of Derrida's trace. The metaphor of writing forces itself upon Kafka as it does upon Derrida, for in the trace, or *Spur,* left by the erasure it is possible to have a narration that is simultaneously present and absent. How else could we have the story of Josefine, the singer who is no singer, told by a member of a folk who practice no *Geschichte* (history or narration) except as a phantom narration, a trace.

Finally, if one wishes to read ''Josefine'' as an autobiographical fable, as Kafka's own swan (or mouse) song, then the final gesture consigning his works to the flames takes on the significance of that mysterious double cunning that prompts Josefine to stop singing. The parallels between story and biography— Kafka's lifelong desire for exemption from ordinary labor, his temperamental recoil from an avid, but misunderstanding public, the persistence of loyal supporters, like Brod—suggest that Kafka's motives may have been far more philosophical and ironic than neurotic. Recognizing the trace structure of works that consume themselves logically and rhetorically in paradox and self-contradiction, perhaps he sensed that in their conceptual insubstantiality his texts were already as spectral as ashes and therefore past losing. With superior cunning he may therefore have wanted to surrender to fate, to absorption in the self-contained, undifferentiated, eternally recurring mass of the folk who practice no history or narration and so forget their heroes. Perhaps at the end of his life, Kafka forgot to tell us that to be happy we must, like Nietzsche's animal, remember to forget.

Kafka's ''Josefine''

7

Max Ernst:
The Rhetorical Beast
of the Visual Arts

Among the producers of pictorial animal images in modern
painting and sculpture, Max Ernst, even more than such practitioners of "animal perspective" as Franz Marc, critiques anthropocentrism with an antihumanistic attack on reason, idealism,
and conventional morality. I also find him enacting the bestial
gestures of Nietzsche and Darwin, a view that challenges two
established versions of the Surrealist genealogy. Neither a
Romantic heritage, like the one Herbert Read and Hugh Sykes
Davies[1] see reflected in the antibourgeois behavior of the Surrealists, nor the neo-Platonic quest for a primal content or a superior reality that Anna Balakian infers from Breton's writings,
seems to me adequately to account for the representational and
technical ruptures in Ernst's works. Both explanations of classical
or Romantic influence seem to me to ground Ernst in an older
metaphysics of idealistic residue that blunts the radical implications of his violent content and form. I hope to show that Ernst,
whose interest in the philosophical and pathological aspects of
the irrational preceded his interest in art,[2] embarked on a
doomed quest to wrest art from reason and culture, where a long
humanistic tradition had enshrined it, and restore it to irrationality, to the libido, to free association, to puns and Derridean
freeplay, to chance—that is, to the human animal itself.

While studying at the University of Bonn as a young man,
Max Ernst read Nietzsche's *Die fröhliche Wissenschaft* ("There,
if ever . . . is a book which speaks to the future. The whole of
surrealism is in it") and was, apparently, profoundly impressed
by its resistance to the domestication of "the fundamental wildness of human nature."[3] Nietzsche may also have adumbrated
for Ernst the radical implications the return of the human beast
poses for art, although Ernst's antiaesthetic theories were equally
influenced by the modern psychoanalysis of his Freudian age.
We see a major shift in the artist's role as early as Ernst's Dada
period, when behavior was given primacy over production and

art became an "act" rather than an artifact. These early experiments in spontaneous and improvised performance were particularly important for the visual artists of the period as attempts to overcome the Apollonian implications (of conscious and rational production, the projection of ideal form, the creation of logic and order, among others) of their media. Restoring the chthonic to art, artists liberated themselves from service to society and culture as repositories of humanistic virtue. Following Nietzsche's revaluation of morality, the artist was no longer a "good" person, an idealist, and indeed, Surrealist artists asserted their return to ferity with the celebration of Violette Nozières, the oedipal criminal whose partly successful parricide represented to them the restoration of libido to the bourgeoisie. Indeed, art became for Ernst, as for many of his Dada contemporaries, a mission of malice.

But insofar as Ernst practices his art as a bestial gesture, and he does so far beyond donning bird masks and investing himself in an imaginary bird familiar, his ontology (and consequently his method) differs somewhat from Nietzsche's. Where Nietzsche "forgets" the "other," cultivating the genuine oblivion of animals toward the consciousness of others as subjects, Ernst practices instead a cunning, and sometimes violent, attack on the "other." Where Nietzsche rebuffs and negates his readers and critics, Ernst teases, traps, discomfits, and shocks them by outraging their expectations and ideals, confronting them with the limitations of their reason, and extorting from them libidinal responses by implicating them as voyeurs in his unholy fantasies. The viewer of *The Blessed Virgin Chastises the Infant Jesus Before Three Witnesses: A. B., P. E. and the Artist* (fig.1), for example, is necessarily embarrassed because Ernst, Breton, and Eluard function as witnesses not only of the scene, but also to our voyeurism in seeing the scene. We are seen seeing. Yet finally Ernst's aims appear to be no more messianic or pedagogic than Nietzsche's as he seems to embrace the same sort of fatalism that renders all efforts to reform or improve mankind pointless and hopeless. His malice is not that of the satirist with moral pretensions, but a purer, simpler, more self-reflexive and literal "beastliness."

As Ernst uses the "other" structurally in his disanthropic enterprise, so he uses the social and the cultural thematically. Because the reclamation of human wildness must be effected through culture, Ernst's efforts produce not naïve or primitive figures like those of Henri Rousseau, but images marked with

Max Ernst

Figure 1. *The Blessed Virgin Chastises the Infant Jesus Before Three Witnesses: A.B., P.E. and the Artist*

psychological crookedness, perversity, and the twisted, devious forms of pornology. This quite corresponds to the psychoanalytical recognition of hallucination as the form of the return of the repressed, of foreclosed thoughts and instincts.[4] Ernst found an excellent precurser for techniques of derangement and estrangement in Lewis Carroll, the master of infiltrating Victorian social rituals (tea parties, croquet games, quadrilles, recitations) with infantile libidinal preoccupations (food, aggression, play, growth). Although Ernst's most direct acknowledgments of his debt to Carroll do not appear until the 1940s,[5] Carroll's influence is already much in evidence in Ernst's work of the two preceding decades. The shocking, and embarrassingly funny,

Beasts of the Modern Imagination

collage novels of Max Ernst[6] particularly echo Carroll's subversions of polite society with madness, metamorphoses, and physical functions (like Alice's deluge of tears). The eruptions of erotic and libidinal behavior are, of course, more explicit in Ernst's collage novels than in Carroll's children's books, and nature's reappropriations of culture are more violent, as in the destructive invasions of domestic interiors by the elemental forces of flood, storm, pestilence, and plague.

If these subversions were purely thematic, then Carroll's and Ernst's aims might be construed as primarily satirical, as moralistic criticisms of one or another human excess or social folly. But Ernst, like Carroll, deranges form, function, relation, and structure as well, and thereby shifts his endeavor from the merely critical to the virtually deconstructive. Even more than Carroll, whose hybrids function as neologisms or new lexical creations ("'toves' are something like badgers; they're something like lizards; and they're something like corkscrews"), Ernst's monstrous zoo reflects a free invention and distortion of form unthinkable in the pre-Darwinian age. Moreover, Ernst's monsters announce no "difference" or "deviation" in their forms, and therefore, like Darwinian "abnormalities," serve to abolish the normative function of form. Giants are "abnormal" only in the context of a convention of size; Ernst's outsize fingers reaching blindly through the windows of *Oedipus Rex* (fig.2) lack any relative measure. Since the very concept of the "ideal" is implicated in such normative thinking, in the fantasy of absolutely abstracting matters of measure and relationship, the endless variability, inconsistency, and incoherence of Ernstian figures refutes any neo-Platonic significance. Indeed, since our critical language is itself thoroughly grounded in normative thinking, the description and analysis of the Surrealist aesthetic (or anti-aesthetic) poses a whole set of discursive challenges that will surface in the course of my discussion.

Finally, in Ernst, as in Carroll, we find a proto-Freudian experiment with semiotic derangement, with the creation of more or less unintelligible messages, whose function is not only to demonstrate the inadequacy of reason when confronted with the irrational, but also to frustrate and dislodge the "other," the reader, the viewer, as subject. If Carroll yet maintains hermeneutical efficacy by having Humpty Dumpty translate or explicate "Jabberwocky" for Alice, Ernst's creation of seemingly unintelligible ciphers and hieroglyphics in the 1970s is a triumph of nonsense, of the irreducibility of his pictorial "signs." These

Max Ernst

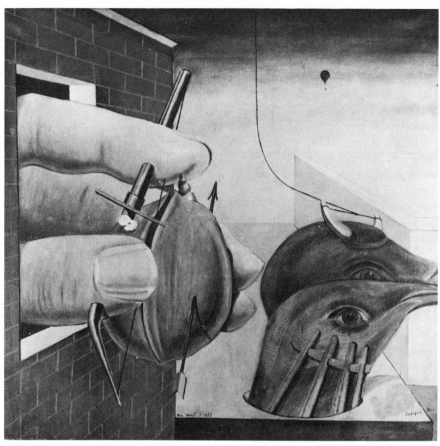

Figure 2. *Oedipus Rex*

extreme later experiments in a kind of negative discourse are
already adumbrated in the collage novels, which must be
"read" not as symbolic productions but as aggressive acts aimed
at the reader's rational faculties. No less than the *frottages* of an
earlier period, the pictorial rubbings created by arbitrary or free
interpretations of the chance features of wood grains and cloth
textures, the collage novels plunge the reader into an oxymoronic "delirium of interpretation"[7] that yields only fractured
sense, uncertain meaning, and conflicting affects. Ernst's picture
books reduce us to illiterate children by frustrating our appropriation of the text. It is in this respect—in neutralizing the useful-
ness of our conventions as a key to understanding, and in deny-

ing us control or authority as readers—that Ernst's collage novels fundamentally differ from the Gothic genre to which they are substantially indebted.[8] For if the Gothic generally reintegrates our deranged perceptions and restores us to a sane grasp of its bizarre behavior and irrational events, then we can see Ernst gradually dismantling the residue of its conventions, as he abolishes it narrative structures (dispensing with the dream frame after *Rêve d'une petite fille qui voulut entrer au Carmel*) and rhetorical devices (deleting all but prefatory texts in *Une Semaine de bonté*).

Firstly, I will explore mainly Ernst's early works, those of the 1930s and before, with special attention to the self-reflexivity inherent in his works. A study of his forms is simultaneously an anatomy of representation, a study of the problems of conceptualizing form. Secondly, in considering the treatment of function in his major formal Surrealist paintings, I hope to show that in the case of such relations as "entrapment," for example, the represented function and the function of the representation are the same. And thirdly, I will explore Ernst's last major collage novel, *Une Semaine de bonté*. I will, of course, be mindful of my own confrontation with Ernst's pictorial texts, and my activity will probably seem less a "reading" than a documentation of Ernst's assault upon the kind of "other" described by Derrida in "White Mythology," the Westerner who believes his own myths and who mistakes his language for divine Reason itself. "A white mythology which assembles and reflects Western culture: the white man takes his own mythology (that is, Indo-European mythology), his *logos*—that is, the *mythos* of his idiom, for the universal form of that which it is still his inescapable desire to call Reason."[9] While scarcely escaping this attack altogether, I expect to expose my own limitations and entrapments in confronting Ernst's art, and thereby to pay the price of a limited authority as critic. Like the other artists of the biocentric tradition, Ernst's own bestial gesture shifts us out of the "human" cultural realm, in which we study art and literature to become better *Bildungsphilister* (to borrow Nietzsche's term) into the fierce but unselfconscious arena of the modern beast.

It is a commonplace in Ernst criticism to assume that his great themes are Paradise Lost and Paradise Regained. Consistent with the psychoanalytic bias of Surrealism, the lost paradise is thought to be as much prenatal as prelapsarian. John Russell finds Ernst's nostalgia for the womb in the image of the German *Wald*.[10] Yvon Taillandier goes even further, attributing Ernst's

Max Ernst

fragmented and hybridized forms to the loss of the prenatal paradise. "(In the voice of an eagle-human hybrid) I commemorate and celebrate Edenic gestation; but, since the distance and the difference between this Paradise and the Gehenna we must cross to reach the open air are as great as those existing between humanity and animality, even when aquiline, my double and antinomic nature is my testimony to the hell of being born, like a perpetual summons and eternal incitement to invent a new world and a new life."[11] Ernst's reputed hallucination of his own conception contradicts this notion. The ingredients of the father's gestating vase or top are already monstrous animal forms, which he creates by drawing with a crayon. "Breathing loudly he hastily traces black lines on the imitation mahogany. Quickly he gives it new, surprising and despicable forms. He exaggerates the resemblance to ferocious and vicious animals to such an extent that they become alive, inspiring me with horror and anguish."[12] Not only Ernst's writings, but his paintings also, contest the notion that prenatal life offers some wholeness or integrity of form. In fact, if the floating forms in *After Us—Motherhood* (fig.3) can be taken to represent fetal forms, then Ernst depicts the phylogenetic process as one of fragmentation and hybridization: birds with lacunae for eyes, elastic arms, webbed feet, clawed paws, cat's whiskers, and transparent tadpole tails. Taillandier's proposed prenatal paradise ultimately represents a valorization of the concept of form that designates the concept of Platonic ideal form or essence as superior, and the concept of forms hybridized, fragmented, deformed, or incomplete (I am forced to use words that themselves reflect the Platonic bias in our language) as inferior. Yet Ernst himself introduces his collage novel *La Femme 100 têtes* with the sentence, "Crime or miracle: a complete man."

Anna Balakian writes that "one of the basic characteristics of the surrealist mind is its uncompromising will to find a foolproof unity in the universe."[13] This premise is echoed by Whitney Chadwick in an article on sexuality and creativity in Surrealist art that proposes the figure of the androgyne as a symbol of precisely such a unity, "the metaphysical fusion of male and female into the perfect being."[14] According to Chadwick, the Surrealists consciously adopted the ideal of androgyny from Plato. Yet again, Ernst's art constitutes an anti-Platonic comment on ideal or classical form.

Although Werner Spies maintains that his extensive documentation of the "sources" of Ernst's collages will not explain

Figure 3. *After Us—Motherhood*

their meaning ("Work with the patterns belongs unequivocally to the realm of production-aesthetic"),[15] I would argue that the "source" is precisely the referent of many of Ernst's distorted and deformed classical figures. Ernst's *donnée,* as it were, appears to be the subversion of the process of idealization itself, for his "sources" include not only Greek and Roman figures but idealized forms as interpreted by later artists (Botticelli, Titian, Ingres, Blake) as well.

In the series of "First Visible Poems" from *Une Semaine de bonté,* Ernst inverts classical forms, quite literally. The male figure in "First Visible Poem, No. 3" (fig.4) appears to be modeled after a classical male figure with the proportions of a Greek *Doryphorus* and the posture of the Roman *Augustus of*

Max Ernst

Figure 4. From *Une Semaine de bonté*

Primaporta (except that in each case the position of the legs is reversed). But Ernst flays the figure and hollows it, to render it incomplete or imperfect. He further replaces the head with a plantlike form, perhaps to mock the Greek ideal of the harmony of mind and body. He once wrote of himself in the persona of a little girl, "He is a brain and a vegetable at the same time."[16] In an early 1920 collage entitled *La Santé par le sport,* the Greek athletic ideal appears to be mocked not only by the contemporary hockey stick in the figure's hand, but also by the crocheted butterfly in place of the face. Not only does the butterfly create a juxtaposition of diverse textures, but it may imply an ambiguity of gender as well, a reference to either Greek homosexuality or the "ideal" of androgyny. This comment is also repeated later when Ernst outfits the burly figure of Hercules ("At eye level / Paramyths," Beverly Hills, Calif., 1949) with a beribboned and ruffled ladies' parasol.

The back view of the female figure in "First Visible Poem, No. 4" likewise recalls the proportions and posture of artistic idealizations of the female body, a Greek Venus, or even Botticelli's more florid goddess, who is particularly evoked by a number of Ernst's inversions in the picture. The figure rises not from the famous half-shell but from a bleached rib cage, suggesting also the unfortunate Eve (in *Histoire naturelle,* Eve is also represented by a view of the back of her head). Instead of the luxuriant hair, Ernst's Venus sprouts an insect or a crustacean and a headdress of fruits and transparent petals, like the adorned figures in Bosch's *Garden of Earthly Delights.* Ernst replaces Botticelli's cool, fresh seascape with an arid, rocky desert strewn with corpses.

Ernst attacks the concept of idealization in art at several levels of philosophical sophistication. At the simplest level, his collages are pictorial parodies of classical forms and figures, their aesthetic harmony and proportion destroyed by alterations that render them unbeautiful and ludicrous. For example, in his picture of the Venus de Milo on p.29 in *Paramyths* (fig.5), he destroys her grace of form by substituting an incongruous, tilted rectangle in place of her face. The butterfly hair or headdress is a recurrent motif in Ernst's work (as we have seen) that suggests either atrophied wings (his pictorial lexicon abounds in winged forms, celestial, satanic, avian, entomological, and reptilian) or infestation (particularly the infestation of monuments, like the rat- or dog-infested Sphinx in "Oedipe" of *Une Semaine de bonté*), elements that diminish and humble the classical form.

But Ernst subjects the Venus to more serious debasement by using in his collage not a direct representation of the statue in the Louvre but an illustration from Bulfinch's *Age of Fable or Beauties of Mythology,* an imitation of "low" art rather than "high" art. Ernst's use of popularized materials (*Le Magasin pittoresque,* Reuleaux's *Buch der Erfindung, La Nature,* and trashy, sensational serials like the *Mémoires de Monsieur Claude*) constitute what Spies calls a *Kulturputsch.* [17] But Ernst's intentions go beyond mere iconoclasm to a philosophical dismantling of form. By using popular illustrations of the *Venus de Milo* he reminds us of the cultural reversions that constitute a hermeneutical spiral in classical art. The sculpture of the Venus in the Louvre itself represents only a representation, a pictorial figure

Max Ernst

Figure 5. From *Paramyths*

of the goddess who is herself only a rhetorical figure, a personification of ideal beauty.

By rendering Venus's drape like a topographical chart, Ernst further subverts the aesthetic image by reminding us that it is invested in a physical form no different in its essential physical features (elevations and angles of curvature, for example) from any other physical object. Furthermore, the representation of that physical image is also subject to a perceptual reversion of forms: the topological chart reminds us that Ernst gives us a two-dimensional form to represent a three-dimensional form. He also reminds us of the ultimate two-dimensionality of his Venus by rendering her face as a circle (not a sphere) superimposed by a parallelogram simulating a tilted rectangle, or the illusion of a rectangle in three-dimensional space. The circular and straight arrows on the rectangle appear to represent an illustration of a magnetic field, an image that might serve several functions. The lines crudely trace a pattern resembling the orbital shape of eyes and an intersecting nose or proboscis, a pattern suggesting the exaggerated and grotesque features of an insect. Ernst might also be using the magnetic field as a scientific analogue of Venus's aesthetic and emotional power to attract and control. Furthermore, the magnetic diagram is itself a pictorial representation of an abstract concept, like Ernst's Venus herself.

In his Venus Ernst gives us a complex semiotic image that virtually self-destructs by parodying and debasing its source, by revealing its own cultural reversions (high art imitating low art imitating high art imitating myth) and formal reversions (copy of copy, representation of representation, illusion of illusion) and by asserting that, whatever their rhetorical intention, aesthetic symbols are mere signifiers of abstract concepts, with no more privileged status as shadows of the Platonic ideal than a scientific diagram or a word like *beauty.*

Ernst's Venus lacks arms, his *Victory of Samothrace* lacks a head, not only in imitation of the originals but, judging from his own "mutilated" or "amputated" figures, as though they were originally armless or headless, like his own *femme sans têtes.* His fondness for the "cut-up" body raises questions about the nature of metonymic thinking that are philosophical rather than psychopathological. Chagall claims to decapitate figures for purely compositional reasons. "If I had the idea of separating her head from her body it was because I needed a space just at that spot,"[18] he writes of *To Russia, with Donkeys and Others.* In contrast, Breton evokes the sadistic intention that informs the mutilation of the body in Surrealist art. "A head adheres to the shoulders only because the blade of the guillotine is withheld."[19] But mutilation and fetishism play different roles in pictorial and verbal art. According to Roland Barthes, Sade needs the fetish in order to overcome the inability of language to describe the whole body except in insipid and perfect terms. "Being analytical, language can come to grips with the body

Max Ernst

only if it cuts it up; the total body is outside language, only pieces of the body succeed to writing; in order to *make* a body *seen*, it must be either displaced, refracted through the metonymy of clothing, or reduced to one of its parts.''[20] Because of the simultaneity of the picture medium, the visual artist suffers no such representational limitation and has therefore no similar need for the fetish. Ernst does not appear interested in either individualizing the parts of the body or investing them with the power to arouse desire for the whole. In "Yachting" (fig.6), a scene from *La Femme 100 têtes,* the serenity of the sailboat-strewn sea, the sailor's apathy toward the two outsize, trussed limbs on which his back is turned, and the extreme discrepancy in size between sailor and limb all undermine the notion that an amputation has occurred, that somehow these limbs were severed from a gigantic figure now hiding its mutilated bulk somewhere outside the picture. Instead, we have the impression that these limbs represent not a mutilation or amputation at all, all of which imply a total body and an original wholeness of form, but that they are objects that are not parts, belong to no whole, and must be viewed as "original fragments," which is a conceptual paradox.

Ernst's body parts, mutilated bodies, hybridized creatures, and otherwise distorted forms betray an intention to challenge the metaphysical framework that gives rise to concepts of wholeness, of the unity of the body, of the expected relations of parts to whole. The process of deconstruction is precisely a thinking of "the structurality of structure," in Jacques Derrida's terms. The deconstructive thinking reveals our entrapment in a language that is embedded with the metaphysics of presence. I cannot even think or describe what Ernst depicts without already contradicting in my words that which I wish to express. I cannot speak of a body without skin (*skinless, flayed*) without implying the original presence of skin.

Perhaps this is why Ernst resorts to words, titles, and captions that circumvent the logical principle of noncontradiction with the rhetorical device of the oxymoron. *La Femme 100 têtes,* with the pun *cent / sans,* hundred / without, expresses simultaneous presence and absence, like the zero suffix in linguistics. Other oxymorons expressing simultaneous presence and absence occur in this work such as "eyeless eye," "flesh without flesh." "Two bodies without bodies lie down alongside their bodies, falling out of bed and bed-curtains like phantoms without a phantom"[21] combines multiple logical contradictions with semantic

Figure 6. From *La Femme 100 têtes*

contradictions, since "phantom" is already constituted semantically of a present absence. *La Femme 100 têtes* is a work
grounded in paradox at all levels. Thematically, it deals with
creation and its opposites, *"l'immaculée conception manquée"*
(rendered by Tanning as "the might-have-been Immaculate
Conception") and infanticide ("to tenderest youth, extreme
unction," "eviscerated baby"),[22] or conversely, with death that
is not death, as in the form of Lazarus—all presided over by the
twin sisters, or *la femme 100 têtes* in her contradictory aspects as
Germinal and *Perturbation*. Technically, Ernst does use the relationship of text and picture in his collage novel to create contradictory expressions, although he sometimes resorts to utterly
conventional techniques to express the inexpressible, for example, representing phantoms with levitating figures, unshaded
line drawings, or figures shrouded in greyish drapes. But sometimes the pictures symbolically present a contradiction found in
the text, as when he sets a pretty drawing of pale, demure Psyche
stepping into her pool (from Thumann to Hamerling's *Amor*

Max Ernst

und Psyche)[23] into a scene of massacre to illustrate "the tranquillity of future assassinations." At other times the captions simply "lie," as when "sea of serenity" is depicted by a violent storm at sea, sinking the large vessel and inundating the hapless survivors on the raft in a maelstrom.[24] Occasionally Ernst uses a complicated "surreal" image to depict a logical impossibility, such as having a single figure occupy two places at once. "Loplop, dumb with fear and fury, finds his bird head and remains motionless for 12 days on both sides of the door" does indeed show a door flanked by a split figure on either side, half male and half female, the male half crowned with the slender neck and head of a swan.[25]

La Femme 100 têtes is an apocalyptic book thematically, but one that reveals the chaos not only at the end of the world but at the beginning as well. "The Eternal Father tries vainly to separate the light from the shadows" reads one of the captions.[26] This inability to separate light and darkness constitutes an interplay of presence and absence (Is light a presence, or an absence of darkness? Is darkness a presence, or an absence of light?) that, according to Derrida, constitutes freeplay. "Freeplay is always an interplay of absence and presence, but if it is to be radically conceived, freeplay must be conceived of before the alternative of presence and absence; being must be conceived of as presence or absence beginning with the possibility of freeplay and not the other way around."[27] In Ernst's works freeplay takes the form of hybridization, for once the artist divests himself of the concept of the body as an integrated and unique presence, then bodies and their parts become mere supplements for absences that can be infinitely substituted, according to Derrida's principle of supplementarity. Ernst's hybrids range from conservative substitutions that retain the "syntax" of the body while playing havoc with the "lexicon" (human bodies with animal heads) to mutations that produce essentially unintelligible forms (human torsos with human legs in place of the head, bodies with vegetable, mineral, and unrecognizable prosthetic parts).

Supplementarity implies a temporal element, continuity, since the possibility of infinite substitutions is realized paradigmatically, that is, in time. It is precisely because of this temporal element that identity, the continuity of form and personality over time, is a more salient concept in literary enterprises than in visual art. Although shape-shifting and identity games always played a large part in Dada and Surrealistic high jinx (Marcel Duchamp's portrait in transvestite attire as Rrose Sélavy, or

Ernst's own identification of his hawk-nosed profile with Loplop, the Bird Superior), Ernst best transcended the formal limitations on identity play in visual art with his generic innovation of the collage novel. He found a number of ways of simultaneously creating and subverting identity, as when he not only gives *la femme 100 têtes* alternate names and functions but endows her with spare heads as well, held in Germinal's lap or carried on a stick, like a mask, by Perturbation's partner. He seems to say that if there is freeplay in the system, a body might just as well have a hundred heads as none, particularly if they do not occupy the shoulders simultaneously but supplement the absence there one at a time.

During his Surrealistic period, Max Ernst exceeded the attacks of Dada and Surrealism on political, moral, and aesthetic establishmentarianism by attacking the conceptual medium itself: the way form is conceived and perceived and the way it is abstracted and valorized. His strategies are varied and ingenious, ranging from parody of classical forms and interplay of high and low art and of presence and absence, to generic and technical developments that reveal the extent to which concepts of form are governed by notions of time, particularly "significant" time. Time is implicated in the way form is valorized, precedence in time being equated with priority in value as form becomes "source" or "model." It is not surprising that during his stay in Arizona following World War II, Ernst grew to admire the Hopi Indians for their "time-less" language, which had so entranced Benjamin Whorf. "Pour eux," Ernst wrote, "le temps à l'état aboli."[28]

Ernst's formal Surrealist paintings (formal because they are full-size, representational oils executed with traditional craftsmanship) invite a naïve response to their content to enhance the effectiveness of their surreptitious attack. We feel the sharpness of their critique of myth the better for having first assumed them merely to *represent* myths. The resonance of earlier paintings quickly reveals itself as parody that de-signifies our idealizations of great art. And Ernst deceives us, with the lure of familiar conventions, into recognizing our deception by convention, as he restores the libidinal matter that traditional representational language represses.

There is nothing subtle about Ernst's subversion of religious iconography and Christian mythology in *The Blessed Virgin Chastises the Infant Jesus Before Three Witnesses* (1934) (fig. 1), a picture he painted at the suggestion of André Breton. By

Max Ernst

shifting his artistic rhetoric from reverence to sacrilege, from devotion to malice, Ernst transforms the icon of Madonna and Child from a sentimental image to a shocking picture designed to disgust and repel the pious and amuse and gratify the malicious. The viewer is forced to abandon a virtuous posture and obliged to contend with an array of libidinal affects: outrage, secret pleasure and recognition, shame, and so forth. Ernst deliberately chose Parmigianino's portrait *Madonna with the Long Neck* as the target for his stylistic parody. The violent agitation of Ernst's scene contrasts dramatically with the artificial postures that constitute the Mannerist excess of this formalistic composition. Furthermore, he translates Parmigianino's elegant elongations of torsos and limbs into nightmarish exaggerations of the Virgin's powerful arms and the infant's long expanse of back extended across the entire breadth of his mother's knees.

Yet by reducing the number of "angels" from five to three (the "bad angels," Breton, Eluard, and Ernst), and emphasizing them as three "witnesses" in the title, Ernst creates two points of reference in the life of Christ that become the subject of his inversions: the Adoration of the Magi, and the Agony of Christ. By inverting the familiar relationships of the Biblical motifs, distorting their "normal" syntax, as it were, he allows certain Freudian elements to emerge from the religious myth. The scene of the Magi's bringing of gifts is changed to a scene of punishment, gifts and punishment serving as a common pair of antonyms (cf. the Wolf Man's dream) in the experience of childhood. The three witnesses in this way change from worshipers of the Infant to voyeurs of Christ's suffering, as representatives of the Christian faithful. The infliction of pain on Christ is itself the central aspect of the salvation myth. Ernst merely displaces the role of tormentor from Roman military to Blessed Virgin, and the role of victim from divine scapegoat to hapless Infant. Other elements are distorted as well. The discarded halo, which so scandalized *Der Spiegel*,[29] evokes the crown of disgrace, the crown of thorns (there are no haloes in Parmigianino's picture). The poignant moment in the *via crucis* when Christ is stripped of his garments is here reduced to its most humiliating infantile counterpart, the child's bottom bared for spanking.

By deranging the traditional iconography of Nativity and Crucifixion scenes, Ernst demythifies the Christian salvation myth by stripping away the religious signification of the actions and representing them in their de-signified secular form. He seems to ask whether it is less perverse to revere an image of an adult

Christ stripped, whipped, and crucified, than of an infant laid across its mother's knee and spanked. His critique of the myth is both psychoanalytical and political, revealing the extent to which religious imagery and belief mask sadism and masochism and, by a similar fraudulent signification of suffering, justify political and social oppression in the name of discipline and self-sacrifice.

Ernst extends his iconoclasm to other religious icons, such as his 1923 *Pietà, or Revolution by Night*. Unlike his Madonna and Child, where he primarily inverts the posture of the figures, here the posture of an older figure cradling a younger is all that remains as an iconographic link to the religious tableau. A bourgeois man, derived from Chirico's *Brain of a Child*, replaces Mary as the grieving parent, and a clothed figure with the head of a statue, also derived from Chirico, replaces the dead Son. Uwe Schneede interprets this painting entirely as an autobiographical allegory. "The father in the picture has given life to the youth, just as Mary has to Jesus. Mary seeks to temper the sufferings of her son through love, although she does not understand them; but this father takes over from her only the gesture of protection. He is holding a dummy; there is no inner bond between father and son. In his father's arms the son is as cold as a statue."[30] I am inclined to interpret only the posture (signifying mourning or bereavement), not the nature or relationship of the principals in relation to the icon of Christ and His Mother. The identity of the principals is perhaps revealed by their literal appearance: the bourgeois man in neat suit, moustache, bowler hat, mourning the grey sculpture whose significance may be not unlike that of the sculpture in Chirico's painting, a fragment of dead and sterile culture, an irrelevant monument out of place in the modern world. If so, the "revolution" in the title is the Surrealist revolution itself, forcing the bourgeoisie to relinquish its inheritance of monumental art and aesthetic ideals. I suspect that Ernst uses the *Pietà* precisely to show that it is a god, or an ideal, that has died, an idol that has fallen, but that such gods or ideals exist only in our icons or representations of them.

Ernst's later painting, *The Robing of the Bride* (1939) (fig.7) may also have a religious source, if not a specific Biblical reference. The female body of the hooded figure unmistakably resembles the figure of Eve from the Van Eycks' panel of *The Ghent Altarpiece*: small rounded breasts, rounded protruding belly, and a graceful hand shielding the pubic region. Furthermore, the elaborately cloaked bride in Ernst's painting may refer

Max Ernst

Figure 7. *The Robing of the Bride*

to the heavily draped woman in Jan Van Eyck's famous wedding picture of *Giovanni Arnolfini and His Bride.* The thin, fur-clad groom in stocking feet bears a vestigial resemblance to Ernst's hybrid, feathered groom, and both pictures have a "mirror" on the back wall. Van Eyck's mirror adds two figures to the scene, while Ernst's subtracts two figures. The grotesque little androgynous, hybrid fetish with exaggerated sexual characteristics may represent Ernst's perverse counterpart to the small domestic dog in Van Eyck's wedding picture. The title of *The Robing of the Bride* is, of course, ironic because the picture will foil our conventional interpretations of its meaning. We might expect the "robing" to symbolize a rite of passage from innocence to experience, a crossing of the boundary of carnal knowledge marked

Beasts of the Modern Imagination

by the assumption of a symbolic garment. Perhaps Ernst chose Van Eyck's Eve for this very thematic reason: because, as the first mythological creature to pass from Nature to culture, Eve was first to come to self-consciousness of nakedness (that is, of being seen by an "other") and to don a garment (or, in Van Eyck's portrayal, to clutch a fig leaf to her groin).

But instead of recapitulating this mythic gesture, Ernst's painting reverses the ritual and produces the opposite of a wedding, a kind of antiwedding. It is the function of the wedding ceremony to repress or displace the sexual act at its center in order to transform biological and animal behavior (mating) into a cultural event. Indeed, Van Eyck's Arnolfini wedding displays in virtually encyclopedic form the whole symbolic language of marriage as a social contract and a cultural act. Ernst's "robing," however, is designed to achieve the opposite effect. The "robe," an animal mask,[31] is donned to delete virtually all human or cultural traces (face, hair, clothing, expression) from the picture in order to restore the "bride" to a purely sexual function that the resemblance to Van Eyck's Eve, a figure with particularly individualized sexual characteristics, makes especially conspicuous. Ernst also substitutes red, pinks, and oranges for the somber blacks, browns, and greens of Van Eyck's domestic interior to introduce yet further erotic conventions into the picture. And yet Ernst's *Robing of the Bride* is not primitivistic but decadent, not a return to nature but an invocation of pornological conventions (particularly the use of theatrical devices, such as the mask that reveals rather than conceals, so central to Sadean costuming) that use culture subversively and hypocritically to deny and conceal their libidinal intent. And as in pornology, in which the "other" reigns supreme and voyeurism is therefore a central mode, we are implicated by the mirror in the picture. It identifies us as "witness" of the perverse wedding (as Van Eyck acts as witness, via mirror, to the Arnolfini wedding) not as seeing subject but as a pornological object, a double of the bride. The scene practically becomes a dramatization of Sartre's argument that if we are seen looking at an obscene object, we become an obscene object: a voyeur. Ernst's picture traps us in its gaze; it sees us, and shows us to ourselves in ways we can scarcely countenance.

If in *The Robing of the Bride* entrapment is a product of pictorial rhetoric, of the manipulation of the viewer, it appears as an explicit thematic content in many other Ernstian works. In the 1923 *There Are No More Real Hydrocycles,* for example, we

Max Ernst

find a bird entangled in a contraption, a prevalent syntax of machine-traps-creature, whose origin may be traced to Ernst's fascination with a nineteenth-century book on bird catching with ruses and mirrors by C. J. Kresz entitled *L'Aviceptologie française, ou traité générale de toutes les ruses dont on peut se servir pour prendre les oiseaux.* But except for the stylized later depictions of birds in cages (the "Aeolian Harps" series), the theme of entrapment is of more than pictorial consequence in his works. Ernst frequently interchanges the subjects and objects of entrapment, to create an ambiguity that is itself a trap, a lure to misunderstanding. His theme of entrapment therefore becomes self-reflexive, moving from the realm of representation to the realm of interpretation.

During the same years that Ernst painted the *Hydrocycles,* he also created metaphors of bird / machine function in the sky, but with far more somber historical overtones. *The Massacre of the Innocents,* a collage produced in 1920–21, depicts a winged, flying thing, which could be either bird, insect, plane, or exterminating angel, threatening silhouetted figures over an aerial view, depicted by photomontage, of towns, buildings, and railroad tracks. If the scene of impending destruction is here presented from the point of view of the bomber, then in *Two Children Are Threatened by a Nightingale* (1924), the danger is perceived from the point of view of the victims on the ground. These figures assume attitudes (prostrate woman, figures fleeing, babes in arms) not unlike those of Picasso's 1937 mural commemorating the bombing of Guernica. The nightingale functions as a metaphor for a military bomber. Ernst exploits the optical illusion of huge planes appearing as tiny as birds in the sky; he exploits also the wonder that such a seemingly harmless flying thing could inspire such fear.

These paintings reflect Ernst's shock after a war of such arbitrariness that he and Eluard discovered afterward they had fought on the same front on opposite sides. They further reflect an awareness of the instability of signs, as the signified of the plane changes from toy to weapon, from the cavorting aerobatic machines that had so delighted Europeans before the war,[32] to the terrible engines of destruction during the war.

In Ernst's 1934 series of paintings called *Garden Airplane-Trap,* the political statement disappears altogether in the interest of inverting the syntactic function of planes once more, from subject to object, destroyer to victim, like the hapless birds of Kresz's book. Furthermore, Ernst renders subject and object

interchangeable, so that the sentence becomes entirely ambiguous and could mean either "garden traps airplane" or "airplane
traps garden."[33] If the *Garden Airplane-Trap* pictures are
thought of as companion pieces to the earlier paintings, then the
inversion of a bomber trapped by a hangar camouflaged with
vegetation lends special credibility to Gilbert Lascault's thesis
that these images of circular entrapment show Ernst's anti-
Platonism in his affinity for Greek *metis,* or wily intelligence.[34]
Although Lascault does not mention him, the great paragon of
Greek *metis* is Homer's Odysseus, whose most famous trap is the
Trojan Horse, a disguised military trap like Ernst's garden.

Like Lascault, I also see Ernst's development of the theme of
entrapment in his paintings as having an ultimately self-reflexive
end, as referring to a devious and illogical way of thinking. This
self-reflexivity is part of the deconstructive process of exploring
and undermining the preconceptions of our way of thinking, of
our language. Instead of exploring the ways in which our language traps us to think of form, Ernst's play with interchangeable functions in his paintings explores the way our language
entraps us to think of relationships. The word *trap* itself necessarily implies a subject and an object. The verb is an obligatory
transitive, as it were: something must trap, and something must
be trapped. As in thinking and speaking of "skinless" and
"headless" bodies, so it is impossible, for example, to think or
speak of "lies" that no one speaks or hears.[35] Since "trap"
cannot be imagined without an implied trapper and trapped,
Ernst again evokes the principle of supplementarity, letting subject and object be supplied by a series of potentially infinite
substitutions: plane, bird, or insect lured by the garden as
though by a carnivorous plant, and putrified plane, bird, or
insect as polluter and destroyer of the garden. Just as Ernst's
trap, the garden, eventually traps itself, so the word *trap* traps us
in the epistemology embedded in our language.

Ernst's most powerful representation of "doubled" entrapment is, of course, the *Oedipus Rex* of 1921 (fig. 2). Bird /
entrapment / machine are organized into new syntactic
arrangements here. The fingers protruding through the window
are skewered by the instrument whose functions, among others,
may be that of a bow for projecting the arrow lodged in the
nut /seed /eyeball-like object held by the fingers. The subject /
object reversal is here ironic, "man shoots bow" having become
"bow shoots man" as well. But although critics note the self-
skewering, generally no one relates it back to the Oedipus myth.

Max Ernst

If Lucy Lippard does so, it is only in the most general sense that the Oedipus myth has something to do with sex.

> Given the title and the myth as the point of departure, each viewer will interpret it in the framework of his own experience and perhaps expertise in Freudian or Jungian analysis. One can mention the "soaring" analogy which appears here, too, or the penetration, the pressure to open the rounded or split female form held by the huge hand of authority, and the painfully misplaced penetration from the sides by the sharper, smaller phallic forms, the "fenced-in" or imprisoned female bird, and so forth.[36]

Yet the Oedipus myth is precisely about trappers trapping themselves, or skewers skewering themselves, if you will. Laius orders his infant son Oedipus skewered by the ankles, an entrapment that doubles back on him when Oedipus later kills him. Ernst clearly had the ankle-skewering motif in mind because one of the plates in "Oedipe" (*Une Semaine de bonté*) shows the bird-headed protagonist holding a naked figure skewered by the foot (frontispiece). Also the companion picture of *Oedipus Rex* appearing in Paul Eluard's *Répétitions* shows protruding fingers holding a microscope clamped on a bird's foot, like a vise. As Laius's attempt to kill Oedipus doubles on himself, so Oedipus's attempt to trap the murderer of Laius doubles on himself. He discovers that he is the murderer, and so traps himself. If Russell and Schneede were correct in calling the nutlike object an eye, then the painting might include a further reference to Oedipus's blinding himself with Jocasta's brooch.

Ernst has some of the same deconstructive aims in *Oedipus Rex* as in his other paintings. Just as it is impossible to think of a hand without a body, so it is impossible to imagine an action without an agent, a deed without a doer. This is the "anthropological reflex" responsible for such syntactic forms as "it rains," "*il pleut*," and "*es regnet*." Yet if we could, we might try to imagine the fingers in *Oedipus Rex* as pure instruments guided by no consciousness, no sight.

By the same token, the wide, glassy eyes of the bird heads stare out of the picture with no apparent object in their sight: "seeing" yet "not seeing," like Oedipus, who is blind when he sees and sees when he is blind. The birds, whose only function is sight, are incapable of action, and yet fail to "see" the action so close at hand. The disjunction between sight and action propels the evil destinies in *Oedipus Rex*. By rendering this disjunction between sight and action, Ernst renders the most compelling psychoanalytic axiom of the Oedipus myth: the tyranny of the unconscious, the ultimate entrapment.

Although Ernst's last collage novel, *Une Semaine de bonté ou Les sept éléments capitaux* (1934), has no text or picture captions, Ernst seems to transform it into a symbolic system, like that of a liturgical or a political calendar (cf. the French Revolutionary calendar) by attaching a series of ostensibly significant categories (day of the week, element, example, color, literary maxim) to each book. But these categories ultimately fail to signify. There is no evidence, for example, that the "water," however destructive, is punitive, like the Biblical deluge; this is a strategy consistent with Ernst's overall de-signifying and demythifying enterprise in this work. He foils and fools the "other" (the reader, viewer, us) by confronting us with a text we cannot read except negatively, as a museum of dysfunctional symbols and fractured significations. I will argue that the elements, animals, viscera, are intended as ironic intrusions of insignificant Nature into a culture stifled in signification, and as failed restorations of the libidinal in the cultural landscape, the libidinal being defined as force that refuses to signify. Both significant time (the heroic past, mythic time) and significant objects (monuments, landmarks, sacred artifacts) will be stripped of their meaning. Ernst uses "novelistic" form subversively, to critique the historian's function that public art is made to serve. The frozen forms (statues, medals, buildings, myths), which bear the excessive signification of the past, are unfrozen and set in motion again, this time according to the postures and actions of bourgeois melodrama, pulp adventure, or old-fashioned pornography, all of which suffer from insufficient significance. "Le Lion de Belfort" fails to narrate the siege and battle,[37] "Oedipe" fails to narrate the myth, and "L'Ile de Paques" fails to reveal the sacred rituals that prompted the construction of the giant heads on Easter Island. Instead, each of the books depicts through a series of private fantasies sordid adventures of the bestial impulse filtered through culture.

If Ernst uses novelistic conventions to render monumental art, myth, and architecture commonplace, he does so only ultimately to disrupt them, as though to remind us that even popular forms can in time become aesthetically elevated and canonized. He therefore develops strategies simultaneously to create and disperse identity so that "protagonists" (of sorts) emerge that can never crystallize into "heroes" of consistent form or purposive

Max Ernst

action. Several of the "protagonists" of *Une Semaine de bonté* are hybrids: the lion-headed man of "Le Lion de Belfort," the dragon-winged woman of "La Cour du dragon," the bird-headed figure of "Oedipe," the rooster-headed male of "Le Rire du coq," and the man with the sculptured Easter Island head in "L'Ile de Paques." The hybridization itself disrupts identity, which Ernst further complicates with variation. As the "narrative" progresses, the lion of Belfort sports not only a variety of costumes in different frames (denoting various occupations and social classes: military uniforms, dress clothes, rags, and the like) but also a variety of heads, though all of them chiefly feline. But Ernst's choice of lion's head does not seem purely arbitrary. Monumental, sculptured lion's heads seem to top military uniforms and distinguished dress, while the ragged street cleaner wears a natural, animalistic head. Appropriately, a figure with a lion's-head door knocker seems to be defending a heavy double gate with battle-ax in hand (or menacing the suspended, half-clad female figure, or inadvertently cutting his own throat)—perhaps a literal dramatization of Colonel Denfert-Rochereau's epithet. This irregularity of pictorial representation from frame to frame, a major departure from traditional picture books, might be attributed merely to the technical conditions of collage art, which require Ernst to use different sources for his lion's heads in order to represent his figure from different angles and with different facial expressions. However, in "Oedipe," where Ernst unabashedly tops his figures with the heads of a variety of species of birds (eagles, crows, turkeys, and so on), it becomes clear that these capital variations are a deliberate attempt to disrupt identity. His purpose may be clearer in "Oedipe" than elsewhere, because the Oedipus myth is about shifts and confusions of identity and includes references to androgyny (Tiresias, made to take male and female form) and hybridization of form (the Sphynx) and function (Tiresias given the ability to understand the language of birds).

One of the deceptions of *Une Semaine de bonté* is that it appears to rupture identity in order to let the beast escape, in order to restore the animal to culture by invoking the literal residues of the metaphors and totemic epithets that define the protagonistic roles, such as the lion-hearted warrior, the priapic cock, and the insinuating dragon. But the beasts that erupt into culture restore no Nature to their denatured worlds, for they are "domesticated" brutes, not in the sense of having their ferocity abolished, but because they have been appropriated by the

Beasts of the Modern Imagination

human. They appear as "received" forms not only technically, as representations of cultural images of the beast, but also conceptually, as human projections and fantasies of what constitutes "bestial" behavior. This, finally, has little to do with the natural behavior of animals. Ernst's lions do not stalk and devour their prey: they kidnap it in carriages and hold it for ransom (plates 1:16, 1:17).[38] Throughout the numerous Orpheus allusions in the "Lion of Belfort" section, there is no Dionysian *sparagmos*, no rapturous surrender to animalistic fate.

If we look at a scene like that of plate 1:2 (fig.8), of a couple strolling through an art gallery, we can see the subtlety with which Ernst exploits cultural conventions to produce a thoroughly denatured Apollonian climate. A beautifully dressed male in cape, sash, saber, and boots strikes a gallant pose with graceful gestures of hands and feet, while a young woman clings adoringly to his arm. But this genteel propriety, however theatrical, is subverted neither by the man's noble lion's head nor by the "art" on display in the gallery: a largely nude female sculpture, and a picture of an enlarged female breast in an oval frame. These artifacts are disturbing not for the sexual element they inject into the scene but because they announce sexuality only as repressed, displaced, and sublimated. They deny the living body, the warm flesh, the procreative instinct, both by their artificiality, and by further conceptual constraints Ernst places upon them. The nude female sculpture is fitted with bands and contraptions, one of which looks like a chastity belt. Her representational function therefore shifts from displaying a natural body to exemplifying its frustration and oppression. She further introduces the "other" into the scene, for chastity belts imply rivals that shift the locus of sexual gratification from the body to the ego, from matters of appetite and pleasure into the cultural realms of competition and prestige, prerogatives, and property. The man ogling the portrait of the breast displays further mediations and displacements of lust with his voyeuristic, vicarious, and fetishistic behavior. The little cultural world of courtship and art appreciation created by the semiotics of clothes and posture in this scene is wholly exteriorized, given over to forms and their viewing, to concealing and fragmenting the body, and to replacing the flames of animal passion with the social drama of human desire.

Une Semaine de bonté is filled with scenes of overwrought behavior, a series of violent actions and motions that, according to Renée Riese Hubert, are consistent with the predominance of

Max Ernst

Figure 8. From *Une Semaine de bonté*

verbs in Surrealistic writing.[39] But in "Le Lion de Belfort," for example, violent and destructive action (so ironically in contrast with Denfert-Rochereau's lifesaving at Belfort) is rendered not only futile and absurd but also emptied of the Dionysian excess of its cruelty. The result is a fragmented recapitulation of the Orpheus myth, in which there is neither retrieval of life from the land of the dead, nor an ecstatic final abandon to animal ferocity and violence. Plate 1:12 (fig.9), for example, depicts the lion-headed figure in motley garb playing the flute or pipe of a snake charmer to a viscus, a chunk of meat (human or animal) that was probably once an organ with muscle attached. In this fragmented, decontextualized state, viscera are not living flesh despite their organic nature, and they lose their metonymic power to represent the whole body, the living body, as they lose their power to respond to music. The female nude in the picture, her pose as artificial and stylized as a statue, wears a heart

Beasts of the Modern Imagination

Figure 9. From *Une Semaine de bonté*

over her genitals, like a fig leaf of feeling and affection repressing the site of sexual activity. But she also will be unable to
respond to the music, for her heart is not a visceral heart, a
living, feeling heart, but the Sacred Heart of Jesus, a purely
symbolic heart signifying the suffering of the mortification of
the flesh. Scapulars, medallions, and sentimental jewelry of the
Sacred Heart function as life-denying fetishes throughout the
chapter, signalling lack and displacement of life; they are often
paired with the ubiquitous medals, whose function, since
medals certify recognition and invite the gaze, is to introduce
the "other" into the scenes. Ernst chooses his representations
carefully for their cultural or acultural functions. In two further
plates of the Lion of Belfort series we see pornological tableaux
given a macabre twist that virtually destroys their residue of
libidinal energy. In plate 1:28 (fig. 10), a lion-headed male tick-
les the soles of a female bound to a bed. This picture could be
regarded as a companion to the Orphic pipe playing of plate

Max Ernst

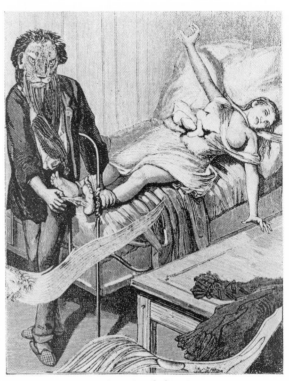

Figure 10. From *Une Semaine de bonté*

1:12 since, in both, the active agent attempts to force an involuntary, living response from an inert creature. But the entrails of plate 1:12 recur here as well, spilling from the body of the eviscerated female on the bed. The gesture is futile and doomed; a corpse cannot be tickled to life any more than it can be beaten to life (cf. the recurrence of viscera in plate 1:29, in which an eviscerated female is whipped). This mad, perverse beastliness of Ernst's Lion of Belfort is not an animal beastliness, and he inherits not the animal kingdom of living creatures that is his traditional portion but, like a doubly failed Orpheus, the lifeless, skull-bestrewn plain of the land of the dead (1:33).

Given the dominant effect of cultural conventions in "Le Lion de Belfort," it is not surprising to find the markings of gender (as the cultural signification of sexual differences) of great importance in this chapter of *Une Semaine de bonté*. But because the content of this section is so markedly androcentric, that is, dominated by male action and male desire, the viewer is put into a curiously female position, like that of the women who hang adoringly on the Lion's arm, or sit obligingly on his lap. We are captured, as viewers, by the "other": invited to admire his medals, to marvel at his feats, to concede his splendor and superiority, to give him recognition and respect. This not only puts us, as viewers, in the castrated position of having yielded all significance to the picture, but it also implicates us unpleasantly as the relatively benign early representations of the Lion become increasingly malevolent and sadistic as the series progresses. By the time we withdraw our recognition and become critical and reproachful, it is too late to avoid all self-incrimination.

In the second book of *Une Semaine de bonté,* the book entitled "L'Eau," the gender perspective changes. The chapter is dominated by the female as much as by the water, and, indeed, the female's kinship with water belongs to the conventional relegation of woman to Nature and her corresponding extrusion from culture, which feminist critics see as characteristic strategies of the androcentric imagination. But its effects in "L'Eau" are interesting to contemplate, because from a biocentric perspective the female's slumbering, passive role becomes curiously empowering. The first three plates of "L'Eau" depict the destruction of all cultural avenues of escape from the deluge: railroad bridges and great suspension bridges are spectacularly destroyed, and even the last sure refuge in times of flood, that of altitude, is denied the victims, as water inundates the tops of cathedral spires in plate 2:30. But the females of plates 2:2 and 2:3 appear oblivious or indifferent to the devastation around them (as do the girls who play with watch chains, balls, or bagpipes in the last three plates), and they thereby establish the major motif of the book, which Renée Hubert calls "Sleeping Beauty": a female figure slumbering in a comfortable bed amid the swirling deluge—clearly cousin to Henri Rousseau's figures in *The Dream* and *Sleeping Gypsy.* But "Sleeping Beauty," with its implication of a passive female dependent upon heroic male rescue, may not be a fitting epithet for Ernst's figure after all. Whether totally alone and unseen as in plates 2:8 or 2:12, or witnessed by the still, gazing men of plates 2:9, 2:10, and 2:11 (fig.11), the sleeping woman is safe from the flood that washes drowned males into her bedroom. The implication of these scenes is that the withdrawal from consciousness and culture, the retreat into oblivion and indifference that restores sleepers and dreamers momentarily to Nature also restores to the female the elemental power that is equal to the flood. The flood

Max Ernst

Figure 11. From *Une Semaine de bonté*

may destroy her (there are a few drowned females in the book) but it does not frighten her, and it seems as though her sleeping form holds it in abeyance. As viewers, we share, this time, the androcentric perspective of the silent men keeping vigil at her bedside. Ours is the only consciousness active in some of these turbulent scenes, but our awareness only makes us vulnerable to the anxiety of understanding the significance of things without being able to do anything about them.

After the agoraphobia of "L'Eau," the claustrophobic little bourgeois rooms of "La Cour du dragon" might seem a welcome haven if they did not threaten to smother us with their fussy wallpapers, carpets, and overstuffed furniture, not to mention the dragon vapor that hangs like so much cigar smoke over some of the scenes. But the human drama of indeterminate intrigue that plays itself out in this building makes one positively long for the nasty individualism of the Lion of Belfort. The ontological space of "La Cour du dragon" is dense with the life of the "other." The violence of the earlier works is replaced in this book with a different kind of power play—the tendering of homage, obeisance, reverence—as figures bow to the "other," grovel, kiss hands and coattails, kneel at people's feet, beg and pray, in gestures of humility and dependence (fig.12). Since many of these gestures are performed by a man in foreign dress (an Algerian, perhaps, given the Parisian setting) this chapter replaces with a racial element the sexual victimizations of the first chapter. Besides exhibiting itself in this semiotics of the master / slave relationship, the "other" recurs throughout the chapter in eavesdropping and spying, tasks in which even the paintings and mirrors in the apartment seem to play a role as they seem, at times, to capture the protagonists in their gaze and betray their hidden emotions and secret passions. Finally, the "dragon" seems to take Manichean forms as satanic or angelic figures, an appropriate antonymy in a chapter given over to overestimation and underestimation. With respect to our role as viewers, Ernst here exploits his medium most effectively to extrude us from the scene. We are indeed voyeurs: we may even be one of the mirrors on the walls that "watches" the figures below like a great eye. But we cannot hear, we are deaf; the rooms and their denizens are dumb to us. The rooms are filled with putative verbal language of which we can infer from the gestural language of the figures only its rhetorical forms: pleas, thanks, reproaches, anguish. The "other" in its most social form, in the intersubjectivity of its discourse, eludes us.

If our perspective in "La Cour du dragon" is restricted by our deafness, then in "Oedipe" it is doubled, as befits the Oedipus myth, which is all about double perspectives or seeing the same set of events from two points of view. The major visual motifs of "Oedipe" are those of pursuit and imprisonment, and using our cultural perspective we readily interpret this as a chapter about crime and punishment, a reading consistent with the Oedipal themes. But when we see a bird shoot a man, the way a man might shoot a pheasant, then it occurs to us that this might merely be "hunting" rather than murder. From an animal perspective, much of "Oedipe" merely reverses roles and does to humans what is normally done to animals: shooting, caging, and beating them, like circus mammals, into tameness. The actions of "Oedipe" are therefore suspended in ambiguity, hovering between fullness and emptiness of signification, presence and absence of morality, the Nietzschean ambiguity of morality as the cicuration or domestication of the beast. The bird-headed

Max Ernst

Figure 12. From *Une Semaine de bonté*

man visiting the jailed woman is like a human attending a caged bird—except for the recurring *corpus delecti,* which adds the signification of crime (fig.13). "Oedipe" has a circus sequence in which trussed humans are transported into large, portable circus cages and trained with a whip by bird-headed figures. The large human hand reaching out of a tiny window over the heads of scurrying birds is a scene from the vantage point inside a birdcage, and we viewers are, at that moment, birds of a feather. The scenes of "Oedipe" are lent a mysteriously affective ambience by virtue of being set at night, under a dark, sometimes moonlit, sky, or in interiors lit by lamplight. This element of the night, too, is ambiguous, for it provides either cover of darkness and the promise of freedom to criminals and fugitives, or a firmament that is itself the dome of a cosmic cage, a prison house of fate, like that encircling an Oedipus who lives in the delusion that he is free.

Beasts of the Modern Imagination

Figure 13. From *Une Semaine de bonté*

By the time we reach the last book of *Une Semaine de bonté*, which combines the last three days of "kindness week" into one volume, we realize that the humanistic title of the work has been a fraud and a trap. There has been no kindness shown *to* man or beast, *by* man or beast, in the representations. Culture has yielded only cruelty and death, as in "Le Rire du coq," the most Gothic of the "tales," whose laboratories and crypts become sites of vivisection and torture. Primitivism provides no alternative, as "Ile de Paques" explores the triangular plays of cultural desire in the jealousies, vanities, and competitions we have encountered in the earlier volumes. Nor does Nature provide a haven, as Ernst transforms the Romantic moonlit landscape of the last plate of "Oedipe" into a land from which living creatures have been extinguished except in their negated form, as skulls, as the dead. Nor has kindness been shown to us as readers

Max Ernst

Figure 14. From *Une Semaine de bonté*

of Ernst's collage novel. None of our talents at deciphering texts, at perceiving conventions and translating gestures, were suffi-cient to overcome the ruptures of these narrative experiments: to separate polyvalent images, to compensate for the missing dia-logue, to adjust to the shifting standpoint of our perspective throughout. The final images of *Une Semaine de bonté,* of a woman tumbling about in a vacuous space in which gravity has been suspended, while the bird, whose aerial role she performs, remains securely perched on the useless ground (fig. 14), surely represent us, as viewers and readers, paradoxically "trapped" in an outer space of semiological freeplay.

But if Ernst is not a satirist bent on preserving a reformed culture, neither is he a nihilist. He yet speaks for the beast, the unconscious, the libido (as does much of Surrealism), not trans-parently, in a primitive language, but deviously, maliciously, negatively, by disrupting the cultural, social, and aesthetic con-ventions that maintain the hegemony of the "other" in the world. His beast creates ruptures in that fabric of understanding and appreciation that knits artists and their public into cultural communities. His beast practices an antirhetoric whose aim is to frustrate discourse and communication and to promote the kind of nonsense that best forces us to confront our flawed and vulnerable apparatus of literacy. If Ernst were an idealist, he would not create forms governed by chance, disruption, fragmentation, and contradiction, which paralyze the conventional idealist rhetoric of reverence and overestimation. If Ernst were a pornographer, he would not disrupt the obsessional formalism of pornographic conventions that make reason the site of the libido. If Ernst were a serious neo-Gothic artist, he would not caricature the density of its cultural exaggerations and its emotional extremes. Instead, Ernst is one of the beasts of the modern imagination, who abide wherever life-denying culture is abolished.

Max Ernst

8

The Ontology of
D. H. Lawrence's *St. Mawr*

In a sense, D. H. Lawrence's novella *St. Mawr* is a Romantic allegory of the salvation of the dark, wild, true, animal self by retreat from modern culture, technology, and enlightenment. Like other "savage pilgrimages" in Lawrence's fiction, its conceptual movement appears to be a simple switch from one axis of a traditional binary system (nature / culture, body / mind, spirit / ideal, Dionysus / Apollo, and so on) to the other. But this naïve interpretation, even when conducted on both thematic and tropological levels, obscures the radicalness of Lawrence's enterprise, which is nothing less than the dismantling of an anthropocentric ontology. In *St. Mawr*, Lawrence does battle with the most fundamental premise of the Western humanistic tradition: that human being is superior to animal being because man thinks, speaks, and differentiates between good and evil.

The savage pilgrimage of *St. Mawr* is an ontological journey into what Lawrence calls "the fourth dimension," the "heaven of existence" where each creature "attains to its own fullness of being, its own *living* self."[1] Insofar as this displacement is symbolized by the traditional narrative device of the mythic journey into a sacral region, *St. Mawr* is allegory. But the term inadequately reflects the ironic relationship between the quester and her object. Since becoming the animal is becoming what one is, the quest has the ironic circularity of Nietzsche's eternal recurrence. But neither is the quest tautological. One can be an animal without *being* an animal, and it is precisely the wedge of difference between these two statements (and the ontological conditions they represent) that is the philosophical object of the novella. The epistemological ramifications of this enterprise constitute the perceptual shift of a Copernican revolution: we must forego our anthropocentric vantage, and seeing "as the animal," from the point of view of our human *animal* being, situates us in the paradoxical realm of knowledge Lawrence oxymoronically calls "blood consciousness." The savage pilgrimage therefore becomes a critical adventure rife with philosophical paradox, an intellectual recapture of noncognitive experience, a representation of "unseen presences," a mimetic critique of mimesis. The biocentric universe Lawrence substitutes for the anthropocentric one is, finally, silent and unconscious, an ontology founded on the negation of the self-conscious subject and therefore inaccessible to literary inscription. Lawrence develops devious strategies to outflank these paradoxes: a complex figurative language to adumbrate states of being that are usually expressed in the negative, and the development of the kind of negative polemic found in Nietzsche's *Zarathustra,* which teaches that one cannot be taught.[2] One cannot learn to live as the animal by reading books (like *St. Mawr*); one can only surrender to the tacit knowledge of the body, the instincts, the blood. Learning to be the animal is surrender to biological fate.

In order to explore Lawrence's dismantling of anthropocentric ontology, I will treat the savage pilgrimage in *St. Mawr* as a metaphysical homecoming (a *Heimkehr,* since the German word better implies the circularity, or re-turning, of the action) with a double irony. The apparent contradiction between the return to the home or origin that is a journey into a brutal, alien wilderness collapses because the animal (the alien, the untamed) is, paradoxically, the true fulfillment of the human being. We sense this thematically when the central implausibility of the plot, the retreat of a nervous, highly strung aristocrat and her purebred horse into a brutal wilderness, is rendered as natural and inevitable as submission to fate. We sense it rhetorically in the inversion of Swiftian satire: Lawrence's normative world is as irrational and feral as Swift's is rational and civilized. Lou is as disgusted by the civility of the Vyners as if they were the vilest yahoos: "Oh, these awful, housebred, house-inbred human beings, how repulsive they were."[3] The collapse of the paradox of the nonhuman as the human "home" (its origin and natural environment) results from a dialectical "revaluation of values" Nietzschean in scope and direction.

As a negated paradox, the *Heimkehr* in *St. Mawr* resonates to the etymological convergence of the multiple and the antonymous meanings of *das Unheimliche* in Freud's 1919 essay on "The Uncanny."[4] The semantic researches with which Freud begins his investigation into this branch of aesthetic sensibility uncover congruent ("familiar, intimate"; "of home and family"; "tame, domesticated"; "gay, cheerful") meanings of the word *heimlich,* as well as the incongruent "concealed, secretive, deceptive." *Unheimlich,* its antonym, opposes only the first set of meanings ("familiar / alien," "comfortable / disagreeable"); with the second it converges in the sense of denoting what is hidden and dangerous. From this etymological evidence Freud infers that *heimlich* and *unheimlich* in their perceptual forms as the familiar and the uncanny must once have been psychologically identical. Their cleavage is temporal and epistemological: the uncanny is the infantile familiar repressed and thereby transformed into something alien and anxiety-producing.

Freud's own analogy of sensibility, place, and being—the uncanny, the unhomely, the infantile—makes this analysis serve as an excellent paradigm for Lawrence's novella. *St. Mawr* is written quite deliberately as an ontological ghost story. The work is replete with the tropology of the supernatural, for example, ghosts, demons, fairies, and the great uncanny stallion himself ("It haunted her, the horse" [15]): a stock of otherworldly imagery whose ironic function is to refer to the alienated condition of the natural world. The sense of the uncanny identifies Lou Witt's alienation from her world as anthroponomic rather than merely cultural.[5] What she experiences is not just disaffection with one or another mode of civilized life but a symptom akin to existential nausea. The phantasmagoria of Lou's transmigration reproduces the psychoanalysand's acceptance of the fabulous world of dream as the authentic site of being, or the site of authentic being attempting to speak itself. The other world embodied in St. Mawr (whom Lou apprehends as "some living background, into which she wanted to retreat" [26]) is the unconscious self, the negated subject, speaking to Lou from "another scene" (Freud's *anderer Schauplatz*): "What was his non-human question, and his uncanny threat?" (14).

Heimkehr in *St. Mawr* proceeds from a plot propelled by an irrationality that is treated like "another sort of wisdom" (26), an "ancient understanding" (13): the paradox of repressed knowledge. Recognizing the generic implications of the uncanny for literature, Freud identified the infantile logic controlling the fiction in the ghost story or the horror tale as a primitive animism. The causal agent of the action is not the plausible motive of a rational character but the spirit of a repressed desire endowed with infantile omnipotence. Lou is governed by intuitions, visions, and nostalgias that precede her ability to formulate them into dialogue and argument. Her animistic universe, in which the fetish and the effigy have important functions,

Beasts of the Modern Imagination

enlivens her, unconsciously and involuntarily, as it were, with her own unsuspected animal life.

The marital, psychological, and cultural conflicts in *St. Mawr* are finally mere symptoms of the greater ontological collision of alien dimensions, "a battle between two worlds. She realized that St. Mawr drew his hot breaths in another world from Rico's, from our world" (19). Since the value systems of the two worlds are totally inverted, or rather, since conceptual categories like value are meaningless in the biocentric universe, each confrontation between them produces the "breaks" or ruptures that constitute the central dramatic events of the plot: St. Mawr's murderous "breaks" in riding, and the women's break with European culture.[6] The clash of a moral (valorized) and an amoral universe also has generic implications for the novella: the misunderstandings, ironies, and incongruities it generates produce comic effects and grotesqueries like those of the Shropshire tea. The Vyners can hardly believe their ears when they realize that Lou and her mother do not value Rico, husband and son-in-law, more than they do their horse. They respond with baffled outrage to this shattering of their self-evident anthropocentric truth. The comedy ceases once civilization is left behind. The work's dissonances, which should be neither discounted nor deplored, are actually felicitous consequences of the novella's philosophic matter.

In attempting to dismantle the anthropocentric ontology, Lawrence confronts the interpretive dilemma that ensues whenever the essential premises of the Western system of thought are challenged. Critical analysis as a rational tool is a specifically human capability belonging to the stock of anthropomorphic resources that are the target of the challenge. The circular dilemma of Lawrence's critical writings (conducting a rational critique of reason) is replicated in the corresponding literary works (where he conducts a mimetic critique of mimesis). How can Lawrence argue, in the conventional rhetoric of argumentation, that being is not subject to argumentation? How can Lawrence represent, in fiction, the falsity of the representation of being produced by conventional fictional technique? Lawrence's problem, like Nietzsche's, is to make his writing constitute an act, a verb rather than a noun, a gesture rather than an object. Lawrence can be the animal, but he cannot speak being the animal except through the duplicity of an experiential fiction that becomes the pretext or "true origin" of the text: the killing of the porcupine that inspires the Nietzschean thoughts of

D.H. Lawrence's St. Mawr

"Reflections on the Death of a Porcupine," the touch of the stallion that awakens the animal self prior to the secondary activity of the discursive critique in *St. Mawr.*

The formulaic nature of Lawrence's fiction conceals the circular and paradoxical direction of his enterprise, that structures are required to dismantle structures, and that to dismantle anthropocentrism, as in *St. Mawr,* requires a complex grasp of the mediations that prevent the reappropriation of original being, the regaining of the "heaven of existence." These mediations constitute familiar Lawrencian motifs: art, money, intellect, synthetic identity as supplements for the fatal lack of natural life and potency in modern society. *St. Mawr,* better than other works, uses a Nietzschean model to demonstrate the function of mimesis as an interplay of presence and absence, of fetishism as an interplay of part and whole. Lawrence's social satire is also structural in its method. Culture is dismantled as a distortion of natural boundaries, confounding race with nationality, natural distinction with social class, natural potency with achievement. The novella's central conflict has the duplicitous psychology of Nietzschean *ressentiment,* in which an anthropocentric ethic belies a natural political struggle. Finally, Lawrence employs instinct as the detector of bad faith, and the visionary faculty as a sharper and truer critical sense than rational epistemology, because it can assume a nonhuman, biocentric perspective.

The tropology of St. Mawr, the stallion, is likewise circular and self-negating. Reading St. Mawr as an archetype,[7] as the fixed and universal symbol of an unconscious meaning (such as the dark god, phallic potency, the life force) obscures his paradoxical function as a self-referential metaphor. The wild animal, or the domestic animal that retains its wildness, already *is* in the fourth dimension without any special dispensation. Lawrence must drive a wedge of difference between our anthropomorphic and a biomorphic perception of the animal by transforming it into a metaphor of itself, by giving it "glamour" (a concept I will discuss later), by casting over it a spell of enchantment. As metaphor, the familiar horse, the domestic hackney, becomes *unheimlich* (untamed, unhomely, alien) to us as his wildness and potency, the fullness of animal being that is ordinarily hidden (*heimlich*), becomes apparent, because it is seen from his own perspective rather than ours. The truth of the metaphor of St. Mawr is its own literal residue, the wild animality of the horse, the fullness of equine being. "Just think of St. Mawr! . . . We call him an animal, but we never know what it means. He seems a far greater mystery to me than a clever man. He's a horse. Why can't one say in the same way, of a man: *He's a man?*" (48)

Reading St. Mawr, the stallion, merely as a Freudian totem of the absent father, a symbolic displacement of all the phallic potency lacking in the modern young men,[8] risks distorting his circular symbolic function by giving him a specifically anthropocentric reference. Lawrence deliberately introduces a shift from metaphor to metonymy in the tropology of St. Mawr, describing the horse in zoomorphic similes, an allotropic practice widely found in the poetry. Lawrence actually negates St. Mawr's totemic function by stripping him of his patriarchal role as the repository of meaning, authority, and law. It is precisely the discursive, social world, the Lacanian Symbolic, that is dismantled in the novella, in order to restore the preverbal, preinfantile, prehuman, presexual universe of the origin, where even the Lacanian Imaginary, with its specular images, is dissolved. "Even the illusion of the beautiful St. Mawr was gone" (137), thinks Lou in the last reference to the stallion in the novella. St. Mawr's metaphoric and metonymic functions are ultimately self-referential and self-negating, serving as clew to the real, and inserting into our anthropocentric apprehension of it a wedge of difference. Once the fourth dimension is reclaimed, St. Mawr, horse and novella, may be lost and forgotten.

St. Mawr, the novella, is "quick" like the stallion insofar as it attempts to constitute an act by the man, the human animal, the asocial, creatural, literal residue of the D. H. Lawrence that precedes the artist. To Lawrence "the artist" is a social entity, a figment of anthropocentric vanity, and "being an artist" (4) is a self-conscious pose rather than an ontological condition. Culture corrupts the artist by making him vulnerable to mediating influences—morality, religion, politics, idealism (not to mention fame and money)—which subvert his "passional inspiration." The result is a distorted perspective, a devaluation of Nature, animal, and body, and a betrayal of "belly and knees," like Tolstoy ("The Judas!") betraying his lionine eponym.[9] For this reason F. R. Leavis's traditional terminology, particularly his insistence on "genius" with a cerebral definition ("supreme intelligence") and its resonances of Romantic privilege and ideality, seems highly inappropriate for assessing the philosophical aim of *St. Mawr*. His condescension to Lou Witt ("He can affirm with a power not given to poor Lou, who is not a genius") barely conceals the anthropocentric chauvinism that is the heritage of

D.H. Lawrence's St. Mawr

the humanistic tradition Leavis defines and defends, and which Lawrence radically subverts.[10] The affirmation, which for Lawrence must be ontological rather than propositional, anyhow, is as much Lou's, or the horse's, or the dandelion's, as Lawrence's. The "genius" of the novella is the self-negating function of its didacticism, its teaching that one cannot be taught, that being in the fourth dimension cannot be imitated, and that neither Lawrence nor Nietzsche can be applied. The ontological status of *St. Mawr*, the work of fiction, is that of a text crossed out, a text we are meant to read and forget, a text that is inscribed, then cancelled, in our conscious mind, so that it may return to haunt us like a dream, to move our affective being, to kindle our nostalgia for wildness and wilderness, to stimulate our instincts and passions from within.

The movement of the *Heimkehr* in *St. Mawr* is inscribed within the narrative and philosophical trajectory that spans Lou's homelessness at the beginning of the story ("She didn't 'belong' anywhere" [3]) and her homecoming announcement (*"This is the place"* [141]) upon her arrival at Las Chivas. The quotation marks bracketing "belong" alert us to the registers of metaphysical meaning Lawrence will tap in exploring the question of home and origin. Lawrence obviates the more superficial interpretations of Lou's rootlessness, as American maladaptation to the European cultural ethos or as temperamental uncongeniality, by generalizing her malaise to the other major figures as well. These figures share a common feature of origin in coming (St. Mawr and Lewis from Wales, Rico and the Manbys from Australia, and Mrs. Witt and Phoenix from America) from lands in which the decadence of civilization is not yet far enough advanced to extinguish their racial capability for vitality. By displacing these figures to fashionable London, Lawrence is able to measure their latent potential for life by the degree of alienation their cicurated environment generates in them. By this criterion, St. Mawr inevitably leads, for the formula inverts the cultural equation of home with domestication. Instead, an implicit definition emerges of home as the site that enables a fullness of life and an intrinsic perfection of being: a site, necessarily, of ferity.

Lou's failure to "belong" anywhere develops an epistemological character as soon as the narration moves more closely into her thoughts and feelings. Yet Lawrence uses the plot to undermine a purely existential interpretation of her alienation. Although Lou's sensation of watching her social world become increasingly oneiric and wraithlike ("Everything just conjured up, and nothing real" [27]) suggests a phenomenological awakening, Lawrence is careful to make its source external to her consciousness. By a skillful interweaving of the symptoms of magic and psychosis, he allows Lou to develop a reality disturbance that is beyond her volition or control.

In Lou's first symptom of unreality, the "nostalgia" for the mews that precedes her first meeting with St. Mawr, the regressiveness Freud associates with the uncanny is reproduced. "She had a funny little nostalgia for the place: something that really surprised her. She had never had the faintest notion that she cared for horses and stables and grooms. But she did. She was fascinated. Perhaps it was her childhood's Texas associations come back. Whatever it was, her life with Rico in the elegant little house, and all her social engagements, seemed like a dream, the substantial reality of which was those mews in Westminster" (10). The "fading" of Lou's social world into insubstantiality is triggered by the eruption of the infantile, which does not recognize the social as real. The regressive impulse toward the site of animal life, toward childhood associations and her own place of origin, is virtually unconscious in Lou, as we see in her whimsical, unpremeditated, and unwitting prediction that she will ultimately take St. Mawr "home" to America. "'But what would your Ladyship do with him, if I may make so bold?' 'I don't know,' she replied vaguely. 'I might take him to America.'"(14)

Lou initially conceals her irrational impulses by cloaking them in socially acceptable motives, pretending (even to herself) to buy St. Mawr for Rico. In the course of the story, the instinctive is revaluated, and the ability to experience magical and psychotic symptoms and to act impulsively becomes accepted as a healthy sign of unextinguished animal life. The intuitive tropism toward the wilderness (and its correlative, the transmogrification of Europe) is replicated in each of the pilgrims. But to preserve the authenticity of experience, to guarantee that it is not mimetic, copied, passed from one to the other, Lawrence limits communication among the figures (except for Lou and her mother) to assure their independent development. He also carefully individualizes their symptoms and tailors them to the peculiarities of each figure: Phoenix, the desert dweller, apprehends London as a nightmarish mirage; Lewis shares the feral vantage of St. Mawr and therefore perceives "the presence of people . . . as a prison around him" (22); Mrs. Witt, the improbable society matron, suffers funny hallucinations of grotesque tea ceremonies. At the

D.H. Lawrence's St. Mawr

last, Lou rationalizes her motives only for the sake of successful dispatch ("You and I are supposed to have important business connected with our estates in Texas" [116]) while allowing her intuitive, biocentric "knowledge" to direct her decisions and actions.

"Instinctive knowledge" is an oxymoron, as Lawrence illustrates in his essay, "The Novel." After defining the ultimate discrimination ("We have to choose between the quick and the dead") he illustrates it with a totally arbitrary classification of the objects in his room: the little iron stove, the sleeping cat, and the iron wardrobe trunk are inexplicably quick, while the table, glass lamp, and books are just as inexplicably dead. In place of criteria or principles of judgment he offers the impudent nonexplanation, "What makes the difference? *Quien sabe!* But difference there is. And I *know* it."[11] Lawrence will not give a logical explanation of the process because to do so would result in a positivistic description of the "flame" (to call it a vitalistic principle is already to appropriate it to scientism): a reduction to its essential elements or constituents, to a law of nature, to something fixed, empirical, repeatable, imitable. Making the difference between the quick and the dead accessible to reason would, furthermore, interject a mediation, an intervention, a rupture, into the "relatedness" of quick objects. Lawrence resorts to figural language ("The quick is God-flame"), tautology ("And the dead is dead"), and paradox (*knowing* without *knowing why*) to resist the philosophical threat to intuition. Finally, in an attempt to evade the metaphysics of presence altogether, to rescue "the flame" from both the substantiality of matter and the abstraction of principle, he resorts to describing it as a structure of structure, as pure "relatedness" itself. "And if one tries to find out, wherein the quickness of the quick lies, it is in a certain weird relationship between that which is quick and—I don't know; perhaps all the rest of things. It seems to consist in an odd sort of fluid, changing, grotesque or beautiful relatedness. That silly iron stove somehow *belongs*. Whereas this thin-shanked table doesn't belong. It is a mere disconnected lump, like a cut-off finger."[12]

This oblique, figurative, structural differentiation between the quick and the dead eventually assumes the consistency of a logic, and, with the support of Nietzschean and Freudian underpinnings, the complexity of a psychology. If quickness is relatedness, then deadness is disconnection and rupture, the creation of the partial object or fetish ("a mere disconnected lump, like a cut-off finger''), or, in the case of an individual, a man, the creation of a doll or mannikin. To Lawrence, the human ego, the *cogito,* is precisely such a partial object consisting only of the accidental features that he calls "the personal" and lacking the essential being that is constituted in its relatedness. "The ego, the little conscious ego that I am, that doll-like entity, that mannikin made in ridiculous likeness of the Adam which I am: am I going to allow that that is *all of me?*''[13] The doll, mannikin, and automaton figure as important elements in Freud's essay on "The Uncanny," where they exercise a function germane to Lawrence's ontopsychology. Refuting Jentsch's theory rooting the uncanny in intellectual uncertainty, Freud builds his own notion, that doubling and repetition belong to the earliest stages of mental life and constitute compulsive functions, on Otto Rank's thesis that "the double" serves as insurance against the destruction of the ego. Freud points out, for example, that the doubling and multiplication of genital symbols serve as a defense against the fear of castration in dreams.[14] By figuring the ego as a doll or mannikin, Lawrence makes the ego itself into the fetish, the partial object, the castrated self.

By making the mannikin or automaton synonymous with the eunuch in the figure of Rico, Lawrence suggests the psychological equivalence of supplements (representations, mimetic figures, effigies) and partial objects (fetishes, metonymies). Both are founded on a lack and therefore constitute a mediation between presence and absence, part and whole. Rico's poses, attitudes, handsome figure, and meticulous dressing and elaborate costume changes ("He has had a couple of marvellous invalid's bed-jackets sent from London: one a pinkish yellow, with rose-arabesque facings. . . . The other is a lovely silvery and blue and green soft brocade" [110]) are supplements for a lack that is defined, and becomes apparent to Lou, in contrast with the animal, St. Mawr. Lawrence alludes to it almost immediately when he describes Rico with a qualified animal trope. He is "the animal . . . gone queer and wrong" (50), tamed and domesticated, the horse "edging away from its master" (3), the horse that dares not make a break, the dog that "daren't quite bite" (10). Rico's lack or deficiency is a purely Nietzschean lack of power, of which his sexual dysfunction or disinclination is merely a symptom. In order to avoid confounding this power with its anthropomorphic supplements (money, social importance, bureaucratic control, and so forth) he has Lou recognize its lack in Rico's eyes by contrast with the eyes of St. Mawr. "At the

D.H. Lawrence's St. Mawr

middle of his eyes was a central powerlessness, that left him anxious. . . . But now, since she had seen the full, dark, passionate blaze of power and of different life in the eyes of the thwarted horse, the anxious powerlessness of the man drove her mad" (15).

Lawrence constructs a pathology for Rico that makes his vocation as artist the figure of his ontological castration. In Rico, Lawrence assimilates to the artist Nietzsche's "dangerous concept of the artiste" (2, GS, 508), equating artist and actor as creators of simulacra that supplement their lack of animal vitality and potency. "But now she realized that, with men and women, everything was an attitude only when something else is lacking. Something is lacking and they are thrown back on their own devices. That black fiery flow in the eyes of the horse was not 'attitude.' It was something much more terrifying, and real, the only thing that was real" (15). Rico belongs also to the uncanny version of the artist as vampire or ghoul who must appropriate the living animal vitality in order to nourish his deadness, like Hoffmann's Sand Man, the object of Freud's analysis in "The Uncanny," who plucks out the eyes of the living in order to make the wooden doll more lifelike. Rico appropriates St. Mawr in this way, using the powerful animal as a prop for the handsome figure he cuts in the Row, apprehending him two-dimensionally, as an aesthetic object, a still life or "composition" together with Lewis: "They'd be *so* amusing to paint: such an extraordinary contrast!" (17). Lou, on the other hand, apprehends St. Mawr without mediation and without ulterior motive: directly, experientially, through a touch sensitive to the texture, temperature, and pulse of life. "She was startled to feel the vivid heat of his life come through to her, through the lacquer of red-gold gloss. So slippery with vivid, hot life!" (13).

The sexual analogue of Rico's artist is the castrating eunuch,[15] a figure that emphasizes the artist's negative and spectral function as reproducer of his own lack, progenitor of his own sterility. Lawrence borrows Nietzsche's mythology and philology to distinguish the chthonic Dionysus from his later Hellenic corruptions in terms of structural concepts (wholeness, originality) relevant to both sexuality and art. "But don't you imagine Pan once *was* a Great God, before the anthropomorphic Greeks turned him into half a man?" (54). Lawrence uses the euphemism for emasculation ("half a man") to emphasize the ontological consequence of the post-Socratic redefinition of the human and the animal as mutually exclusive categories. The Western distortion that defines the human as the nonanimal (the rational, the virtuous, the civilized) makes *homo sapiens* tautological and synecdochic. To Lawrence, *human* is synonymous with *limited*,[16] and post-Socratic man (in contrast to the comprehensive Pan, the All, the human with his animalism intact) is a partial object, a synecdoche, a fetish. "The ego! Anthropomorphism! Love! What it works out to in the end is that even anthropos disappears, and leaves a sawdust mannikin wondrously jazzing."[17]

Lawrence recognizes that the artistic function is inherently fetishistic, that art is inevitably a secondary creation of the object in a reduced dimension, miniaturized, like the Priapus on Rico's intaglio; reduced to two-dimensionality, like Rico's portraits; and trivialized, like the gods appropriated from the realm of religion and faith in order to serve decorative functions. "The world always was a queer place. It's a very queer one when Rico is the god Priapus. He would go round the orchard painting lifelike apples on the trees, and inviting nymphs to come and eat them" (111). Lou's interpretive function does not reverse the fetishism of art and restore the object to wholeness; her interpretation of Rico as a painted / painting phallic god, a perpetually regenerating effigy, only recognizes the fetish as fetish, the object as partial, by situating it contextually in relation to its lack. Nowhere is the structural complication of Lawrence's ontological rhetoric more brilliantly in evidence than when he resorts to a metonymic metaphor for Rico. "If his head had been cut off, like John the Baptist's, it would have been a thing complete in itself, would not have missed the body in the least. . . . The head was one of the famous 'talking heads' of modern youth" (18).

When Lawrence adopts the arts as a metaphor for ontological mediation, he preserves Nietzsche's generic distinctions, for example, those between ritual and realistic drama, and updates them to accommodate modern technological invention. Lawrence's *Lost Girl* is, in a sense, a modern recapitulation of Nietzsche's philological argument about the decadent transition from Greek tragedy to New Attic comedy, from the Dionysian festival to the bourgeois realism of the plays of Euripides. The Natcha-Kee-Tawaras' vaudeville act, with its continuity in offstage, private life, is nonmimetic and dithyrambic, not a reenactment but a ritual *becoming* of primitive figures, as Alvina becomes Allaye. This Dionysian art form is replaced by the modern cinema. In *St. Mawr*, the cinema reproduces the mediations of European painting in America, and Lou feels as appro-

D.H. Lawrence's St. Mawr

priated by the one as by the other. Where once she felt "as if I too were nothing more than a painting by Rico" (111) the cowboys of Texas make her feel like an Eastern lady in a Zane Grey Western (131). Moreover, the cinema's influence on life creates an infinite mimetic regress in America, as the cowboys mimic the mimetic films, which result in a visual labyrinth of "life enacted in a mirror" (130). Lawrence gives this phenomenon a social aim whose philosophical roots may be found in Hegel's distinction between animal and human desire. The Texas ranch boss is a paragon of human self-consciousness, playing for recognition or "pure prestige"—"existing for the time being purely in his imagination of the sort of picture he made to her" (131).

The psychology of the castrating eunuch is founded on Nietzschean *ressentiment*: a defensive psychology of the weak who take revenge on the strong by making their own lack, their deficiency, normative. Rico and Flora Manby display just such a democratizing instinct in their plan to geld St. Mawr. But what of St. Mawr? Lawrence establishes the distinction between two kinds of aggressiveness as the ethical crux of the novella. "But St. Mawr? Was it the natural wild thing in him which caused these disasters? Or was it the slave, asserting himself for vengeance?" (73). The difference between the two is precisely one of mediation. The wild thing's aggressiveness is autotelic, referring only to itself, to the potency of its life flowing forth unchecked and dangerously. The slave's aggressiveness is social, intersubjective, self-conscious, and devious. The slave's vengeance is not active but reactive, its source is not in the self but in the perception of the "other," its motive is extrinsic (aggressiveness not for its own sake but for an ulterior, self-conscious motive), and, because it is born of weakness, its tactic is one of inflicting secret harm in order to maintain itself in safety. This is the doubled psychology of Lou's apocalyptic nightmare vision of evil with its obsessional theme of betrayal.

> But she thought with horror, a colder horror, of Rico's face as he snarled *Fool!* His fear, his impotence as a master, as a rider, his presumption. And she thought with horror of those other people, so glib, so glibly evil.
>
> What did they want to do, those Manby girls? Undermine, undermine, undermine. They wanted to undermine Rico, just as that fair young man would have liked to undermine her. . . .
>
> Mankind no longer its own master. Ridden by this pseudo-handsome ghoul of outward loyalty, inward treachery, in a

game of betrayal, betrayal, betrayal. The last of the gods of our era, Judas supreme! (70)

In Rico, Lawrence combines the doll, the mannikin, with its emotional correlative of secondary, reactive aggressiveness (anger) to produce the automaton. "Rico's anger was wound up tight at the bottom of him, like a steel spring that kept his works going, while he himself was 'charming,' like a bomb-clock with Sèvres paintings or Dresden figures on the outside" (26). The metaphorics of mechanized and remote-control violence (bombs, dynamite, guns) serve to distinguish the various kinds of mediated, human aggressiveness from the spontaneous, autotelic power of wild animals. "I always felt guns very repugnant: sinister, mean,"[18] Lawrence writes in "The Death of a Porcupine." The meanness refers, no doubt, to the instrumental function of weapons that spare their users all risk except that of reciprocal fire. Lawrence's military pacifism and existential militancy are in no way self-contradictory; he believes in the right and duty to kill but mocks the Italian hunters (l'uomo è cacciatore)[19] training their rifles on tiny songbirds. Wild things possess courage commensurate with their intrinsic power ("the wild thing's courage to maintain itself alone and living in the midst of a diverse universe" [73]), while Rico, like the Italian hunters, like a terrorist, conspires "to live in absolute physical safety, whilst willing the minor disintegration of all positive living" (73).

Lawrence uses Mrs. Witt as a version of Rico in order to establish subtle differences in the causality of fetishism. She shares Rico's mechanical aggressiveness ("Mrs. Witt was *so* like a smooth, levelled gun-metal pistol" [9]) although its source is not a lack but an intellectual displacement, a misunderstanding. She devalues and represses her own real power ("In her strong limbs there was far more electric power than in the limbs of any man she had met" [95]) in favor of Mind, an instrument and supplement in Lawrencian ontology, a fiction compensating for a lack. In Mrs. Witt's fetishism, her mania for trimming shrubbery, her voluptuous response to hair, her fondness for shoes ("She was a demon in shoes. . . . Yes, she had brought ten pairs of shoes from New York. She knew her daughter's foot as she knew her own" [44]) we see not only the castrating tendency, the need to "cut up" the body because it cannot be apprehended whole, but also the possibility of vitality kept alive and unextinguished, however misdirected and cathected. Mrs. Witt's

D.H. Lawrence's St. Mawr

pathology is not ontological, like Rico's, but purely epistemo-logical. As a "pure psychologist, a fiendish psychologist" (30) she knows only analysis and vivisection, the ability to apprehend the Lawrencian body in fragments, in its dead parts ("If you cut a thing up, of course it will smell" [30]). The apprehension of wholeness, of structures in their proper relations of presence and absence, eludes her precisely because it must be found in the instinctual subject (the body electric as perceptual organ) rather than in the object of contemplation or analysis. Mrs. Witt does not suffer from Nietzschean resentment because the Mind she envies is partial and inconsequential, and intuitively, in her body's instincts, she "knows" it. "Her own peculiar dynamic force was stronger than the force of Mind" (95).

The epistemological metaphor of castration in *St. Mawr* is ocular fragmentation and disintegration, like the "alert argus capability of the English matron" (9) in Rotten Row, or Mrs. Witt's Medusa face ("She stared at everything and everybody, with that stare of cold dynamite waiting to explode them all" [21]). Lawrence extends the distinction between mechanical aggressiveness and organic potency to his ocular metaphorics, contrasting the hostile, prying, analytical vision of Mrs. Witt with the animal eyes of Lewis, "the eyes of a wildcat peering intent from under the darkness of some bush" (17), to which all anthropomorphic or social mediations are transparent. The animal perspective is, like the infantile, a point of view that does not recognize the social and therefore dissolves supplements and discloses the lack they conceal. Under Lewis' gaze, people are "found out" (17). Title, money, clothes, or profession fail to mediate Lewis's judgment of Rico's "merits as a man, alone without a background: an ungarnished colonial" (18). St. Mawr's stare has the same effect of stripping social identities and appurtenances from Lou. "And she felt that it forbade her to be her ordinary, commonplace self. It forbade her to be just Rico's wife, young Lady Carrington, and all that" (15).

Lewis and St. Mawr do not have a wicked eye, as Laura Ridley supposes (123–24), an eye with psychic or hypnotic powers, because the will to power in Lawrence, as in Nietzsche, does not consist in a Hegelian capture of the other's desire, in the "bully-ing" that is an appropriation of the other's consciousness and will.[20] In Lawrence, as in Freud's essay on "The Uncanny," the "evil eye" is a projection of envy by the victim onto another, who is then endowed with the animistic power to take revenge by doing harm. Lawrence rather formulates the function of St.

Mawr's eyes as the posing of "a non-human question" (14), as a clew, like that of a Freudian free association, that leads to an unsuspected knowledge in Lou, unsuspected because external to the anthropomorphic and anthropocentric perspective that defines her human self-knowledge. St. Mawr's "uncanny authority" is the authority to dissolve the self-conscious subject, to insist that life and power exist external to the thinking self, and to transform the Greek "Know Thyself" to the presubjective "Be Thyself."[21]

Since the Lawrencian body "knows," holistic vision, predicated upon power and fullness of life, is possible only for the strong: Mrs. Witt is capable of it; Rico is not. Mrs. Witt's first signs of recuperation are expressed in epistemological terms, as a revision (re-vision) of her thinking, a seeing of things not from a different angle but in a different structural relationship. This recuperation is therefore also rhetorical or poetical, as when she dissolves the metonymic organization of the figure of the body. "But—do you know?—it hadn't occurred to me that a man's beard was really part of him. It always seemed to me that men wore their beards, like they wear their neckties, for show. I shall always remember Lewis for saying his beard was part of him. Isn't it curious, the way he rides? He seems to sink himself in the horse. When I speak to him, I'm not sure whether I'm speaking to a man or to a horse" (23). Her second observation, abolishing the discontinuity between the human and the animal, is clearly intended to serve as an analogue to her first observation abolishing the fetish. The implication is that the fetish, even when it is a part of the body, or the body itself, is always a cultural object (the beard as a necktie), and that a holistic vision therefore depends upon seeing the human (generic "man") as a natural rather than a cultural entity, namely, as an animal.

In order to give his concept of holistic vision a prerational heritage, and to define instinctive or irrational perception as a visionary plenum to which rationality represents an occlusion, Lawrence borrows from early Greek mythology the ocular metaphor of the "third eye." "Pan was the hidden mystery—the hidden cause. That's how it was a Great God. Pan wasn't *he* at all: not even a Great God. He was Pan. All: what you see when you see in full. In the daytime you see the thing. But if your third eye is open, which sees only the things that can't be seen, you may see Pan within the thing, hidden: you may see with your third eye, which is darkness" (54). This "third eye" is an ocular version of Nietzsche's "ears behind the ears" (3, *TI*, 387),

D.H. Lawrence's St. Mawr

a nonpositivistic instrument that distinguishes immaterial realities on the basis of their wealth or dearth of life: the European phantasmagoria from "the unseen presences" of the sacral wilderness, the impotence of decadent men from the celibacy of the atavistic Vestal Virgin. The relationship between Lawrence's ocular and sexual imagery constitutes the epistemological equation: human sight or cultural perception is to castration as the "third eye," feral sight or natural fullness of vision, is to animal potency. In Lewis's juvenile Celtic cosmos, the ferity of the mystical vision becomes explicit: humans may see the Pan-like creatures in the moon only upon observing the feral taboos of avoiding fire, cooked food, and clothing.

The irony of having the mythology of the "third eye" imparted to the company of arch and gay young Edwardians ("Our late King Edward" is invoked in the company that includes an "Eddy Edwards") by the goatish artist and philologist Cartwright,[22] serves to draw a sharp distinction between knowledge and recognition. "Isn't it extraordinary that young man Cartwright talks about Pan, but he knows nothing of it all?" (56). Recognition (re-cognition) implies the repetition of an earlier cognitive experience, in Lou's case the experiential knowledge acquired through St. Mawr. Lou knows what Cartwright is talking about because she has already seen through her "third eye." Mrs. Witt has not, but she could. "'But what do you know of the unfallen Pan, mother?' 'Don't ask me, Louise! I feel all of a tremble, as if I was just on the verge'" (56). The unconscious basis of knowledge is also evident in its relation to wit rather than erudition. When Lou blurts out that she just sees a sort of "pancake" in contemporary young men, the pun on Pan identifies, with the unconscious quickness, accuracy, and wit of a free association, the source of the young men's corruption in domestication and harmlessness.

The circularity of the *Heimkehr* in *St. Mawr* entails a phylogenetic journey through animal history because the animal, too, has been repressed, domesticated, and corrupted and does not, in its modern form, constitute a prelapsarian paragon. St. Mawr's atavism therefore serves a function analogous to the Freudian infantile, demonstrating the persistence of the primitive type: the Eocene lord of creation surviving in the modern hackney as surely as the omnipotent infant survives in the repressed adult. "With their strangely naked equine heads, and something of a snake in their way of looking round, and lifting their sensitive, dangerous muzzles, they moved in a prehistoric twilight where all things loomed phantasmagoric, all on one plane, sudden presences suddenly jutting out of the matrix. It was another world, an older, heavily potent world. And in this world the horse was swift and fierce and supreme, undominated and unsurpassed" (19). St. Mawr's atavism, with protean fluidity and potency as its chief features, constitutes the complex structural paradigm for the redemption of modern man. The rapprochement between the human and the animal ("But half-way across from our human world to that terrific equine twilight was not a small step" [20]) requires originality and wholeness, the reestablishment of both linear and lateral continuity with the life force. Lou enunciates both of these principles, the need to get life straight from the source and the need to escape the generic fixity of the species, when she tells her mother: "'A pure animal man would be as lovely as a deer or a leopard, burning like a flame fed straight from underneath. . . . He'd be all the animals in turn, instead of one fixed, automatic thing, which he is now, grinding on the nerves'" (50).

Lawrence, who had extended his equation of immobility and fixity with death to psychological theory as early as his famous letter to Garnett in 1914,[23] in *St. Mawr* extends the principle to phylogeny as well. Having translated the allotropic states of the ego into inconsistent novelistic characterizations in *The Rainbow,* Lawrence translates the allotropic states of species into the richly transmogrified animal tropes of St. Mawr. He transforms descriptive imagery into generic metaphors as the aqueous attributes of St. Mawr ("slippery," his color "a bright, red-gold liquid . . . his head lifted like the summit of a fountain," running with "that luxurious heavy ripple of life") are replaced by a marine typology of reptilian and ichthyic forms. Lawrence's phylogeny is not, strictly speaking, Darwinian, for the evolutionary prototype of St. Mawr is not the tiny eohippus but a mythological hippocampine form, a monstrous equine-reptilian hybrid evoking the fluidity of genera in its transitional life form. "St. Mawr gave a great curve like a fish, spread his forefeet on the earth and reared his head, looking round in a ghastly fashion. . . . He rested thus, seated with his forefeet planted and his face in panic, almost like some terrible lizard, for several moments" (67).

The fall of St. Mawr, a brilliant moment of poetic compression, is structured like a palimpsest that inscribes in the contemporary moment of a prosaic riding accident a perverse version of

D.H. Lawrence's St. Mawr

classical, medieval, and apocalyptic emblems of the Manichean struggle of man with the animal and with his own animal nature. Foreshadowed by an earlier allusion (19), Hippolytus appears to be there, the horse tamer and devotee of the virginal Artemis punished for his denial of life by the hippocampine Poseidon, god of the sea and god of horses. The reptilian St. Mawr also conjures up the dualistic dragon of Lawrence's *Apocalypse* ("the grand divine dragon of his superhuman potency, or the great demonish dragon of his inward destruction"[24]), the dragon of aboriginal life in contest with the St. George of civilized and christianized England.

Allotropism, a version of wholeness in Lawrencian morphology, functions as an antidote to the fetish because it describes a metonymy without a lack: relatedness and contiguity without substitution. The Lawrencian cosmos (Nature) is a plenum full of interrelated creatures and things that are neither equal nor fixed as a result of differences in degree and kind of power. Lawrence's political theories are firmly grounded in the natural politics of Nietzsche and must therefore be read without anthropomorphic distortion. Although Lawrence's great chain of being sounds deceptively progressionist ("And man is the highest, most developed, most conscious, most *alive* of the mammals: master of them all"[25]) it does not have an anthropocentric teleology or eschatology. In Lawrence's cosmology man is neither the end of creation nor the measure of all things ("One would think, to read modern books, that the life of any tuppenny bankclerk was more important than sun, moon, and stars"[26]), and although as a species, a creatural form, the human is more vivid than other species, individual humans may be deader than dandelions. Since for Lawrence, as for Nietzsche, strength and weakness are vitalistic concepts emptied of their anthropomorphic residue, the cardinal distinction between the human and the animal is erased and replaced by the transgeneric distinction of the wild and the domesticated. The master / slave relationship between Rico and St. Mawr becomes reversed on these grounds, with the stallion, "Lord St. Mawr," as the master not by preordination but by default. "St. Mawr, that bright horse, one of the kings of creation in the order below man, it had been a fulfilment for him to serve the brave, reckless, perhaps cruel men of the past, who had a flickering, rising flame of nobility in them" (75).

The long denouement following the fall of St. Mawr is designed precisely to demonstrate that the opposite of social hierarchy is not democracy but natural hierarchy. Lawrencian aristocracy is founded on neither birth nor money but on vitalism and a kind of "soul"—the nonideational, nonidealistic "flame" of a deanthropomorphized theology in which God is the sum of all quickness.[27] The conceptual pairing of upper-class women and lower-class men does indeed obliterate the old social barriers as the ladies and their grooms head for America, but their new relationship does not constitute a new democratic social realignment. Phoenix, a servant in England, remains a servant in America, although on the entirely different grounds and criteria of the natural order. Although he is more potent than Rico (Lord Carrington) since he subdues St. Mawr after the first trouble in the Row, and more vitally connected to Nature, he traffics in mediated objects and is too materialistic. According to Lawrence, "the providing of food, money, and amusement belongs, truly, to the servant class. The providing of *life* belongs to the aristocrat."[28] Phoenix, offering Lou an implied prostitution more degrading than her marriage to Rico ("He was ready to trade his sex, which, in his opinion, every white woman was secretly pining for, for the white woman's money and social privileges" [136]) is rejected and relegated to the function of groom and chauffeur.

To describe his hierarchical Nature rife with inequalities, Lawrence uses a vocabulary redolent of the emotional connotations of social class. The polarity of Lawrencian Nature at its best and at its worst is inscribed in the antonymy of the words *glamour* and *squalor*, both pertaining to the wilderness and marking the subtle distinction between its soul and its matter. *Glamour* resides in the deanthropomorphized fourth dimension. "The flying-fishes burst out of the sea in clouds of silvery, transparent motion. Blue above and below, the Gulf seemed a silent, empty, timeless place where man did not really reach. And Lou was again fascinated by the glamour of the universe" (128). By penetrating to its etymological root in Scottish and Welsh usage, Lawrence strips the word *glamour* of its resonances of meretricious beauty and restores it to the realm of magic and enchantment. Glamour, then, once more connotes an animistic universe where power radiates from natural things and exerts itself on the irrational and intuitive sensibility of the human.

Squalor and *sordidness*, also attributes of the savage wilderness, refer to the materiality of nature, particularly to the excess of inert and lifeless matter best characterized by the filth that accretes to the overcrowded welter of indiscriminate life. Exces-

D.H. Lawrence's St. Mawr

sive fecundity resulting in the herding, lumping, and cohesion of living things overwhelms their vitality with materiality. Lawrence shares Nietzsche's repulsion by the herd, recapitulating the mildly nightmarish welter of babies in the Brangwen household in the sordid infestations of goats and pack rats on Las Chivas. But whereas the violence of the natural competitive struggle restores ecological balance to the wilderness, the democracy of civilization produces the evil of Lou's nightmare. "Creation destroys as it goes, throws down one tree for the rise of another. But ideal mankind would abolish death, multiply itself million upon million, rear up city upon city, save every parasite alive, until the accumulation of mere existence is swollen to a horror" (71).

The *Heimkehr* in *St. Mawr* entails the return to an ontological ferity: not just a return to the wilderness, but a virtual, if practicable, abolition of the social. The result is a curious paradox that resonates to Freud's unhomely home, a community that is not a community but a misanthropic ménage of people and animals marked by mutual indifference, separation, and solitude, but related in quickness and power. Lou's misanthropy betrays its ferity in her analogy: "A sort of hatred for people has come over me . . . and I feel like kicking them in the face, as St. Mawr did that young man" (115). Indifference is not predicated upon a lack (a "human" deficiency) in this new order of relationships. Humans now relate to each other as animals do, without social consciousness of each other, without intersubjectivity, without concern for impressions or prestige, without concern for each other's conscious response, without malice, seduction, envy, supplication, or love. Lewis all along relates in this way to humans and animals alike. Lou, whose relationship to St. Mawr has been pulsating, instinctive, and mystical from the first, only later recognizes this as the natural order of things. "He knew her and did not resent her. But he took no notice of her. He would never 'respond.' At first she had resented it. Now she was glad. He would never be intimate, thank heaven" (53).

Originality, getting life straight from the source, is also possible only in the wild state in which the mediation of the social, the cultural, the intersubjective, the rational, and the communicative are abolished. Lawrence uses a distaff metaphor, "knitting the same pattern over and over again" (49), to describe rational thought as divorced from feral origins and from natural power. Because it is submitted to convention, tradition, and influence, that is, to synthetic and man-made structures and laws, rational thought is mechanical, repetitive, and artificial. The "thought" of feral humans like Lewis is the paradoxical process of animal instinct: "He has a good intuitive mind, he knows things without thinking them " (49). To Lawrence, artistic imagination is subject to the same limitations and cultural conditioning as reason and is therefore as incapable of originality. "Every possible daub that can be daubed has already been done, so people ought to leave off" (114). Like Nietzsche, Lawrence would subscribe to a notion of aesthetics as "applied physiology," to an art whose function vis-à-vis life is to serve as a stimulant rather than a simulacrum.

Lawrence likewise views language as a cultural entity with the power to appropriate life and assimilate it to culture. The self consequently becomes victimized by idle talk and transformed into a purely social (that is, mediated) object, as Mrs. Witt recognizes to her sorrow. "I seem to have been a daily sequence of newspaper remarks, myself. . . . I never had any motherhood, except in newspaper fact. I never was a wife, except in newspaper notices. I never was a young girl, except in newspaper remarks. Bury everything I ever said or that was said about me, and you've buried *me*" (86). The self's natural residue, the creatural animality or vitality of its body, is ejected from the ontological sphere by language. But Lawrence does not intend to privilege literary or fictional language over journalistic writing either. Bad novels merely multiply a language that does not speak vitality and consequently succeeds only in camouflaging its own void: "I feel as if the sky was a big cracked bell and a million clappers were hammering human speech out of it" (154). Lawrence used the bell image elsewhere to contrast with human speech the sound of wild and unmediated animal life in the neighing of St. Mawr: "the powerful, splendid sound . . . like bells made of living membrane" (75).

As we know from the experience of Alexander Selkirk (though hardly from the anthropomorphic fantasies of Defoe) the wilderness can rob human beings of their speech and restore ("reduce," from an anthropocentric perspective) them to ferity. The recuperative power of the wilderness is precisely its ability to extract and reclaim wild, natural life from socialized, acculturated human beings. On Las Chivas this power takes the form of the ability to induce aphasia in the New England woman who is Lou's predecessor. "At the same time, the invisible attack was being made upon her . . . she could not keep even her speech. When she was saying something, suddenly the next word would be gone out of her, as if a pack-rat had carried it off. And she sat blank, stuttering, staring in the empty cupboard of her mind, like Mother Hubbard, and seeing the cupboard bare" (149). America is not, geographically, an originary site, and where civilization has made inroads, originality is no longer possible. *"Plus ça change, plus c'est la même chose"* (128), Mrs. Witt says, watching the American tourists in Havana. Lou echoes the phrase in Santa Fe, another tourist haven. Civilized America easily replicates European mediations and produces some of its own, replacing horses with motor cars, for example (75). The "more absolute silence of America" (74) is possible only in a brutal wilderness, like that of Las Chivas, which can repel the social and cultural imperialism of its human invaders and thereby preserve a feral ethos for Lou's misanthropic ménage.

Lou's *Heimkehr* is possible only upon completing her abdication of the social, the domestic, the homely, a process begun upon her first meeting with St. Mawr and concluding when, with the overcoming of her last temptation (Phoenix) she renounces all sexual intercourse that could implicate her in an interpersonal or social relationship. "'I am not a marrying woman,' she said to herself. 'I am not a lover nor a mistress nor a wife'" (139). Lou ultimately forecloses the human, social world as she does her home in Westminster, shutting it down like a museum, separating herself with finality from cultural artifacts that are extruded from life, salvaged from fate and time, immobilized in the stasis of death. "She felt like fastening little labels on the furniture: *Lady Louise Carrington Lounge Chair, Last used August, 1923.* Not for the benefit of posterity: but to remove her own self into another world, another realm of existence" (118).

The concluding description of the wilderness, one of the most splendid pieces of Lawrencian topography, is analogous in its epistemological and ontological functions to the visions earlier induced in Lou by St. Mawr. Before producing forms or images, these visions produce an affect. The first "split some rock in her" (14) and released a torrent of tears; in another, Lou "breathes" St. Mawr's great animal sadness like a terrible sigh. The first sight of Las Chivas likewise triggers a desire ("Yet it was the place Lou wanted") and an emotional response ("Her heart sprang to it" [141]). Her vision is also preceded by a recognition; her *"this is the place"* carries the conviction of one who knows because she has been there before, as though Lou were the atavist or reincarnation of the defeated little New England

Beasts of the Modern Imagination

woman whose heart had nonetheless absorbed the magic of the monstrous land. This accounts for the narrational rupture represented by the description: although its narrator exhibits the extreme omniscience of prehistoric knowledge (the miserable pioneering failures scarcely merit record or attention), Lou (who does not know the history of the place) responds *as though* she knew, as though the omnisciently narrated description displayed her unconscious knowledge. She echoes the prosopopeia of the topography in alluding to the spirit of the place ("I can't tell you what it is. It's a spirit. And it's here, on this ranch. It's here, in this landscape" [158]), and she predicts for herself an experience like that of the New England woman, who is unknown to her ("I don't know what it is, definitely. It's something wild, that will hurt me sometimes and will wear me down sometimes. I know it" [158]). Lou's instinctive fullness of knowledge gains discursive expression only at the price of logical fracture and inconsistency: "I don't know . . . I know it."

Born experientially of Lawrence's Kiowa Ranch, this remarkable description of Las Chivas subverts the traditional rhetorical function of description, which is allied to that of the museum (to erect monuments, to fix grandeur for posterity, to submit Nature to the conditions of the Institution).[29] His enargia (and Lawrence might have approved the metaphysical propriety of this allusion to "vividness" of style) is above all devoted to the kinetic landscape, the vivid and destructive firmament, the vegetation as sensitive and protean and dangerous as a wild animal. "Strange, those pine-trees! In some lights all their needles glistened like polished steel, all subtly glittering with a whitish glitter among darkness, like real needles. Then again, at evening, the trunks would flare up orange-red, and the tufts would be dark, alert tufts like a wolf's tail touching the air" (146). This landscape is unlike the pastoral or Romantic landscape in that humans with their consciousness and their aesthetic sensibility are excluded from this wilderness unless they are assimilated to its ferity. "The great circling landscape lived its own life, sumptuous and uncaring. Man did not exist for it" (148). The little New England woman is seen from the vantage of the grey squirrel "as if she were the alien" (150) and feels herself a trespasser on her own land, which negates all concept of property. "The berries grew for the bears, and the little New England woman, with her uncanny sensitiveness to underlying influences, felt all the time she was stealing" (152). The description represents the settlers' failure to domesticate the wilderness (even their plumbing is described in the metaphors of cicuration, "the wild water of the hills caught, tricked into the narrow iron pipes, and led tamely to her kitchen" [149]), as a grateful repulsion of cultural achievement in favor of the living feral world. Lou has no plans to imitate the pioneer endeavor: "I was rather hoping, mother, to escape achievement" (156).

The dialogue between Lou and Mrs. Witt that concludes *St. Mawr* shares the function of other Lawrencian endings: to frustrate faith in communication and rational discourse, to confirm that the quest for the origin must be original (singular and inimitable) and that the text must be negated as a didactic instrument since it can do no more than stimulate an affect, kindle a latent desire, trigger a memory or a nostalgia. But the interlocution also has a certain psychoanalytic significance because the two women are mother and daughter, and Mrs. Witt (not the individual, the social entity, but the body, the animal) constitutes Lou's own vital origin.[30] The *Heimkehr* is also the reconciliation with the mother, in their special relatedness that survives the paradoxes of their situation ("I want to be alone, mother: with you here" [156]) and of their figural language (the disjunction of sexual and religious metaphors in their dialogue) to coincide in a commonality of desire. Their end is a Nietzschean *amor fati,* and Lou's submission to the God that is the sum of all quickness, the spirit of the wilderness, the secret, feral home of her animal self, is no more than Mrs. Witt's desire to surrender to a positive death, to die into the unconsciousness of the pulse of life, "to be folded then at last into throbbing wings of mystery, like a hawk that goes to sleep" (97).

9

The Animal and
Violence in Hemingway's
Death in the Afternoon

I had expected Hemingway to be a beast and found, instead, an aesthete in beast's clothing. But the process of locating Hemingway outside the biocentric tradition proved extremely valuable for illustrating what, besides the representation of animal and Nature imagery, constitutes biocentric art. Hemingway's agon with the animal might well be construed as libidinal activity had he not produced a philosophical argument to rationalize it in his nonfiction works on bullfighting and safari hunting. That literary gesture demonstrates, through the cultural teleology of his violence, the mediation of animal and Nature, and the manipulative functions of his rhetoric and pedagogy, that Hemingway's contest is with the "other," not the animal, and that his quest is for mastery, not for animal power. The possibilities of demonstrating biocentric activity through a process of negative inference from Hemingway's enterprise seemed useful enough to justify such a counterpoint chapter.

But clearly my own position as a critic would be different in this chapter from what it had been in the others. There I had been presenting a critique of anthropocentrism; here I would be practicing such a critique. It occurred to me that I would be repeating the critical gestures I had been tracking in the other writers and thinkers and that I escaped the dangers inherent in this enterprise (of imitating my subjects and behaving like a disciple) only because I had been ambushed by my own analysis: my expectations had been foiled and I was surprised and disappointed that Hemingway did not "fit." Other critical dilemmas proved less tractable, especially those concerning my own rhetorical motives and strategies. I had to purge myself, however imperfectly, of female *ressentiment* against Hemingway *machismo*. I had to eschew humanistic premises for my judgments and act *not* from pity for the animals. I had to focus the writer's posturing, hypocrisy, and perversity as my target, not Ernest Hemingway, the man. And I had to avoid apologizing for the imperfect execution of these obligations. But the objective that eluded me most fully was the invention of a bestial "voice" or "style." I had to content myself with possessing a bestial "eye," and speaking *for* rather than *as* the animal, in a polemical tone not entirely free of tinges of antivivisectionist bitterness. Yet my criticism (reflecting the more existentialist implications of biocentric thought) is aimed not at the bullfight, but at Hemingway's particular defense of it. My target is not violence per se (in the face of which a biocentric position can only be fatalistic) but the aesthetic and idealistic rationalization of violence.

At the beginning of *Death In the Afternoon,* Hemingway announces pedagogy as the first twist of the teleological spiral by which violence—and the animal that is its object—is forever displaced, repressed, and abolished until only the residue of a writing marked by bad faith remains. "The only place where you could see life and death, *i.e.,* violent death now that the wars were over, was in the bull ring and I wanted very much to go to Spain where I could study it. I was trying to learn to write, commencing with the simplest things, and one of the simplest things of all and the most fundamental is violent death" (*DA,* 2). Not only is the bullfight a substitutive experience, an ersatz for the superior but unavailable wars, but its very violence is reduced to a heuristic function, a field trip exhibit mounted for the education of the fledgling writer. Consciously or not, Hemingway here reenacts the primordially displaced origin of the bullfight. According to Collins and Lapierre, the later conquistadors awaiting military campaigns that never came to pass "kept sharp the skills of war" by killing wild bulls from horseback.[1] The bull is doubly mediated at the very origin of tauromachy: killed neither for his own sake nor even as a substitutive enemy or sacrificial victim,[2] he is negated altogether as a significant object in favor of a pure instrumentality. His function as a victim of violence is abstracted; he serves as a proleptic device, an exemplary or model opponent, a paradigm of danger. His pain and death are stripped of significance except as the incidental expenditure of a deferred violence.

Hemingway's subjectivist praxis of "writing truly," in which truth pertains only to the emotional and sensational fidelity of the writing, requires that all experience serve the ends of the writer's tutelage. But Hemingway primordially confuses the intrinsic significance he would like to impute to violent experience with its representability. When he writes of violent death, "it is death nevertheless, one of the subjects that a man may write of" (*DA,* 2), he soberly misses the joke: that he may write of it only if he eludes it, if he experiences it vicariously, as a witness or a spectator. *Death in the Afternoon* is therefore justified by an ocular ethic that forbids the wince, the reflexive occlusion of the violent moment ("the author had never seen it clearly or at the moment of it, he had physically or mentally shut his eyes" [*DA,* 2]), in favor of a necroscopy with the scholarly authenticity of "the observations of the naturalist" (*DA,* 133). But by failing to interrogate the metaphysical status of *the spectacle,* by failing to perceive the repression and denial of Nature at the heart of its function, Hemingway's "writing truly" is vulnerable to the bad faith of mistaking the voyeur's spurious objectivity for the writer's desire for the truth.

Hemingway's function as a pedagogue in *Death in the Afternoon* is more than just the harmless egotistical posturing Dos Passos referred to as "where Old Hem straps on the longwhite whiskers and gives the boys the lowdown."[3] Although teaching is polemical in nature, Hemingway uses its rationalistic methods and assumptions to lend authority to his argument that the *corrida de toros* can be justified on aesthetic and athletic grounds. By imputing to the bullfight the intellectual attributes of both art and science, he assimilates the violent killing of the animal to such traditional humanistic values as beauty, harmony of composition, symmetry of form, logical development, eloquence of gesture, precision of execution, and the personal virtues of valor, discipline, and integrity. But the pedagogic function used as a means of rationalizing violence in the interest of culture has the devious and hypocritical coloration not only of the priestly enterprise, according to Nietzsche, but also of pornological writing, according to Deleuze. The problem at the heart of *Death in the Afternoon* is that by refusing to confront the irrationalities and perversities of tauromachy, Hemingway's writing becomes implicated in them. The book shows us not only the bullfight through Hemingway's eyes, but also Hemingway writing to be seen seeing. Hemingway *performs* not as biocentric artists perform, for the sake of the activity itself, but as a spectacle.

As professor of tauromachy, Hemingway presumes to externalize the hidden interiority of the bullfight, to decode its mysterious and unintelligible signs. The bullfight is revealed to have a logical narrative in which each moment has a plausible rationale, a cause and effect that are never obvious but must be inferred

Hemingway's Death in the Afternoon

from the teleological function of the spectacle as a whole. Thus sticking the bull with banderillas exceeds mere cruelty; the bull is greatly hurt not for the sake of causing him pain, but in order to modify his performance in the ring, to make him slower, and more deliberate and accurate in his horn work, to transform him into a more valuable "artistic property" (*DA*, 89). Suffering Nature, concealed in the black, dense, vital mass of the bull's flesh, eludes the light-drenched exposure of the solar spectacle, and is therefore elided. In the context of the modern tradition that demystifies the Western cultural hermeneutics of suffering—an enterprise extending from Nietzsche's *Genealogy of Morals* and Freud's *Beyond the Pleasure Principle* to contemporary studies by Barthes, Bataille, Deleuze, and Girard—Hemingway's *Death in the Afternoon* stands as a distinct retrogression.

Notwithstanding his derision of writers who mystify instead of sticking to straight statement (*DA*, 54), Hemingway performs a priestly function when he lays his 1,500 sacrificial bulls on the altar of art. The priest gives pain and violence a spiritual teleology in a betrayal of the body that assimilates living Nature to the exigencies of abstract values, for example, sacrifice, atonement, redemption, and sublimation. Hemingway's ephemeral moment of candor, when he writes of the matador, "A great killer must love to kill"(*DA*, 232), is betrayed instantaneously by a valorized, idealistic vocabulary that removes autotelic killing (that is, killing as an unconscious, instinctive act committed in an effusion of animal power and excitation) from the realm of the bestial to the plane of virtue. For Hemingway, the pleasure of killing entails consciousness of its "dignity," of "a sense of honor and a sense of glory, . . . a spiritual enjoyment of the moment of killing, . . . aesthetic pleasure and pride," and assorted other "spiritual qualities" (*DA*, 232–33). But dignity, honor, pride, and glory are values of an intersubjective and social origin, values conferred by the consciousness of the recognition of the "other": in short, cultural values rather than intrinsic ones. Hemingway claims that "killing is not a feeling that you share" (*GHA*, 120), and yet the entire safari cult of competition and trophies, celebration and largesse, photography and taxidermy, externalizes the experience for consumption by social consciousness.

Hemingway acts the pornologist's part (the masochist justifying cruelty in the name of art and Platonic ideals, the sadist justifying it in the name of science and rationalism) when he writes, "There is no manoeuvre in the bullfight which has, as object, to inflict pain on the bull. The pain that is inflicted is incidental, not an end" (*DA*, 195). If, to correct for our anthropocentric bias, we were to substitute *woman* or *child* for *bull* in the preceding sentence, the perversity of the language would become immediately apparent. The language itself enacts an order of mental or rational cruelty by stripping the inflicted pain of any intrinsic importance, by denying its centrality to the event, by dismissing it, with a sadist's arrogance, as a mere detail in a larger, abstract project. Hemingway's sadism does not lie in his capability for violence and cruelty, his willingness to hurt people and animals, his interest in seeing soldiers killed, and killing game. Indeed, when he acknowledges his pleasure in violence and aggression (both verbal and physical), he achieves the disarming innocence of a Nietzschean *Übermensch*. "There are no subjects I would not jest about if the jest were funny enough," he wrote in *The New Yorker* in reply to criticism of *Death in the Afternoon*, "just as, liking wing shooting, I would shoot my own mother if she went in coveys and had a good strong flight."[4] Sadism resides in the displacement of pleasure from the commission of cruelty to its contemplation, description, and rationalization. It is not constituted by actions but by attitudes that are founded on a lie, on the denial of the importance of pain. Sadism betrays *physis* in the interest of *technē*, subordinating the claims of Nature to those of culture. We see it in Hemingway's studied apathy toward the pain of the bull "cruelly punished" by pronged harpoons driven forcefully into his neck muscle. "I kept my admiration for him always, but felt no more sympathy for him than for a canvas or the marble a sculpture [*sic*] cuts or the dry powder snow your skis cut through" (*DA*, 99).

Hidden in the patently false analogy, which equates sensate being (bull) with insensate being (marble, snow) in order to negate the bull's pain, lies an invitation to penetrate Hemingway's hypocrisy, to expose the shamming masquerade of "logic" implicit in his pedagogy. Like Deleuze's pornologer, Hemingway is on the side of violence, not only against the bull but against the reader as well. His malicious treatment of the fictional "old lady" who serves as our proxy reveals his sadistic ulterior motives. Beneath the ostensible purpose of educating her about the ultimate material reality of death, his "Natural History of the Dead" has the scarcely concealed aim of assaulting, shocking, and discomfiting her.

Hemingway's Death in the Afternoon

Old lady: I don't care for the title.
Author: I didn't say you would. You may very well not like any of it. But here it is.

(*DA,* 133)

He subjects her again to the painful anecdote of the Greeks breaking the legs of their mules at Smyrna before drowning them in the shallow water, not in order to deplore the violence, but in order to contrast (and justify by contrast) the functional and purposeful cruelty of the bullring with the Greeks' gratuitous act. At the same time, he assaults her (and us) with the specious reasoning that two wrongs make a right.

Because Hemingway separates prejudice and expertise, malice and critical acumen *organizationally* in the text of *Death in the Afternoon* (by relegating the more egregious gossip and opinion to the ends of chapters) he is able to protect his credibility as an expert technical witness to the bullfight. His glossary ultimately enjoys an authority that deflects our attention from the partial, contrived, and censored nature of the information we are given. For example, the mechanical definition of the *estoque* or killing sword diverts us from recognizing that the technicality of his description of the weapon's shape and trajectory addresses exclusively the problem of human expediency and technical efficiency while suppressing all reference to the living, sensate body that the sword wounds, hurts, and destroys.

> The blade is about seventy-five centimetres long and is curved downward at the tip in order that it may penetrate better and take a deeper direction between the ribs, vertebrae, shoulder blades and other bony structure which it may encounter. Modern swords are made with one, two or three grooves or canals along the back of the blade, the purpose of these being to allow air to be introduced into the wound caused by the sword, otherwise the blade of the sword serves as a plug to the wound it makes. (*DA,* 406)

The lexicon of feeling and emotion is expelled from the glossary along with the bull's perspective and subjectivity until Hemingway's rhetorical demonstration is conducted in a vacuum of theory and abstraction, as though referring to a mere model of a bull, an artificial construct of a bull delineating only the mechanical obstacles to a perfect kill rather than the living and feeling flesh, nerves, organs, and arteries that are severed, penetrated, and destroyed by the steel.

Hemingway ultimately demystifies the bullfight by creating a

Beasts of the Modern Imagination

new myth. He solves the mystery of how the killing of the animal can be great art by creating its tautological opposite: the mystery of how great art can be founded on animal torture and killing. Hemingway's specious answer, that killing can be done with courage, skill, and technical brilliance to create a spectacle of incomparable beauty, masks another answer, that the bull-fight epitomizes the anthropocentric bias upon whose conse-quent suppression of Nature (the animal, the body, pain) the Western tradition has founded culture and art. Hemingway is enthralled not merely by violence, which could be found in purer, more spontaneous form in the town square *capeas,* but precisely by the mediated, formalized, acculturated violence of the corrida. It is this violence alone that allows him to play the sadist's part: that of the exponent of violence tricked out in the seemingly legitimate, cultural role of the art critic, who recog-nizes the aesthetic composition created by man and bull at the moment of killing; that of the scientist, who analyzes the psy-chology of tormenting the bull into courage; and that of the pedagogue, who overcomes the ignorance and prejudice of his shrinking readers and brings them to an enlightened acceptance of violence.

In writing *Death in the Afternoon,* Hemingway reverses the function of the traditional playwright, which is described by Derrida (in his essay on Artaud) as the creation of a text whose language, in the form of the written word, precedes, deter-mines, and dominates the *mise en scène* of classical theater.[5] But the *mise en scène* of the bullfight, a staged event without words, precedes and determines Hemingway's text, which becomes a supplement, a language, a writing supplied and poured into the volume of mute space in which the tauromachian gestures are enacted. When Scott Donaldson writes of *Death in the After-noon,* "it stands, more than forty years after it was written, as the best book in English on its subject,"[6] he assumes that Hemingway's text represents, stands for, "speaks" the bullfight. But does it?

Death in the Afternoon represents neither the existential event that transpires in the ring nor its unmediated (open, unconditioned, true) perception by the trained or untrained spectator. Hemingway's book represents not the bullfight but the modern myth of the bullfight as the triumph of the hero-artist. He gives the spectator a language and a conceptual frame-work that constitutes a pretext (justification and script) through which to read and interpret the spectacle. He superimposes on

Hemingway's Death in the Afternoon

the seemingly spontaneous dispersal of actions and images in the arena the anthropocentric drama of the matador. The spectator's attention and affect is diverted from the materiality of the violence to its abstract significance, and from the animal to the man, who is transformed by Hemingway's argument from the *Mata Toros* (bull butcher) to the matador or formal killer of bulls. The matador combines, as it were, the feats of Theseus and Dedalus, hero and artist of Cretan tauromachy. At the moment of killing, the matador embodies the function of the mythical killer of the Minotaur, and, as he forces the living beast into heroic and aesthetic postures, the function of the mythical sculptor of bovine effigies.

In his negative evaluation of *Death in the Afternoon,* Nemi D'Agostino exposes Hemingway, earlier the critic of decadence in *The Sun Also Rises,* as himself a decadent. "This passion for the bull ring, this over-subtle primitivism, this craving for sensation which finds vent in moments of morbid and bloodthirsty ecstasy, actually springs from a cultured and detached pleasure in the primitive and the barbaric."[7] But D'Agostino goes on to interpret this development in essentially Nietzschean terms, as a "renunciation of culture and of that conquest essential to human progress, the suppression of the blood instinct." I would argue that, on the contrary, far from renouncing culture, Hemingway uses culture in its traditional Western humanistic function of exalting art over Nature and man over animal, of displacing violence, of subordinating the body, pain, and death to ideals and abstractions, of building an anthropocentric, cultural, spiritual kingdom upon an animalistic and biological hell. In the remaining portion of this chapter I will explore in greater depth Hemingway's philosophy of Nature, of killing and death, and of art and representation in *Death in the Afternoon.* But I will do so by restoring the foreclosed perspective of the animal to the ring, in order to subject Hemingway's anthropocentrism to a critique.

Both *Green Hills of Africa* and *Death in the Afternoon* represent violent death, "one of the simplest things of all and the most fundamental" (*DA,* 2), cognitively, subjectively, that is anthropocentrically, as a phenomenon that presents itself to the human perception, the human imagination, as something observed and studied rather than something experienced in the flesh and felt in the nerves, in the senses of the sensate body of living creatures whether animal or human. The protagonist of an encounter with violent death is consequently the witness rather than the victim, who is rendered negligible as a mere object: "as the mere fact of the child being about to be struck by the train was all that he could convey, the actual striking would be an anti-climax, so that the moment before striking might be as far as he could represent" (DA, 3). In the safari, likewise, the significant experience of violent death resides in the drama of the hunter, his laudable control and state of impersonal calm before a good kill, or his excitability, dispersed concentration, and remorse at a bad kill. The moment of violent death itself at the impact of the shot is indeed an anticlimax because it is merely mechanical, one sort of unnatural motion or another. "As I started to squeeze he started running and I swung ahead of him and loosed off. I saw him lower his head and jump like a bucking horse as he comes out of the chutes and as I threw the shell, slammed the bolt forward and shot again, behind him as he went out of sight, I knew I had him" (GHA, 118).

It is precisely the mechanical nature of the kill in the hunt, its cause and effect of good shot / clean kill and bad shot / messy kill, that makes even a lion hunt inferior to the contrived heroic drama of the bullfight. "I was so surprised by the way he had rolled over dead from the shot after we had been prepared for a charge, for heroics, and for drama, that I felt more let down than pleased. It was our first lion and we were very ignorant and this was not what we had paid to see" (GHA, 41). However, Hemingway, imputing an audience of aficionados, insists so much on technical expertise, aesthetic appreciation, and moral approbation of bravery as the source of pleasure at the bullfight that he represses the specter of an audience excited by blood, pain, and cruelty. Both D. H. Lawrence and Norman Mailer describe the Mexican bullfight audience as bloodthirsty riffraff, Lawrence with contempt, and Mailer with affection; Mailer's Mexicans love to see the bull vomit blood: "later I learned the crowd would always applaud a kill in the lung—all audiences are Broadway audiences."[8] Similarly, Hemingway describes P.O.M. at the gut-shooting of the buff: "She was like some one enjoying a good musical show" (GHA, 102). The occlusion of pain and its subordination to the requirements of heroism, technique, and beauty, make the bullfight the sadistic obverse of wrestling, described by Roland Barthes as the perfect vulgar entertainment, a purely mimetic spectacle that offers audiences an exaggerated iconography of torture and suffering.[9] The difference

Hemingway's Death in the Afternoon

between wrestling and the bullfight is analogous to the difference between a "stag" film, where perverse activity is faked, and a "snuff" film—one of an actual torture and killing.

Hemingway realizes that unlike a sculptor (for example, Brancusi, who depicts movement in static form), the bullfighter creates his art with living flesh, as does the dancer or singer. Consequently, the bullfight is a minor art, ephemeral and impermanent, one where, "when the performer is gone the art exists only in the memory of those who have seen it and dies with them" (*DA*, 99). *Death in the Afternoon* is therefore written not only in the paradigmatic style of the handbook or manual, but also in the personal, subjective style of the memoir, preserving for us memories of individual matadors and specific performances. Hemingway gives us both *langue* and *parole* of the bullfight. Yet, if only permanence were needed to make tauromachy a major art, why not simply record the bullfight on film, a perfectly feasible technical possibility in the 1920s? Perhaps it is because unlike Barthes's wrestling match—of which he writes, "It is not true that wrestling is a sadistic spectacle: it is only an intelligible spectacle"[10]—the bullfight, in which the pain and suffering are internalized and concealed in the animal, is unintelligible without the explication of an expert narrator. Yet in Hemingway's book, this explication invariably functions as a rationalization for repressing, discounting, and negating the pain and death that give the spectacle its significance.

Hemingway *can* tell the difference between the exterior and the interior of a moment of suffering, between its representation and its inimitable sensation. "The numbers of broken-legged mules and horses drowning in the shallow water called for a Goya to depict them. Although, speaking literally, one can hardly say that they called for a Goya since there has only been one Goya, long dead, and it is extremely doubtful if these animals, were they able to call, would call for pictorial representation of their plight but, more likely, would, if they were articulate, call for someone to alleviate their condition" (*DA*, 135). But he chooses, in the rhetoric of his narration, to focus on the wit of the narrator, on the aesthetic sensibility of the artist witness, on visual or verbal representation rather than cruelty and suffering, on figurative language (*called for* as "deserving" or "constituting a fit topic") whose literal residue (*called for* as "screamed for help" or "pleaded in despair") is dragged in as an afterthought, a little joke, a humorous concession to the repressed pain that can no longer remain censored in the passage. The joke, like much of Hemingway's humor, depends on the embarrassing intrusion of bodily exigencies and mortality (the agony of the animals, the dead Goya) into the artist's aesthetic theorizing.

The externalization of pain, of bodily damage and its somatic consequences, always scandalizes Hemingway, who responds nervously by either laughing at it, dismissing it as unimportant, or seeking its abolition through euthanasia. In a rather daring polemical maneuver, he opens his book on the bullfight with an attempt to make the reader accept its most shocking visual element, the goring and disembowelling of the horses by the charging bull, as a comic spectacle. His first stratagem is to make us feel foolish about regarding the animal's pain as a serious matter and empathizing with it. He does this by dividing people into two classes, those who identify with animals and those who identify with human beings, and by denigrating the "animalarians" by imputing to them hypocrisy ("The almost professional lovers of dogs, and other beasts, are capable of greater cruelty to human beings than those who do not identify themselves readily with animals"),[11] aesthetic callowness ("They get no feeling of the whole tragedy"), and overreaction ("They will suffer terribly, more so perhaps than the horse" [DA, 5–9]). Having put us on the defensive, he then proceeds to ridicule the horses in order to make them unworthy of sympathy and in order to make us forget that they are horses, large, warm-blooded mammals with bodies, organs, and somatic sensations not unlike our own. "They are so unlike horses; in some ways they are like birds" (DA, 6). The description of these "parodies of horses" in the simile of "awkward birds," monstrous creatures with "strange-shaped heads" like "wide-billed storks," is intended to reduce rhetorically their bodily presence by making their bodies lighter, frailer, less substantial and by identifying them with a more alien, less homologous, less sympathetic species. Having established the horses' ridiculous and comic character, their disembowellings become "burlesque visceral accidents," more embarrassing than painful, and very funny, like shitting. "I have seen it, people running, horse emptying, one dignity after another being destroyed in the spattering, and trailing of its innermost values, in a complete burlesque of tragedy" (DA, 7).

In order to pull us from the inside to the outside, to disengage us from our site of empathy inside the terrified body of the blindfolded horse, dazed with pain, plunging desperately to expel the horn tearing at its bowels, Hemingway conjures up the

Hemingway's Death in the Afternoon

metaphor of comic theater, of circus, in order to make us apprehend only the visual exterior of the spectacle, "the most picturesque incident" in the bullfight, and to distance us emotionally by making us laugh, as though the pain, fear, injury, and death we see were no more real than in a theater performance. The comedic language is not in itself inappropriate, for the *suerte de varas* abounds with formal and thematic elements of low comedy: surprise, accident, acrobatic falls, unnatural bodily contortions, anal humiliations, and the like. But Hemingway outrageously begs the question in pressing his logical equation of the goring of horses and its burlesque imitation by clowns as equally funny events. "There is certainly nothing comic by our standards in seeing an animal emptied of its visceral content, but if this animal instead of doing something tragic, that is, dignified, gallops in a stiff old-maidish fashion around a ring trailing the opposite of clouds of glory it is as comic when what it is trailing is real as when the Fratellinis give a burlesque of it in which the viscera are represented by rolls of bandages, sausages and other things. If one is comic the other is; the humor comes from the same principle" (*DA*, 7). The principles are, of course, as radically different as life and art. We can laugh at a clown being beaten in the circus because we know that the performance is voluntary and the blows are faked, like those in Barthes's wrestling match. But the same scenario with an involuntary victim and real blows would be a cruel exhibit whose spectators would be implicated in the violence. If they were amused by seeing live cruelty, their laughter would be perverse, whether its motive were a primitive pleasure in the cruelty itself or a more decadent pleasure in the "rational violence" of studied apathy toward cruelty. That the victim is an animal only increases the perversity, for the horse's oblivion to its role in the cultural drama contrived for it makes Hemingway's critique of its "performance" the *reductio ad absurdum* of his theatrical analogy. By requiring the horse to do something "tragic, that is, dignified" in response to being gored, Hemingway imposes on it his own idiosyncratic repressions and taboos. He is scandalized by the trailing of "the opposite of clouds of glory"—viscera, excremental entrails, mortality, and death—and the "dignified" gesture he demands is one of self-control, reserve, denial, internalization, concealment, and retention: like Joselito's ("gored through the lower abdomen so his intestines came out [and he was unable to hold them in with both hands]" [*DA*, 242]), or the brave bull's, "his mouth tight shut to keep the blood in" (*DA*, 124), or Papa's

Beasts of the Modern Imagination

own, as he bravely treats his prolapsed rectum (no laughing matter!) on safari ("Already I had . . . experienced the necessity of washing a three-inch bit of my large intestine with soap and water and tucking it back where it belonged an unnumbered amount of times a day" [*GHA*, 283]). Hemingway (unlike Joyce and Lawrence) despises the body because its instinctive and somatic activity is beyond control of the mind and will and therefore betrays pride, dignity, and vanity by depriving the individual of a "noble exit" (as though life were a theatrical performance). "The only natural death I've ever seen, outside of loss of blood, which isn't bad, was death from Spanish influenza. In this you drown in mucus, choking, and how you know the patient's dead is; at the end he shits the bed full" (*DA*, 139).

Hemingway's vehement objections to the introduction of the peto, the quilted mattress shield protecting the horse's underside (and "dignity"), betrays his fear that any formal humane concession, any official admission, as it were, that brutality and pain exist in the ring, may inaugurate a wider challenge of the rationalization of violence that makes the bullfight possible. "These protectors avoid these sights and greatly decrease the number of horses killed in the bull ring, but they in no way decrease the pain suffered by the horses; they take away much of the bravery from the bull, this to be dealt with in a later chapter, and they are the first step toward the suppression of the bullfight" (*DA*, 7). The illogicality of Hemingway's objection is that, by his own admission, the motives behind the decree are not humane but commercial ("'to avoid those horrible sights which so disgust foreigners and tourists'"), a cynical bid to increase the number of spectators at the corrida and to save expense through the recycling of injured horses (*DA*, 185). If anything, the decree seems designed to neutralize opposition in order to perpetuate the bullfight. But Hemingway's objection is philosophically shrewd: he knows that outright denial is better than censorship, and that the horse's peto becomes the mark that hides something horrible, unspeakable, and filthy, a reminder not only of the erstwhile goring of the horses, but of the guilt and shame it should inspire. Hemingway prefers to this the outright denial, the blunt confrontation of the trailing entrails and the insistence, in flat contradiction to his statement above, that *the goring does not hurt*. "A man who has been wounded knows that the pain of a wound does not commence until about half an hour after it has been received and there is no

Hemingway's Death in the Afternoon

proportional relation in pain to the horrible aspect of the wound; the pain of an abdominal wound does not come at the time but later with the gas pains and the beginnings of peritonitis" (*DA,* 9). The horse, presumably, is dispatched with a *coup de grace* of the puntillas before its suffering commences, and the bull, likewise, suffers minimally (in spite of later talk about the "cruel punishment" of the banderillas) because "all wounds he receives are in hot blood and if they do not hurt any more than the wounds a man receives in hot blood they cannot hurt very much" (*DA,* 220).[12] Although Hemingway proffers his promotion of euthanasia as a moral and humane gesture, it clearly serves him well as a neutralizer of violence that legitimizes any sort of cruelty on the ground of humane brevity.

The final polemical stratagem of Hemingway's apologia for the goring of the horses is an appeal to the reader's critical and aesthetic vanity by making a holistic vision the *sine qua non* of the cognoscente. "The aficionado, or lover of the bullfight, may be said, broadly, then, to be one who has this sense of the tragedy and ritual of the fight so that the minor aspects are not important except as they relate to the whole" (*DA,* 9). Aficionados are thus defined by their deliberate apathy toward the suffering of the horses because the structural requirements of art for harmony, proportion, the formal relations of its parts to the whole, supersede the claims of living Nature, the living body, to maintain its formal integrity, the harmony of its organs, muscles, bones, nerves, and sinews, that constitutes it as a living whole. To support this argument Hemingway resorts to a series of false analogies including tragic drama (presumably Shakespearean, since, in spite of the classicism he imputes to the bullfight, classical tragedy admits neither comic interludes nor onstage violence), the symphony, and fine wine. The fallacy in the analogies is that none of these cultivated pleasures requires a price paid in bodily pain and death by an involuntary participant. When Hemingway writes, "If the auditor at a symphony concert were a humanitarian as he might be at the bullfight he would probably find as much scope for his good work in ameliorating the wages and living conditions of the players of the double bass in symphony orchestras as in doing something about the poor horses" (*DA,* 9), he quite suppresses the much more obvious and accurate comparison with the castrati, Italian youths castrated to maintain the purity and beauty of their prepubescent soprano and contralto voices. Would Hemingway, perhaps the most phallocentric and homophobic modern writer (who treats

Beasts of the Modern Imagination

homosexuals as eunuchs),[13] expect the aesthete to dismiss as insignificant and unimportant the incidental detail of the castrato's sexual mutilation in the interest of art? This deliberate foisting of faulty logic upon his readers is part of Hemingway's strategy for achieving authority not on his own intellectual merits but on his opponents' insecurities, their fear of being called philistine. His is the mastery of the bluff and the authority of default, which can be maintained only as long as investigation and challenge can be inhibited with ridicule and preemptive denigration.

Hemingway embeds in the text of *Death in the Afternoon* its antithesis, *Toros Celebres,* "a book, now out of print in Spain" (*DA,* 110) that celebrates chiefly rebel bulls, insurrectionists, as it were, bulls willing to kill but not to play according to the rules of the corrida, who crash through the *barrera,* goring carpenters, policemen, and random spectators. Hemingway mentions *Toros Celebres* in order to cancel it, for his political metaphor betrays that he recognizes it as the subversive counterpart of *Death in the Afternoon.* "It is the difference between street fights which are usually infinitely more exciting, portentous and useful, but out of place here, and the winning of a championship in boxing" (*DA,* 112). *Toros Celebres* marks the return of the repressed, of the bull's point of view and interest; it celebrates the autonomy of the animal, its use of its power for its own ends, and the uncontrollability of its aggression rather than its manipulation. Hemingway must discredit such rebel bulls if he is to preserve an essential element of the sadist's posture, namely, the fiction that the victim colludes in the sadistic spectacle, that the victim's participation is voluntary, that the victim's role accords with his nature and is therefore pleasurable. "A bull that jumps the barrera, unless he makes the leap while pursuing the man, is not a brave bull. He is a cowardly bull who is simply trying to escape the ring. The really brave bull welcomes the fight, accepts every invitation to fight, does not fight because he is cornered, but because he wants to. . . . The bull is a wild animal whose greatest pleasure is combat" (*DA,* 112–113).

Toros Celebres is also a descriptive rather than a prescriptive work, and it thereby helps to illuminate (by contrast) Hemingway's hidden idealism, his preoccupation with the hypothetical and the theoretical, his commitment to the triumph of pure science (the realm of the mathematically and the geometrically *possible* [(*DA,* 21)]) and applied science, strategy and technique, over the spontaneity of living Nature. He gives us a fascinating glimpse into the semantic texture of the Spanish *suerte* or "act" of the bullfight, with its double sense of the uncontrollable ("chance, hazard, lots, fortune, luck") and control ("skillful manoeuvre; trick, feat, juggle" [*DA*, 96]), of peril and strategy, danger and defense as permanent, inevitable, fated conditions or states of life; but he elaborates the philosophical implications of this linguistic content only obliquely. In the bullfight, it is the spontaneity of the animal that produces the element of chance and thereby creates the danger; the man's ostensible defense is really an offense and it is abstract and cerebral, a matter of science, or mathematical and geometrical calculation ("He should deliberately, as now, try to pass the points of the horn as mathematically close to his body as possible without moving his feet" [*DA*, 68]), of intellectual, technical, and mechanical control of the material conditions of the ring. At times Hemingway replaces his secular and mechanical definition of killing with an inflated, quasi-mystical language, in which killing becomes "one of the Godlike attributes" (*DA*, 233) (rather than one of the bestial or predatory attributes) and death is something "given" or "administered"—"Because they have pride they do not mind killing; feeling that they are worthy to give this gift" (*DA*, 264). He treats death as though it were a grace and killing a sacrament, a spiritual transaction, a generous yielding of the self rather than a bodily assault whose end is the material deformation and putrescence he describes for us so vividly in "A Natural History of the Dead." When he transforms killing from a physical into a metaphysical phenomenon, Hemingway becomes guilty of uttering (as he himself calls it, and defines it) horseshit: that is, "unsoundness in an abstract conversation or, indeed, any overmetaphysical tendency in speech" (*DA*, 95).

Hemingway's famous definition of the bullfight as tragedy ("the death of the bull, which is played, more or less well, by the bull and the man involved and in which there is danger for the man but certain death for the animal" [*DA*, 16]) supports neither an Aristotelian interpretation, like those inflicted on us by some of his later imitators,[14] nor quite a colloquial, nonliterary sense of the word as a great catastrophe or pitiable event. Hemingway himself stresses as the salient element of his definition not the certain death of the bull (the unvanquished bull's mandatory slaughter after the fight is, in any event, merely a legal expedient) but the element of play, the contest with chance—the ludic structure of the spectacle. In spite of his disclaimer that the bullfight is not a sport or equal competition,

Hemingway is at his best (and least philosophically corrupt) in *Death in the Afternoon* when he explicates the bullfight as a primitive gaming sport or form of gladiatorial combat. Had he confronted the violence of the bullfight honestly without attempts to sugar it over with talk of art and brilliance and dignity and honor and immortality, he might have captured for it the same horrific symbolic significance that film writer / director Michael Cimino invested in the game of Russian roulette in *The Deer Hunter,* that of a formalized, rule-governed, ludic version and a compulsive reenactment of and obsessional alternative to the dispersed, random, corporate violence of war.

When Hemingway writes, "The matador must dominate the bulls by knowledge and science" (*DA,* 21), he makes of the corrida a battle of wits, a form of "intellectual" and psychological combat between the man and the animal so complex and fascinating that his explication becomes as seductive to the reader as the muleta to the bull. The theoretical rules of the game, the narrative sequence of the three coherent phases of the bull's progressive physical and psychological modification, the use of psychological force (provocation, fatigue, deception) over physical injury (laming, loss of blood) as a controlling device, the variety of honorable and dishonorable options available to the matador in specific quandaries—all of these explications are so intellectually rich and complex that they indeed divert us from the pain and violence they repress as much as the lure diverts the bull from the man. We easily become as embarrassingly enthralled by the details of tauromachian form and strategy (veronicas, mariposas, naturals, and so forth) as Sterne's Uncle Toby, whose intellectual obsession with military minutiae occludes the crippling, killing, and gelding produced by the battle of Namur.

Since the nature of the "play" produced in the corrida varies with the behavior of the bulls, Hemingway oscillates between the metaphors of gambling ("playing cards" [*DA,* 147]) and musical performance ("So the pipe organ and the steam calliope are the only musical instruments whose players can be compared to the matador" [*DA,* 150]). Both are false because they are benign analogies that deny the gladiatorial elements of coercion and violence in the bullfight. The ludic metaphor is altogether flawed in that only one participant in the game actually "plays" or understands the rules ("It is up to the bullfighter to make the bull play and to enforce the rules. The bull has no desire to play, only to kill" [*DA*, 147]). But the musical metaphor brings to the fore the actually philosophical object of the bullfight, which is one of reification, of reducing the spontaneous power, aggression, and vitality of the bull to a set of conventional movements, gestures, and postures, of transforming the dangerous living creature into a tractable object, an artistic property, a "prop." Hemingway's goal of having the matador "perform brilliantly" with the bull evokes the metaphor of instrumentality, of the matador's activity and volition against the bull's passivity and mediation. The "play" of the bullfight depends upon an inverse relationship between the man's and the bull's intelligence and therefore requires an abolition of the bull's experience, spontaneity, and autonomy.

The major contrivances of the bullfight, the rules and laws that make the matador's "victory" possible, are those assuring a vacant taurine mind, a tabula rasa ("The ideal bull is one whose memory is as clean as possible from any experience of bullfighting" [*DA*, 126]) by prescribing the bull's age, guaranteeing his novitiate by mandatory slaughter of veterans, and fixing a temporal terminus for each fight to limit the bull's acquisition and accumulation of fighting knowledge in the ring. Paradoxically, Hemingway's explication and defense of these suppressions of the animal's intelligence pay greatest tribute to it ("female calves . . . after a few sessions, become so educated, the fighters say, that they can talk Greek and Latin" [*DA*, 107]) by stipulating the inevitability of the bull's victory if the corrida were indeed a sport in which the knowledge of bull and bullfighter were equal. "If the bulls were allowed to increase their knowledge as the bullfighter does and if those bulls which are not killed in the allotted fifteen minutes in the ring were not afterwards killed in the corrals but were allowed to be fought again they would kill all the bullfighters, if the bullfighters fought them according to the rules" (*DA*, 21). The knowledge and science of the matador is therefore optimally pitted only against the danger inherent in the bull's body, that is, of its bulk and horns, rather than against the danger of his mentality.

To the extent the matador uses "science" to dominate the bull, he requires, in the form of the bull, a scientific object, that is, a knowable, explicable, predictable phenomenon. Consequently, the adjectives borrowed from the lexicon of military virtue (bravery, nobility) to describe the good bull refer to qualities defined anthropocentrically, in terms of their advantage to the matador. Bravery becomes the willingness to charge, without which there could be no bullfight ("The bravery of the bull is the primal root of the whole Spanish bullfight" [*DA*, 113]), but in a perfectly consistent and predictable manner that the matador can anticipate, control, and use to create plastic or sculptural effects. What Hemingway finds "unearthly and unbelievable" (*DA*, 113) in the bull's bravery is its foolish perversity, the implicit gluttony for punishment that seems to impel the animal to behave unnaturally, against its own best interest. But the cause of this seemingly unnatural behavior is the contrived inexperience of the bull, its simplicity or gullibility (the noble bull is described as "brave, simple and easily deceived" [*DA*, 426]), which makes it initially confused and unable to determine the precise origin and agent of its pain. Were it allowed more time to make this determination, it would become "almost unkillable" (*DA*, 107). The ideal bull for the matador is one that is least like a living animal (spontaneous, autonomous, unpredictable) and most like an object, a prop, a mechanical bull, "a bull that charges as straight as though he were on rails" (*DA*, 6, 160). Matadors want perfect Pavlovian animals with behavior governed by simple stimulus-response mechanisms. But although virtually mechanical bulls are wished for combat, living bulls with easily penetrable and yielding arteries, organs, and muscle ("If the man leans after the blade the bull will seem sometimes to pluck the sword out from his hand") are wished for killing ("Other times, hitting bone, it will seem as though he had struck a wall of rubber and cement" [*DA*, 237]). As usual, Hemingway's description represents the standpoint of human expediency rather than animal sentience.

The tension that informs all of Hemingway's prescriptions for the bullfight is the need to determine precisely the locus of control, the center of power that, in the nature of all games, inevitably shifts from one site to another. The reification of the bull therefore poses a vexing problem because, although Hemingway accepts the Darwinian premises that make of the animal a plastic organism, a malleable object subject to the genetic modifications of natural and artificial selection, he wants the bull transformed into a tractable object in the arena, not on the range, through the psychological domination of the matador rather than the eugenic control of the breeder. Genetic control is necessary to keep the bulls feral ("They are bred from strain that comes down in direct descent from the wild bulls" [*DA*, 105]) yet without the "crescient" intelligence of the "old deadly Miuras . . . the curse of all bullfighters." "Similarly there are

Hemingway's Death in the Afternoon

certain strains even of bulls in which the ability to learn rapidly in the ring is highly developed. These bulls must be fought and killed as rapidly as possible with the minimum of exposure by the man, for they learn more rapidly than the fight ordinarily progresses and become exaggeratedly difficult to work with and kill" (*DA,* 129). Artificial selection is necessary because the ludic nature of the bullfight requires some control of randomness and chance. But although the game is intentionally stacked in favor of the matador, a pernicious degree of contrivance is introduced when players are given control over the condition of their adversaries. "The bull is the main element of the fiesta and it is the bulls that the highest-paid bullfighters are constantly trying to sabotage by having them bred down in size and horn and fought as young as possible" (*DA,* 164). The matador's impact on taurine eugenics corrupts the bullfight for it internalizes the element of control, displacing it from the arena to the range, from the psyche of the bull to his body, and thereby removes it from spectacle.

The idealism and prescriptiveness of the bullfight, its "standards" and rules, are founded on the suppression of Nature, the animal, the body, in the ostensible interest of culture. But the double system of enforcement Hemingway describes—the matador enforcing the rules upon the bull and the spectators enforcing them on the matador—reveals that there are, after all, two animals in the ring rather than one, and that the matador's instinctive nature, like the bull's, must also be disciplined. The idealistic fiction Hemingway creates is virtually Nietzschean in its assumptions: that both man and bull are driven by a will to power, that they fight because they love to fight, because it is "natural" to them, because it gives them pleasure. But the bullfight could be such a Nietzschean event only if it were truly spontaneous, if it were free of contrivance, if it were unselfconscious and, therefore, if it were not a spectacle but were fought purely for the autotelic benefit (aggression, excitation, pleasure) of either or both of the participants. Yet because the corporeality, the sentience, the mortality of the matador give him conservative and self-protective instincts and reflexes, he requires idealistic supplements (virtues) to counteract them. Like the bull's bravery, the matador's honor (the Spanish *pundonor,* "as real a thing as water, wine, or olive oil" [*DA,* 92]), ensures his willingness to behave unnaturally and perversely against his own best somatic interests, to betray his body in the interest of ego and vanity.[15] Consequently, "to be gored was honorable" but to

seek safety was not; "any attempt to control the feet was honorable" (*DA*, 19) but to surrender to the natural reflex to run and
avoid danger was not. Indeed, technique itself, as a substitute of
intellectual and mechanical physical control for biological
instinct and physical reflex, becomes honorable. The man's
honor, like the bull's bravery, is an internalization of the spectator's desire, a voluntary courting of danger and disregard of
consequences of the sort the audience wishes to see. If the matador fails to internalize the public's desire for his brave and haz-
ardous behavior (in the form of honor), Hemingway condones
external measures ("the throwing of cushions of all weights,
pieces of bread, oranges, vegetables, small dead animals of all
sorts" [*DA*, 163]) that will override the matador's fear of the
bull with fear of the crowd. The corrida is a combat between two
animals whose natural behavior is dominated, hierarchically, in
the order of abstract power (the crowd's political and economic
power, the matador's intellectual and technical power, the bull's
physical and instinctual power) by the spectator. "But if the
spectator did not impose the rules, keep up the standards, prevent abuses and pay for the fights there would be no professional
bullfighting in a short time and no matadors" (*DA*, 164).

When Hemingway writes, "It is one hundred to one against
the matador de toros or formally invested bullfighter being
killed unless he is inexperienced, ignorant, out of training or too
old and heavy on his feet" (*DA*, 21), his rhetorical structure
misleadingly implies that under optimal professional circumstances the matador incurs minimal risk in the ring. In fact, one
hundred to one, given optimal conditions for a well-trained,
experienced, fit bullfighter, are not particularly good odds (especially as they pertain only to deaths and exclude nonfatal gorings) and Hemingway's own statistics belie his ruling fiction
that, theoretically, science triumphs over Nature in the corrida,
and technique neutralizes chance. By means of a circular logic,
the gorings themselves become negative proofs of the correctness
of theory and the efficacy of technique ("The confident
unsoundness of his technique gives you a feeling that he may be
gored at any time" [*DA*, 217]). Hemingway inflicts upon the
matadors the same intellectual violence he inflicts upon the
other animals, displacing the significance of the goring from
man to abstraction; from physiological experience to deviant
calculation ("they would only have to move up an inch or two to
gore" [*DA*, 209]); from violence to the criterion of courage
("Bienvenida . . . should not really be judged until his ability to

dominate his nerves and reflexes after his first serious wounding has been proven" [*DA*, 216]); from object of empathy to disciplinary device ("He is the only bullfighter I have been glad to see gored; but goring him is no solution since he behaves much worse on coming out of the hospital than before he went in" [*DA*, 252]).

The matador as animal is sacrificed upon the altar of art as surely as the bull, if not as inevitably or totally. Goring is a necessity in the bullring because it serves as proof of the lethal instrumentality of the horns and the reality of the danger: "Joselito should die to prove that no one is safe in the ring" (*DA*, 158). Goring as an intrinsically physical experience, internalized in the animal flesh of the man, becomes totally insignificant and unimportant aside from its abstract uses as a "proof" (a sign, a material substitute for an abstraction, a guarantee of certain realities) and as a proleptic device, a warning to other matadors, an intimation of mortality: "El Gallo . . . never admitted the idea of death and he would not even go in to look at Joselito in the chapel after he was killed" (*DA*, 159). El Gallo's gesture of avoidance is characteristic, and it is repeated again in the photograph of the dead Granero, who is cancelled through avoidance and disregard as his mourners look out at us, and we (under the direction of Hemingway's caption) look back at them, extruding the corpse from the lines of our vision.

The matador, as animal, as living body, is doubly betrayed. He must be injured and killed in order to preserve the meaning of the bullfight, to prove the reality of the risk and danger; yet his mortality as a physical fact must be negated and denigrated in the interest of protecting the theories, myths, and fictions that sustain the bullfight.

> Now the essence of the greatest emotional appeal of bullfighting is the feeling of immortality that the bullfighter feels in the middle of a great faena and that he gives to the spectators. He is performing a work of art and he is playing with death, bringing it closer, closer, closer, to himself, a death that you know is in the horns because you have the canvas-covered bodies of the horses on the sand to prove it. He gives the feeling of his immortality, and, as you watch it, it becomes yours. (*DA*, 213)

The feeling of immortality is, of course, a fraud, a lie, an abstract fiction diverting us from the material reality, which is the censored obscenity on the periphery of our vision, the canvas-covered horse, with its guts torn and spilled—like Jose-lito, the day he was killed, or like Montes and Varelito gored in the rectum and suffering lethally perforated intestines, or like Isodor Todo vomiting blood from a chest wound, or like Gitanillo, whose sciatic nerve was pulled out "by the root as a worm may be pulled out of the damp lawn by a robin" (DA, 219). Or like Alcalareno II, whose literally unspeakable fate is censored by Hemingway for us ("That was too ugly, I see now, to justify writing about when it is not necessary" [DA, 227]), as he censors other violence for his little boy: "She would substitute the word umpty-umped for the words killed, cut the throat of, blew the brains out of, spattered around the room, and so on, and soon the comic of umpty-umped so appealed to the boy . . . I knew it was all right" (DA, 228).

The matador as animal, as bodily creature, is most deeply betrayed because, since Hemingway will not accept the great frequency of goring as a rupture of his theory, as a concrete refutation of the scientific possibilities he imputes to bullfight-ing, he is obliged to transform the *cornada* into an ambiguous sign: simultaneously a badge of courage and a mark of transgres-sion. It is both necessity and embarrassment: testimony of risk taking and evidence of its failure, an unsuccessful effort, a fool-ish bravery. Not only are matadors inevitably wounded in spite of their science, but Hemingway makes their wounding a matter of blame: Hernandorena is guilty of "a simple technical error" (DA, 19); "Joselito should die . . . because he was getting fat" (DA, 158); Luis Freg is gored seventy-two times because he is heavy on his feet and unskillful with cape and muleta (DA, 263). There is a definite literal residue in Hemingway's euphe-mism of goring as "punishment" by the bulls. If a goring is purely a matter of chance, a freak accident rather than a personal or technical failure, then the matador gets neither blame nor credit, and the goring is dismissed altogether, as without signifi-cance, a moral cipher. "True, he has been gored, but each time through an accident such as a sudden gust of wind that left him uncovered when he was working close to a bull that he believed safe" (DA, 252). The pain and damage of goring is existentially the same for Cagancho whether occasioned by flawed technique or by bad luck; but in Hemingway's moral economy of the bullfight, the latter is extruded and negated, like the "visceral accidents" of the horses.

Lawrence Broer's statement, "What the bullfighter accom-plishes with the sword and muleta becomes the corollary of what

Hemingway wishes to accomplish with words" is virtually a parody of Hemingway's own specious reasoning in *Death in the Afternoon*.[16] Broer presumably means that for Hemingway the two professions are analogous (similar in function rather than logically sequential) because honesty and killing both involve degrees of risk that can be avoided by trickery or faking. But not only are the risks of honesty and physical courage different in kind, with different consequences (censure versus goring), but the matador's very act of candor and integrity, when he genuinely exposes his body to the horn as he guides the bull past him with the muleta, is itself (ironically) a moment of deception, the deception of the bull. The bullfight is founded on the deception of the animal, and the animals deceived are both taurine and human. The matadors are as much unwitting suicides as the bulls, deceived into thinking they act offensively and autonomously as they deliver their lives and bodies to the charnel house of the arena in pursuit of a false target or decoy—an "honor" as meaningless as a piece of red serge—while the real danger to their very being is not dishonor but the crowd's irrational thirst for blood, its repressed and sublimated lust for violence, its disguised passion for torture and killing. *Death in the Afternoon* is itself such a lure, such a textual cape or muleta with powers to mesmerize and hypnotize its readers as we are led into intellectual collusion with violence and torture while assuming we are pursuing beauty and tragedy. Hemingway's posture of candor and courage in the opening pages of the book is a sham. Instead of speaking the truth and reaping the whirlwind by openly taking the side of violence, he is most deceptive (logically and rhetorically) when he is ostensibly most confessional, bravely owning up that he loves the bullfight because it is great art and great science.

Ultimately, Broer is right in his analogy: Hemingway's writing does resemble the matador's art—but we are its victims unless we become renegade critics who refuse to salute every time the word *art* is run up the flagpole. We can take our cue from the renegade bulls who escape the game by crashing through the *barrera*. I have tried to challenge Hemingway's basic assumptions by abjuring his anthropocentrism and cultural chauvinism. I choose to speak for the animal (human, taurine, equine) and for Nature, including the natural violence of animal predation and fighting bulls on the range rather than contrived gladiatorial combats tricked out as art and tragedy. I side with the cowardly bulls who upset the order of the game by acting in their own best interests, and the defensive bulls in their *querencias* who defend their lives "seriously, desperately, wisely, and ferociously" (*DA,* 154). My hero in *Death in the Afternoon* is the gypsy Cagancho, whose "cynical cowardice is the most disgusting negation of bullfighting that can be seen" (*DA,* 250), because he obeys his instincts, he protects his body, he serves his own ends, and he refuses to buy into Hemingway's (or any other) perverse ideology. Hemingway would like us in reading *Death in the Afternoon* to imitate his own enthrallment with the *cornada* of Hernandorena.

> For myself, not being a bullfighter, and being much interested in suicides, the problem was one of depiction and waking in the night I tried to remember what it was that seemed just out of my remembering and that was the thing that I had really seen and, finally, remembering all around it, I got it. When he stood up, his face white and dirty and the silk of his breeches opened from waist to knee, it was the dirtiness of the rented breeches, the dirtiness of his slit underwear and the clean, clean, unbearably clean whiteness of the thigh bone that I had seen, and it was that which was important. (*DA,* 20)

It is representation of violence that is important to Hemingway, not the violence itself, and he demands from us, therefore, a purely aesthetic response to the *cornada,* to the visual and textural and conceptual contrasts of the double wounds (surface and essence, embarrassing and unembarrassing, dirty and clean, gray and white), while the shock and pain, the interior sensation of Hernandorena is occluded. But as renegade critics we can refuse to stare in wonder at the aesthetics of the bullfight and instead ask, as I did, why the blood does not flow, and why Hernandorena does not scream.

10

Conclusion:
The Biocentric Tradition
in Context

Regarded from a conventional historical perspective, the "biocentric tradition" I have attempted to explore and analyze in this book could be said to have spanned a century (from Darwin's *Beagle* voyage in the early 1830s to Max Ernst's collage novels in the 1930s) or three major generations, a more appropriate measure, grounded in the metaphor of biological reproduction and transmission. Although I have tried throughout to analyze the curious nature of the influence that connected these generations more by denial and repudiation than by debt and obligation, I wish to conclude my study by rehearsing once more the "evolution" of this antianthropocentric critique. One peculiarity of the historical development of this critique that is worth exploring more closely is its disciplinary shift from science to art, a shift that entails a changing conception of history, a confrontation with the problem of representation, and increasingly tortured discursive practices. Discussion of these matters has been dispersed throughout the text, but a more concerted historical recapitulation will reveal the paradoxically regressive evolution of the antianthropocentric critique. I shall speculate on the reasons for this regressiveness by placing the biocentric tradition in the context of other antihumanistic currents in nineteenth- and twentieth-century thought.

It is no historical accident that the critique of anthropocentrism shifts from natural science through philosophy into the realms of literary and artistic expression. I would argue that the nature of biocentric discoveries, that i   their destabilization of the very concept of form, triggered a confounding and softening of the generic boundaries that separate categories of thought within and among traditional disciplines or fields of knowledge. Like Darwin, who reaped from the older, preprofessional role of "naturalist" the freedom to range broadly from paleontology to comparative anatomy to human psychology, his biocentric successors also eschew conventional aims and functions in defining their intellectual enterprises. Nietzsche thus aestheticized his science and biologized his aesthetics; Kafka dramatized his purely rhetorical narratives; and Ernst created pictorial "novels." The mutability of natural and intellectual form that is a central discovery of biocentric thought produces a corresponding disciplinary and generic blurring, if not an outright collapse.

It is virtually inevitable that the antianthropocentric tradition I have described originated in the realm of natural science, in the study and contemplation of Nature as "real" rather than as a symbolic projection of the human. Given its unflattering implications for human nature, natural selection as an explanation for biological development and human origin is not likely to have been produced by human desire (with its cultural configuration and aims) but required the most impartial and disinterested response to exotic and alienating Nature of the kind Darwin encountered on his travels. Given the reluctance of much of his own scientific community, and the outrage of the public, it is not surprising that the sociologists and utilitarians of Darwin's own day (Herbert Spencer with his synthetic system is a notable example) would appropriate his theories to an optimistic determinism and a practical ethics that would blunt its most radical implications. That historical moment required a Nietzsche, a thinker unencumbered by any need or desire to promote general human happiness who could reinterpret human culture as a survival strategy whose consequences for the human biological organism were devastating. In this he maintained the biocentric perspective inaugurated by Darwin: the ability to see man as a *Naturwesen* or creature, and to value his life from the point of view and interest of his living organism.

Nietzsche adapted Darwinian psychology to continue his own program for tracing the infinite continuities between Nature and culture. But if he was able to treat even abstract philosophical activity as a form of irrational organic behavior, Nietzsche was also able to do what Darwin's lack of Hegelian background prevented him from doing: to identify the *dis*continuities between Nature and culture in activities whose end is not survival but prestige. By emptying Hegelian intersubjectivity of its idealism, Nietzsche was able to identify in the enthrallment to the symbolic "other" the precondition for consciousness, social interaction, and cultural ambition, all quintessentially "human" states that depend on the devaluation of the material body, the repression of instinct, the oppression of the animal, and the obliteration of creatural or "animal" man. Nietzsche's

The Biocentric Tradition in Context

redefinition of the animal metaphor to reflect not a new system of values but a model of a natural world in which the very concepts of value and significance are abolished as cultural inventions sets the philosophical agenda for his artistic heirs of the next generation: Kafka, Ernst, and Lawrence.

Nietzsche recognized, as well as or better than any of his successors, that a biocentric vision plunges writers, thinkers, and artists into ontological crisis about their work. The question of how to transform intellectual and artistic creativity into a biocentric act poses, at the least, a technical dilemma that requires solution both at the representational and at the rhetorical level. The solutions to this problem constitute some of the most brilliant, if little recognized, productions of modern creativity: mysterious, puzzling texts and pictures that strive to be interpreted as spontaneous performances. This guise is, of course, disingenuous. Biocentric artists cannot reclaim their animal innocence without a double ingenuity, a double wit: the wit to outwit themselves. Hence the hidden irony of their enterprise: that biocentrism produces a most cerebrally convoluted art of multilayered obliquities and self-destructive feints, while brawny, "frank," and simple prose like Hemingway's conceals the most anthropocentric of cultural aims.

Because their recognition of the Darwinian antianthropocentric legacy was filtered through Nietzsche, the modern biocentric artists elaborated its most radical implications in their work. The wild technical experiments that resulted were grounded in an extreme affective or emotional reorientation that gives their work much of its alienating quality. Wary of the trap of a humanistic appropriation, which could transform their critique of anthropocentrism into an array of self-deprecating and selfless virtues, their art required an unromantic, unsentimental (though not entirely unsympathetic) fidelity to the animal's alien otherness. They embraced libido as the inhuman (that is, the "animal") principle of life without attempting to domesticate or idealize it. They escaped Romantic subjectivism by shifting their focus away from feeling and sentiment toward irrational action and antirational behavior. They explored illogical ways of assaulting logic and devised ways of frustrating rather than refining artistic expression. With Nietzsche as an unwilling and inimicable predecessor and no specific whetstone (like classicism) to react against, these modern artists (unlike their Romantic ancestors) returned to a site of Nature on which no values exist, no symbols mean, and no humans communicate in conventional ways.

However, I mean less to claim an ahistorical origin for these modern artistic experiments than to argue that their development depended less on any genealogical continuity with earlier traditions than on the kind of revaluations that affected the very concept of history itself. Biocentrism began with a reformulation of natural and animal history that greatly modified modern historical thinking. Darwin replaced Hegel's idealistic and teleological concept of history with a vitalistic and autotelic model in which time, force, and form were uniquely related. The result was a subtle but definite shift in the hidden values imputed to historical process itself. Notwithstanding the many progressive appropriations of Darwin's evolutionary model even in his own time, recognition of its truly conservative impulse—that the passage of time produces neither incremental quality in living organisms nor proximity to a superior final form—has prevailed. Among the conceptual casualties of Darwinism was ultimately the notion of "progress." Not only was faith in the ameliorative effects of progress eroded, but the fundamental value implicit in change was also now interrogated. This prepared the way for the regressive historicism of biocentric art.

But beyond this general philosophical reevaluation of change and progress, I would argue that a more significant metahistorical regression, that is, the abolition of history as an intellectual practice, has ontological aims. History is collective human remembering, and even Darwin's animal history retains an anthropocentric residue in its subject, if not its object. Nietzsche's application of psychology to the problem of history quickly yielded the analysis (evident in the Strauss critique) that the uses and abuses even of racial history are prompted by hidden conservative motives whose aim is the protection of the human ego and the preservation of certain cultural myths. A human appropriation of animal history could escape its internal contradictions only by abolishing memory in the interest of being: forgetting one's animal development in order to become one's animal being in the eternal now.

But because, for humans, zoomorphic forgetting must be preceded by racial memory, the metahistorical course of the biocentric tradition runs from history to its abolition: Darwin remembers the animal origin and development; Nietzsche remembers the importance of forgetting it again; the biocentric artists forget

The Biocentric Tradition in Context

as well, but only after having first remembered. In Kafka, this historical play can be traced as a theme over the course of his *oeuvre:* for example, the ape's painful recital of his cultural evolution is negated by the antihistorical mouse folk. Lawrence's protagonists remember and forget within a single work, as Lou Witt's intimations of an animal prehistory and kinship lead her to an aphasic existence in the wilderness. Ernst practices biocentric remembering and forgetting simultaneously, in a form that approximates human lying: he promises a historic "week" in *Une Semaine de bonté* but abolishes the time of his narrative, and the atavistic appearance of his human-animal hybrids is a sham. Ernst uses the atemporality of visual art for the purpose of antihistorical statement.

This repeal of historical thinking in the biocentric tradition was motivated by the ontological imperative to *internalize* all new knowledge of animal life and animal history. Behind the cultural roles of the scientist, philosopher, and artist contemplating the implications of evolutionary process, the human animal experiences the process itself in perfect oblivion. The task of finding a language and voice for that animal and its interior life became the great rhetorical challenge of biocentric thinkers. To that end they adopted an analogy to history and its repeal, to memory and forgetting, in the repression of metaphorical thinking. The literary equivalent to the ontological recuperation of the animal was achieved by turning metaphor on its head: repressing its abstract meaning and retrieving the material reference, the literal residue, that is treated as the symbolic equivalent to unconscious animal life.

The biocentric thinkers recognized that, although Nature remains largely inaccessible to language (that is, it is impossible for language to speak Nature), figurative language can nonetheless function as an arena for biocentric performance. As the material reference or the literal residue of metaphorical language is appropriated, irrational impulses are often liberated, there is a display of joking and wit of the kind that signals a return of the repressed, the zoomorphic libido has opportunity to act. But while this is perhaps truer of the later artists (Max Ernst, for example, uses metaphor, pun, and all forms of conceptual doubling as opportunity for bestial play), one finds even Darwin interrogating the metaphorical nature of the scientific language bequeathed to him by tradition and predicting its collapse. Nietzsche uses etymology to trace in metaphysical language the *Leitfaden des Leibes,* the clew that leads the philosopher back to the language of the body. Kafka misleads readers into creating allegories whose collapse reveals the truth concealed at the repressed literal level. And, like Kafka, who uses the animal figure in fiction only to collapse its tropological meaning, Lawrence restores the animal qua animal to metaphor as the predominant reference.

By presenting the repeal of history and the practice of metaphorical repression as analogous forms of regressiveness, I hoped to show that the biocentric agenda of reappropriating the animal in the human challenged thinkers to devise intellectual equivalents for the ontological condition of animal life. To these strategies (historical and metaphorical regressiveness) one could add a third, discursive repression, which was born out of the realization that speaking as the animal requires the abolition of human speech and the repeal, if not entirely of the intention to communicate, then certainly of the intention to mean and signify. But the solution to this dilemma could not simply be silence: it had to be silence with a difference, silence that signaled the renunciation (not merely the absence) of speech. Only Kafka and perhaps Ernst, in their repeal of reason and logic and in their strategies to frustrate meaning and communication, approximated this condition. Nietzsche and Lawrence opted for a different, but equally regressive, solution. They produced a libidinal speech, a discourse charged with aggressiveness, exuberance, delirium, recklessness, with inarticulate qualities that signify no meaning but only the vivid aliveness of the speakers.

This discursive regression inevitably disturbed the conventional relationship between author and reader, producing a philosophy that refused to instruct and an art that refused to please. The authors abdicated authority, the claim to have produced truth and meaning, and the artists repudiated aesthetics. Instead of valuable artifacts, they produced autotelic activity in the form of performances or exercises analogous to the instinctive activity of animal life, and therefore of benefit only to their own organisms. Because biocentric thinkers and artists must preserve their autonomy from the "other," they make no concessions to the audience, whose needs and desires are disregarded, whose approval is rebuffed, whose understanding is frustrated, and whose pleasure is stimulated only at the most libidinal level, if at all. The result, not surprisingly, has been a chronic misunderstanding of biocentric literary and visual texts, which, it seems to me, owe their degree of acceptability in the modern intellectual canon to the extent to which they have been mis-

The Biocentric Tradition in Context

prised or distorted as humanistic documents of one sort or another.

The regressiveness of the biocentric tradition makes it unique among intellectual enterprises—or uniquely perverse, one might say, if one imputed to philosophical developments the self-interest of human individuals that impels them to consolidate and aggrandize their position in the world in order to exert influence and achieve some degree of cultural hegemony. I am, here, deliberately caricaturing the anthropocentric assumptions and metaphors we routinely apply to the nature and behavior of collective intellectual enterprises in order to make possible a different mode of evaluating the apparently self-destructive role of biocentric thinking in modern intellectual life. Since "biocentrism" was not a movement at all, let alone a movement with worldly ambitions, its regressive course can be seen as analogous to the misanthropic retreat from the world by its various practitioners: Darwin hiding away in Down House, Nietzsche ensconced in the Alpine retreats of the Engadine, Kafka withdrawn and reclusive in the midst of urban society, Lawrence and Ernst seeking the stillness of the alien American wilderness. Rather than compete with, borrow from, or react to earlier and contemporary modes of thought, biocentric thinkers seem to aspire to spontaneous intellectual activity that guarantees them some autonomy from their cultural milieu. The metaphor of "evolution" to describe their historical development may therefore be appropriate only to the extent that it suggests surrender to irrational and organic principles of development, an urge to embody the irresistible logic of their thinking in the flesh. Its implications of adaptation to an intellectual and social environment may be misleading.

However problematic the antimimeticism of biocentric thinking makes its intertextual relations with other "traditions" in the same century, these relationships ought nonetheless to be clarified for the sake of extricating biocentric thought from false genealogies that would blunt its originality. But given the fertility and diversity of the intellectual landscape in the Victorian period and its succeeding decades, only the most cursory survey is possible, and my very brief analysis makes no claim to anything more than an indexing of gross similarities and differences. I will at the outset confine myself to three major currents in nineteenth- and early twentieth-century thought that appear to anticipate or reflect important premises of biocentric thinking: the positivistic scientific tradition, the phenomenological philosophical tradition, and literary, artistic, and philosophical Romanticism. There is ample critical justification for choosing to focus on these three movements, since each of the biocentric figures whose work I have been exploring has been variously identified with one or another of these: Darwin as a positivist; Nietzsche and Kafka as existentialists; Nietzsche, Lawrence, and the Surrealists as modern Romantics. I will suggest, however, that the antiidealism that positivism, the antimetaphysical stance that phenomenology, and the antirationalism that Romanticism bring to bear on Nature may suggest a kinship with biocentric thought that is ultimately imperfect at best, and even illusory. For virtually every other intellectual movement exhibits humanistic residues or an anthropocentric teleology that only the biocentric thinkers seem to have eluded with any degree of success.

The age of philosophical idealism that preceded the emergence of biocentric thinking, particularly the Absolute Idealism of Hegel, produced a philosophy of culture that I have found useful for defining biocentric thought negatively, as its non-dialectical opposite. Not only does the period of positivism that follows overlap biocentric thought chronologically and historically, extending during the time of its greatest influence from the latter nineteenth to the early twentieth century, but its scientific view of Nature and society promises, but fails, to produce and sustain a biocentric philosophical tradition. Perhaps this is because the sociological orientation of Comte (with its roots in the reformist practice of Saint-Simon and Fourier) continued to direct even the theoretical discoveries of evolutionary positivism into sociological directions, as we see in the work of the English utilitarians in the late nineteenth century and the American pragmatists in the early twentieth.

Both social and evolutionary positivism ultimately share two major anthropocentric premises that distinguish them from biocentric thought and that help to clarify Darwin's paradoxical place within both traditions. I have previously referred to these in my discussion: an underlying faith in progress (with its residual idealistic implications of a linear movement of history and a hierarchical politics of Nature) and a tendency (which becomes more prominent in its later neopositivistic forms) to subordinate the science of Nature to the science of mind. Together, these presuppositions signal positivism's faith in the power of mind to produce truth (in its early commitment to scientific verification, empirical facts, and experimental proofs perhaps more than in its consequent interest in logic and language) and we see in its optimistic orientation, its faith in gradual but continuous advancement, the devious play of human desire and aspiration.

Darwin's ambitious collecting and classifying projects, conducted according to principles of inductive rigor, seem to combine with his reluctance to speculate upon what he could not prove to make him the classic positivist. Yet he shares neither of the previously mentioned premises, having bought his freedom from teleological thinking at the price of a possibly painful agnosticism, and having subordinated throughout his speculative career the power of mind to the power of Nature, thereby virtually placing the epistemological superiority of the scientist into question, as we see at times in the notebooks. Darwin's ability to resist the humanistic seductions of progressive thinking resulted, I believe, precisely from his ability to separate anthropomorphic fictions and desires from the facts of his discoveries. He recognized that the autotelic character of living organisms severely limits the ramifications of evolutionary "progress," since organisms adapt not to future goals or models but to present environments and circumstances. The organism is therefore not a product of engineering (the breeder's power notwithstanding, as I discussed in chapter 2) with its implied possibilities of increasingly improved design, and we find little emphasis in Darwin's own work on the inevitability of progressive structural complexity that so strongly marked Herbert Spencer's biological model of social development.

Darwin does not serve as a protoutilitarian as Spencer does precisely because he interprets the relationship between biology and morality retrogressively while Spencer interprets it progressively. Darwin demystifies morality and robs it of its intrinsic sanctions, by exposing the bestial vestiges of human behavior and betraying the instinctual bases of virtue and vice. His is therefore a proto-Freudianism that prepares the way for the usurpation of ethics by psychology, while Spencer revalidates ethics with the new authority of biology and physics. The utilitarians ultimately privilege human behavior in a way Darwin does not: Spencer, with his grounding in evolutionary theory does so, of course, less than Bentham and Mill, in whom the practical (Bentham's interest in legislation and jurisprudence) and the theoretical (Mill's interest in ethology) direction of utilitarianism is shaped by an anthropocentric ideology.

Expressed in the largest terms, positivism distinguishes itself from biocentric thought because of its historical pursuit of the

philosophy of science rather than the philosophy of Nature.
(Biocentric thought also fails to produce a "philosophy" of Nature, but only because it could not proceed without questioning
and undermining the intellectual aspect of its enterprise,
thereby putting "philosophy" in quotation marks, as it were,
and stipulating the performative rather than the speculative nature of its activity.) This epistemological bent is already clearly
evident in Mill's emphasis on logic and on the science of mind,
and perhaps even in the Humean association psychology of his
paternal predecessor, James Mill. And it characterizes, too, the
modern offshoots of nineteenth-century positivism: both logical
positivism on the one hand, and American pragmatism on the
other. But although Darwinian evolutionary theory does exert an
important impact on the empiriocriticism of Avenarius and
Mach, and on the instrumentalism of Dewey and Bergson, the
focus of modern positivism becomes increasingly metacritical
and metascientific: concerned with the nature of concepts, causality, laws, logic, propositions, mathematics, and language.
There remains consequently not even a vestigial connection
between certain modern forms of positivism (the logical empiricists of the Vienna Circle, for example) and biocentric thought.
Such a paradoxical exception as the curious and controversial
"friendship" of Bertrand Russell and D. H. Lawrence in no way
bridges this discontinuity; it rather clarifies their untimely alienation and disaffection.

The remaining positivists I will discuss, Dewey, Avenarius and
Bergson, exhibit, in their focus on the function of "experience"
as a natural and organic phenomenon, the biocentric residue of a
Darwinian legacy. I did not include the American Pragmatists in
the biocentric "tradition" because their concern with questions
of value, meaning, and belief commits them ultimately, in vary-
ing degrees, to the Symbolic Order. This is true of Charles
Sanders Peirce's semiological theories to a greater extent than of
William James's psychology of belief, which is embedded in a
Darwinian explanation of the adaptive function of human
thought. Dewey's Instrumentalism likewise subordinates
thought to Nature and gives reason a mediative function. But
Dewey's humanism is less clearly anthropocentric than James's.
Dewey's intellectual genealogy was complicated by his original
attempt to produce a synthesis between Hegelian idealism and
Thomas Huxley's physiology, a failure resolved in favor of a
naturalistic and antiepistemological analysis of experience.
Although criticized for its anthropomorphization of Nature,

The Biocentric Tradition in Context

Dewey's organic classification of human experience as action, suffering, and enjoyment bears a biocentric stamp. Even his later epistemological work on the nature of inquiry seemed to retain its experiential focus both in his theoretical work on instrumental logic and in his practical enterprises of implementing an experiential pedagogy in the educational reforms of his laboratory school in Chicago. I excluded Dewey from among biocentric thinkers less on theoretical than on political grounds: because his theories, however biocentric in many of their premises, are blunted in their subversive impact because he eschewed them as tools of cultural critique except in limited, anthropocentric ways, and because they are finally placed in the service of conventional humanistic ends.

The premises of Richard Avenarius's empiriocriticism also exhibit a strong Darwinian influence. Although interested almost exclusively in problems of human cognition, he determined to explain these in the context of a "natural" concept of the world, eschewing metaphysical explanations in favor of a biology of knowledge. Like the Pragmatists, he gives epistemological processes a vital function: interpreting the modes of human knowing in the light of the organism's interaction with its environment. But he takes the implications of his cognitive theory far enough to argue for a collapse of the ontological distinction between mind and matter. However, his complex mathematical formulations of these interactions among metabolism, external stimuli, and the expenditure of vital energy (for example, $f(R) + f(S) = 0$), suggest in their conspicuous scholasticism a rationalistic appropriation of biocentric premises. Avenarius thinks biocentric thoughts, but he is not, himself, a "beast."

To clarify Henri Bergson's status in relation to the biocentric "tradition" is as problematic as ascertaining his place among positivists, a dilemma only imperfectly solved by calling him a new positivist. Bergson's concept of the *élan vital* is a genuinely vitalistic and, therefore, biocentric contribution to modern intellectual history, and his curiously indebted critique of Lamarck, Darwin, and Spencer for putatively mechanistic models of evolution has the ring of the kind of biocentric *méconnaissance* I have earlier described in Nietzsche and Lawrence. Bergson's own concept of "creative" evolution (*L' Evolution créatrice*, 1907), propelled by a vital impetus, strikes me as a biocentric gloss on Darwinian theory in its major premises, which is only partially betrayed by the anthropocentric teleology implicit in some of the earlier works on time, memory, and freedom, as well as the later works on mind and morality. My exclusion of Bergson from the biocentric tradition is perhaps more arbitrary than that of other figures, for even the metaphysical and mystical elements of his thought are not conspicuously more anthropocentric, perhaps, than those of a thinker like Lawrence. But I excluded figures with essentially biocentric theories (Freud is an even better example) who do not internalize the implications of these theories in the form of bestial gestures.

Other figures, not necessarily positivists, but who belong to the tradition of modern Continental vitalism (Driesch, von Hartmann, Becher, and Klages, for example) deserve mention for their critique of "transcendental" philosophy in the interest of articulating a contemporary *Lebensphilosophie*. Among these Ludwig Klages has a special relevance to my project not only because his characterological psychology is explicitly founded upon a "biocentric" metaphysics, but also because the strong Nietzschean influence upon his writing (see *Die psychologischen Errungenschaften Nietzsches*) gives him legitimate standing in the "tradition" I have attempted to identify. Nor does his philosophical writing lack a histrionic energy that I have elsewhere construed as a kind of biocentric rhetoric. But Klages is primarily Nietzsche's disciple rather than Darwin's, and although he appropriates a narrowly defined Dionysian Nietzsche as his master, his dualistic model of the human being as the battleground of *Leib* and *Seele* strikes me as a conventionalization of Nietzsche's complex physiological psychology.

My discussion of the relationship between biocentric thought and modern phenomenology will be even briefer and more compact than that of positivism's impact because, it seems to me, any argument of reciprocal influence would be historically untenable. But, without attempting to establish a genealogical relation, I do think it is worth pointing out that biocentric thinking depends upon an epistemological stance that resembles a phenomenological approach to Nature in its nonrational, nonempirical, nonmetaphysical method. A zoocentric view of the animal, grounded in the perception of the interiority of life, requires an ability to separate mind and world and to extrude from human seeing and knowing the pervasive philosophical assumptions, the logical and rational procedures, and the emotional colorations of subjectivity, all of which constitute an anthropomorphic bias. Biocentric thought reflects a phenomenological immediacy of experience whose alienating impact (for

The Biocentric Tradition in Context

example, the ensuing isolation from the Symbolic Order) makes possible an ontological authenticity, an ability to perceive and embrace our animal being. When Nietzsche and Kafka are identified as existentialists, what is being commended is precisely their ability to formulate an original, undistorted, alienated vision of human existence—their function as what Lacan (borrowing metaphors from Merleau-Ponty and Sartre) calls the "gaze."

Because their extirpation of philosophical assumptions leads to that leveling of values that renders the Symbolic Order transparent, phenomenology and its existentialist elaborations provide uniquely effective tools for the modern critique of anthropocentrism. Yet this philosophical tradition never, in itself, produces a biocentric vision, perhaps because its historical roots (evident, for example, in Husserl's "Cartesian meditations") turned its focus toward the study of mind with special emphasis on the interplay of the human consciousness and ego with its Husserlian *Lebenswelt*, or personal everyday life. The resulting emphasis on attitude and comportment (involving a complex interplay of perception, intuition, and mental "action") inevitably leads toward such specifically human concerns as the shaping of the modern existentialist ethic. But even when this ethic depends on the abolition of the significance of the Symbolic Order, for example, when Camus deconstructs (in *L'Étranger*) the sentimental bourgeois encrustations that give parricide its symbolic cultural significance, its end is to define, if not prescribe, certain constituents of social and communicative (that is, human and cultural) behavior. Even a thinker like Heidegger, whose ontological notions depend upon unreflective and unconscious behavior much more than does Sartrean intersubjectivity, for example, betrays in his preoccupation with such comportment as *dread* and *care* an anthropocentric (albeit not humanistic) orientation.

But Heidegger's lectures on Nietzsche's aesthetics illustrate the very slippery status of even that residual anthropocentrism. Heidegger places Nietzsche at the culmination of the Western philosophical tradition. Yet even as he identifies Nietzsche as the last great metaphysician of that tradition, the philosopher who explores the Being of beings, he redefines metaphysics in nonidealistic terms by dissolving spiritual categories, abstract concepts, and privileged words into various forms of ontological activity. This produces, I believe, a curious circularity of argument with respect to Nietzsche's biocentrism. Heidegger preserves Nietzsche's physiological metaphors only to adjure their physiological reading. In this way he retains their ontological value without delivering them to what he fears would be a positivistic reading, the reduction of art to the functional level of gastric juices, as he puts it. At the same time, he transforms the idealistic realm into the arena of life and living being by translating cultural (art) and ideal (truth) concepts into ontological categories as kinds of activity of living being.

Although Heidegger does not produce a biocentric theory of human ontology, neither does he constitute being within the Symbolic Order. His assessment of Nietzsche follows the same paradigm. He makes no concessions to Nietzsche's vitalism, suppressing the broader range of biological, zoomorphic, and organic metaphors and attributing them, when they cannot be ignored, to Nietzsche's conscious exaggeration, to his attempt to create a detour to the real ontological issues, to his desire to speak to his contemporaries in a familiar and respected language. The language of biology, he argues, must not be read from the perspective of the field of biology. Yet he traces the ways the vitalistic language prevents a humanistic or cultural reading of Nietzsche's ontological ambitions, making art and truth dissonant activities of the perceiving organism rather than strictly anthropoid aspirations. Adopting the procedures of his own work, Heidegger therefore explores the fluid nature of Nietzschean discourse, tracing his way through the unconscious knowledge embedded in language to lead *being* from Nietzsche's sense of the biological, to the sensuous, to the perspectival, to the shining forth or disclosure that constitutes for Heidegger the essential metaphysical activity. By thereby dismantling the equation of being with presence or any of its philosophical substitutions (to borrow the Derridean formulation), he becomes incapable of any centrism, whether anthropo- or bio-.

Finally, the last movement with enough similarities to biocentric thought to be mistaken as its "double" is Romanticism, whose philosophical heterogeneity makes a systematic separation difficult. Further, it is difficult always to determine if differences between the two are in degree or in kind, whether, for example, the biocentric retreat from culture is only a more extreme form of Romanticism's rejection of bourgeois ideology, or if it constitutes a different order of critique. I will retain the criteria I have used throughout this study to argue that residues of idealism (the overestimation of the mental, spiritual, and subjective), humanism (the assumption that human values constitute an order of the real), and anthropocentrism (the dominance of the perspective of the human ego) separate much Romantic philosophy and aesthetics from biocentric thought. Since Nietzsche's own critique of libertarian socialism (rehearsed in chapter 4) can be extended beyond the French Romantics, I will confine myself here to a brief exploration of the philosophical differences that underlie such apparently common commitments as those to Nature, individualism, primitivism, and irrationality.

The Romantic interest in Nature does indeed appear in biocentric guises, notably in the protovitalism of Herder's theory of the universal activity of *Kraft,* and in Schelling's disengagement of Nature from subjectivity in his *Naturphilosophie.* But although these theories reflect the same reaction found in Darwin against Enlightenment models of mechanical-materialistic Nature, they exhibit a quasi-pantheistic undercurrent not found in biocentric thought. Although both departed from the idealism of their mentors in significant ways, Herder retaining the antirationalistic emphasis of Hamann over the influence of Kant, and Schelling establishing the independent reality of Nature in direct opposition to Fichte's subjectivist epistemology, Herder's vitalism is not built on an agnostic premise, and Schelling restores to his independent Nature a Platonic world-soul. The idealistic taint of theories of Nature with notions of divine immanence creates the "natural supernaturalism" that carries notions of the sublime into both aesthetic theory and artistic practice, infusing the natural realism of both British landscape painters and the French Barbizon school with mystical strains. Wordsworth, likewise, expressing his love of Nature in stylistic oscillations between the bucolic and the sublime, succeeds neither in expelling the ideal from his contemplations of Nature, nor in abolishing the perceiving subject.

This subordination of Nature to its perception is characteristic of Romantic subjectivism: an emphasis on the perceiving subject that results, for example, in the inflation of the human ego, the cult of genius, and the idealization of the artist. The anthropocentric features of this type of individualism are easy to identify. Goethe's Werther, for example, betrays in his human desire, his enthrallment to the "other," anthropoid features reflected also in the reciprocal mimetic behavior of his readers, mimicking his clothes, his *Weltschmerz,* and (it is believed apocryphally) his fate. Nor is Faust's restless, titanic striving of the same teleological order as Zarathustra's yea-saying fatalism. But Byron, for example, poses a genuine problem. For Nietzsche's acknowledged kinship to Manfred does indeed suggest the possibility of construing the Byronic hero as a beast, impelled to burst the bounds of convention with an excess of libido and vitality. If the Byronic hero is not a compensatory fantasy of the crippled poet, nor a defensive poseur capturing the world's sympathy and admiration by making a spectacle of his brooding melancholy, then he might indeed be regarded as a form of biocentric *Übermensch*. But the function of "romantic irony" betrays in its attempt to control the perception of the "other" by ameliorating the egoism of the Romantic hero in literature, a degree of self-consciousness incompatible with Nietzschean ambition.

When Romantic individualism is elaborated into a supernatural sympathy with Nature, its function can also be analyzed from a more semiological perspective: as an attempt to incorporate Nature into the Symbolic Order. The expressionistic function of Nature in Goethe's Romantic fiction, for example, is precisely an attempt to make Nature signify the human, to transform it into a language or code of human conflict and feeling. For the same reason the value of the primitive in Romanticism will mark a divergence from biocentric thought, as Romantic primitivism marks Nature as a site of significance and signification. The figure of natural man, whether idealized as Shelley's prototype (and female antitype), Keats's poet, or Rousseau's *naïf*, represents the human outside of culture as nonetheless the repository of highest human value. The biocentric primitive, in contrast, is stripped of virtue, value, and significance and restored to an objective status beyond the reach of the censure or admiration of the "other." The Nietzschean *Übermensch* is neither an ideal type nor a hero. His ontological plenitude, in its profound indifference, bears no reference to others and therefore rebuffs their interpretation and judgment. The counterweight to the idealism of the primitive, the dark side of Romanticism that Mario Praz identifies as the obsession with erotomania and algolagnia, confounds the semiological relationship between Nature and culture even further. Sade's devious manipulations of the libidinal as rational and the rational as libidinal succeed in encoding the erotic and the criminal and encrusting them with cultural significance, while protesting their natural status. This procedure is effectively reversed in modern biocentric art, whose enterprise (in Kafka and Ernst, for example) is to extricate the animal body from its Gothic matrix by decoding the pornological functions in which culture entraps it.

Romanticism's interest in the irrational is often thought to

The Biocentric Tradition in Context

make it the forerunner of the modern psychoanalytical thought of Freud and Jung and its artistic expression in Surrealism. But even in its most "scientific" phase—the forms of faculty psychology (notably physiognomy and phrenology) that became Herder's point of departure in his quest for the integrated personality—we see the attempt to coax irrationality into significance, to make it meaningful. Faculty psychology coexisted comfortably with mysticism, as in the case of Lavater, who was, after all, a theologian. Romantic irrationality also took mystical form in art, notably in the poetry, engravings, and philosophical system of Blake, in whom it was inspired by Swedenborg, among others. But even the most biocentric manifestation of Romantic irrationality, Schopenhauer's essentially vitalistic Will, is betrayed (as Nietzsche bitterly complained) by his attempt to circumvent its pessimistic cultural implications by surrendering the living body to the debilitations of Oriental asceticism.

If this historical survey has revealed some blurring of the boundaries between biocentric thought and the more vitalistic elaborations of other modern intellectual movements, I hope it has also brought its specific features into sharper focus. My selections inevitably betray some arbitrariness because my criteria consist of a wide range of philosophical concerns (an antiidealistic, antirational, antimetaphysical conception of Nature; a self-referential critique of anthropocentrism, a vitalistic equation of life with power and energy rather than with matter, and so on) married to an equally wide range of stylistic strategies (performative prose; devious logic or aggressive polemic; the use of animal or organic metaphors amid perspectival shifts; the text's refusal to seduce, concede, or ingratiate, and so forth). After these admissions it may be fitting to conclude this survey with the most ambiguous figure in the biocentric menagerie, Sigmund Freud, whose psychoanalytic theories abound with biocentric implications, and whose exclusion from my discussion was based, finally, on pragmatic rather than intellectual grounds.

The groundwork for a critical rehabilitation of Freud as a biocentric thinker would certainly seem to have been laid by Frank J. Sulloway in his acclaimed biography, *Freud. Biologist of the Mind* (New York: Basic Books, Inc., 1979). Sulloway impressively documents the professional repressions of the contribution of nineteenth-century biological theory (including Lamarckian theory and much faulty biogenetics) to modern psychoanalysis, as well as the historical distortions that transformed Freud into a "crypto-biologist" ever masking the true scientific path of his discoveries. But Sulloway's Freud is no "beast" in my sense of that term, for the motives imputed to him and to his followers are essentially intellectual (the need to make the history of psychoanalysis conform to psychoanalytic theory) and mythopoeic, giving psychoanalysis an autochthonous origin in Freud's self-analysis. Sulloway argues that the early psychoanalytic establishment was profoundly implicated in the manipulation of its professional and historical reception, and that Freud himself was moved by psychological necessity to mold his professional life in conformity to a deeply rooted "hero-complex." Such a Freud is the antithesis of a biocentric thinker, yet Sulloway's evidence clearly provides much invaluable data for the exploration of biocentric and vitalistic traces in his work. Sulloway does not encompass the neo-Freudianism of Jacques Lacan, which relies almost exclusively upon Freud's anthropogenetic theories. Lacan's interest in representation and signification, that is, his detailed and complex explorations of the realms of the Imaginary and Symbolic orders, respectively, seems inversely proportional to his occlusion of the function of the biological in the realm of the Real, a gap only partially remedied by the work of Laplanche. A biocentric reading of Freud (and I believe that one is possible) would provide an alternative to the Lacanian debiologizing of Freud, on the one hand, and the sociobiological interpretations of Freud's work that Sulloway's biography is sure to spawn, on the other.

My purpose in placing biocentric thought into the context of a historical survey of intellectual and philosophical movements seemingly related to it has been to show that its regressiveness was as much a matter of the function and aim of its theories as of its thematic content. This personification of "theories," as though they exhibited behavior, may be better understood if we remember that, just as books, discourse, images, and so on can function as mediators or models of human desire (that is, can inspire recognition, agreement, and imitation, and may therefore play a role analogous to human consciousness in intersubjectivity), so also can theories. My argument, then (stretched just a little for the sake of provocation) has been that even if they appear to resemble one another, anthropocentric theories "behave" progressively and impressively, like cultural humans, while biocentric theories "act" regressively, like beasts. Romanticism, for example, exhibits in some of its forms an idealistic desire that essentially imitates an older theology in its aim to ameliorate and ennoble. Its progressiveness is inherent in the constitution of its object, which is desire itself, always deferred, always abstract or ideal: "the desire of the moth for the star." Biocentric thought, on the other hand, constitutes an oxymoron, a conceptual paradox, for its thought "acts" as life does. It breaks out of its mediated role in human intersubjectivity by its ability to dispense with an audience (as Kafka tried to do) and to survive misprision (as Nietzsche felt he did). The theories of the biocentric thinkers prove nothing, demand nothing, and thereby abolish their own role in the play of human desire. Since biocentric theorizing is an autotelic act, it aims to reverse the traditional philosophical enterprise of substituting thought for life. And because it teaches nothing, explains nothing, and creates effects only by the most indirect and accidental means, biocentric thought is gratuitous: an excess, a superfluity. Unlike the striving for transcendence, improvement, and enlightenment that characterizes much Western philosophy, biocentric thought aims only to have us become what we already are, to give up striving and surrender to fate, to return from our imaginative life in deferred dreams and aspirations to the eternal now of our bodies and our living vitality. The beasts of the modern imagination teach us only what we already know and what is, in any event, entirely tautological: that life is, above all, life.

Notes

1. INTRODUCTION: THE BIOCENTRIC TRADITION

1. "The 'real' emerges as a third term, linked to the symbolic and the imaginary: it stands for what is neither symbolic nor imaginary, and remains foreclosed from the analytic experience, which is an experience of speech. What is prior to the assumption of the symbolic, the real in its 'raw' state (in the case of the subject, for instance, the organism and its biological needs) may only be supposed, it is an algebraic x" (translator's notes to Jacques Lacan, *Ecrits,* trans. Alan Sheridan [New York: W. W. Norton & Co., 1977], ix). Although I borrow the term from Lacan because I make use of his distinction between the Real and Symbolic Order, I also intend the Symbolic to refer to its early formulations in the writings of Claude Lévi-Strauss as the ensemble of systems of symbolic exchange (language, kinship, economics, art, religion, and so forth) that together constitute culture.

2. The genealogy of this notion of mediated or triangular desire, with its prominent role in the theories of René Girard and Jacques Lacan, includes derivation from Hegel's discussion of the Master / Servant dialectic (Georg Wilhelm Friedrich Hegel, *Phänomenologie des Geistes,* "Selbstständigkeit und Unselbstständigkeit des Selbstbewusstseyns; Herrschafft und Knechtschafft," *Gesammelte Werke,* vol. 9, herausgegeben von Wolfgang Bonsiepen und Reinhard Heede [Hamburg: Felix Meiner Verlag, 1980], pp. 109–16) via the interpretation of Alexandre Kojève, *Introduction to the Reading of Hegel,* ed. Allan Bloom, trans. James H. Nichols, Jr. (New York: Basic Books, 1969).

3. Francis Darwin, ed., *The Life and Letters of Charles Darwin* (New York: D. Appleton & Co., 1919), 2: 27.

4. *The Autobiography of Charles Darwin 1809–1882,* with original omissions restored, ed. Nora Barlow (London: Collins, 1958), p. 87.

5. All translations from the German in this book are mine unless otherwise indicated.

6. Sigmund Freud, "Das Unheimliche," *Gesammelte Werke,* vol. 12 (London: Imago Publishing Co., 1947).

7. D. H. Lawrence, *Reflections on the Death of a Porcupine* (Bloomington: Indiana University Press, 1963), "Blessed Are the Powerful," p. 157.

8. Nietzsche argues that sexual desire increases power that, in turn, spawns new forms. "Not only is the *feeling* of values displaced: the lover *is* more valuable, is stronger. In animals this condition produces new weapons, pigments, colors, and forms: above all, new movements, new rhythms, new allurements and seductions. It is no different with humans" (4, *PW*, 344).

9. "How One Philosophizes with the Hammer" is the alternate title to *Twilight of the Idols* (*Götzen-Dämmerung*).

10. Jacques Derrida, "White Mythology: Metaphor in the Text of Philosophy," trans. F.C.T. Moore, *New Literary History* 6, no. 1 (Autumn 1974), 5–74.

11. *Die Philosophie im Tragischen Zeitalter, Friedrich Nietzsche-Werke*, 3: 1098.

12. Karl-Heinz Fingerhut, *Die Funktion der Tierfiguren im Werke Franz Kafkas* (Bonn: H. Bouvier u. Co. Verlag, 1969). Fingerhut states (p. 1), "Every relationship to animals is conditioned at the outset by an 'image' that the collective or individual phantasy of humans substitutes for the real biological creation."

13. Lawrence, *Porcupine*, "Aristocracy," pp. 230–31.

14. The most interesting exception, and there are several, is Wilhelm Emrich's work, *Franz Kafka* (Frankfurt am Main: Athenäum Verlag, 1961), which uses Heideggerian philosophy to explore the animal's alienating function as the "other" and as otherness.

15. For the genealogy of this concept (its appropriation by Jacques Derrida from Martin Heidegger's *Zur Seinsfrage*) see translator's introduction to Jacques Derrida, *Of Grammatology*, trans. Gayatri Chakravorty Spivak (Baltimore: The Johns Hopkins University Press, 1974), pp. xiii–xx.

16. Sigmund Freud, *Studienausgabe*, Band 1, *Vorlesung zur Einführung in die Psychoanalyse Und Neue Folge*, ed. Alexander Mitscherlich, Angela Richards, James Strachey (Frankfurt am Main: S. Fischer Verlag, 1976), p. 283.

17. Thomas H. Huxley, *Man's Place in Nature* (Ann Arbor: University of Michigan Press, 1959). Retold in the introduction by Ashley Montagu, p. 3.

2. DARWIN'S READING OF NATURE

1. Sir Frederic Bateman, M.D., *Darwinism Tested by Language*, with a preface by Edward Meyrick Goulburn, D.D. (London: Rivingtons, 1877), pp. iii–iv.

2. These suffixes, originally used in the words *phonemic* and *phonetic*, refer to the ability or inability of a difference to produce semiological signification. For example, the hand raised in class to get the teacher's attention and to obtain permission to speak

is an "-emic" gesture in contrast to the "-etic" hand raised inadvertently as part of a stretch and yawn.

3. Bateman, *Darwinism,* p. 112.

4. Ibid., p. vii.

5. Ibid., pp. 187–88.

6. Ibid., p. 53.

7. Thomas S. Kuhn, *The Structure of Scientific Revolutions* (Chicago: University of Chicago Press, 1970).

8. Near the end of the "M Notebook," Darwin speculates on the anthropomorphism behind theories of special creation. "This unwillingness to consider Creator as governing by laws is probable that as long as we consider each object an act of separate creation, we admire it more, because we can compare it to the standard of our own minds, which ceases to be the case when we consider the formation of laws invoking laws & giving rise at last even to the perception of a final cause" (Gruber, 296).

9. Michael Ruse, *The Darwinian Revolution* (Chicago: University of Chicago Press, 1979), p. 57.

10. "The term 'natural selection' is in some respects a bad one, as it seems to imply conscious choice; but this will be disregarded after a little familiarity. No one objects to chemists speaking of 'elective affinity;' and certainly an acid has no more choice in combining with a base, than the conditions of life have in determining whether or not a new form be selected or preserved" (*V,* 1:6).

11. Bateman, *Darwinism,* p. 199.

12. Michel Foucault, "What Is an Author?" in *Textual Strategies,* ed. and trans. Josué V. Harari (Ithaca, N.Y.: Cornell University Press, 1979), p. 141.

13. Darwin to Lyell, 10 April 1860, *The Life and Letters of Charles Darwin,* ed. Francis Darwin (New York: D. Appleton & Co., 1896), 2: 95.

14. Darwin to Lyell, 17 June 1860, *More Letters of Charles Darwin,* ed. Francis Darwin and A. C. Seward (London: John Murray, Albemarle Street, 1903), 1: 154.

15. Ibid.

16. Loren Eiseley, *Darwin's Century* (New York: Doubleday & Co., 1961), p. 148.

17. Stanley Edgar Hyman, *The Tangled Bank* (New York: Atheneum, 1962), p. 64.

18. Ibid., p. 76.

19. Peter J. Vorzimmer, *Charles Darwin: The Years of Controversy* (Philadelphia: Temple University Press, 1970), p. 270.

20. Hyman, *The Tangled Bank,* pp. 52–53.

21. Eugenio Donato, "The Museum's Furnace: Notes toward a Contextual Reading of *Bouvard and Pécuchet,*" in Harari, ed. and trans., *Textual Strategies,* pp. 213–38.

22. Stephen Jay Gould, *Ever Since Darwin* (New York: W. W. Norton & Co., 1977), chap. 1, "Darwin's Delay." Gould argues that Darwin delayed publication of the *Origin* because he feared the censure its philosophical materialism would unleash upon him. But I find in Darwin's similarly protracted method for the perfectly noncontroversial study of barnacles, which cost eight years of labor, persuasive evidence that he was impelled by a sense that only compendious research validated the inductive method.

23. Arthur O. Lovejoy, *The Great Chain of Being* (Cambridge: Harvard University Press, 1936), chap. 7. "The Principle of Plenitude and Eighteenth Century Optimism," pp. 208–26.

24. David L. Hull, *Darwin and his Critics* (Cambridge: Harvard University Press, 1973), p. 36.

25. Jacques Derrida, "White Mythology: Metaphor in the Text of Philosophy," *New Literary History* 6, no. 1 (Autumn 1974).

26. Page du Bois, *Centaurs & Amazons* (Ann Arbor: University of Michigan Press, 1982).

27. Michel Serres, "The Algebra of Literature: The Wolf's Game," in Harari, ed. and trans., *Textual Strategies,* pp. 260–76.

28. Donato, "The Museum's Furnace," p. 448.

29. Hull, *Darwin*, p. 39.

30. Hyman writes of *Variations under Domestication,* "In an important sense the whole book is erroneous genetics. Mendel's demonstration of particular inheritance had been published for three years, but no one was aware of it until 1900, and Darwin was the prisoner of the genetic theory of his time," (Hyman, *The Tangled Bank,* p. 45). But he concedes that Darwin anticipated such concepts as dominance ("prepotency") and mutation ("saltation").

31. Ibid., p. 54.

32. Gould, *Ever Since Darwin,* chap. 4, "Darwin's Untimely Burial," pp. 39–45.

33. Charles Darwin, assisted by Francis Darwin, *The Power of Movement in Plants* (London: John Murray, 1880), p. 571.

34. In spite of his general debiologizing of Freud, Lacan appears to retain some aspect of the Imaginary Order as operative in animal life. See Anthony Wilden's commentary in Jacques Lacan, *The Language of the Self,* trans. Anthony Wilden (Baltimore: The Johns Hopkins University Press, 1968), pp. 159–60.

35. Hyman, *The Tangled Bank,* p. 61.

3. DARWIN, NIETZSCHE, KAFKA, AND THE
PROBLEM OF MIMESIS

1. Aristotle, *Poetics,* trans. Leon Golden (Englewood Cliffs, N.J.: Prentice-Hall, 1968), chap. 4, p. 7.

2. According to Stephen Jay Gould, the problem of "creativity" of natural selection continues to generate vexing controversies that he would resolve by describing it as "good design," the criterion of the engineer (*Ever Since Darwin* [New York: W. W. Norton & Co., 1977], pp. 41–42). I produced a much more antirationalistic and vitalistic reading of Darwin because I included his entire *oeuvre,* not just the theory of natural selection, as my focus, and because I wished to stress his "influence" on Nietzsche, who interprets, in the complex, devious ways I will describe more fully in the next chapter, Darwinism as a vitalistic philosophy, emptied of its metaphysical elements.

3. Paul Ricoeur, *Freud and Philosophy: An Essay on Interpretation,* trans. Denis Savage (New Haven, Conn.: Yale University Press, 1977), p. 32.

4. William C. Rubinstein, "A Report to an Academy," in *Franz Kafka Today,* ed. Angel Flores and Homer Swander (Madison: University of Wisconsin Press, 1958), pp. 55–60.

5. Klaus Wagenbach, *Franz Kafka in Selbstzeugnissen und Bilddokumenten* (Hamburg: Rowohlt Taschenbuch Verlag, 1964), p. 30.

6. Wagenbach, *Kafka,* pp. 71–72.

7. Franz Kafka, *Sämtliche Erzählungen,* pp. 289, 359.

8. Entry for 1 February 1922, Franz Kafka, *Gesammelte Werke: Tagebücher 1910–1923,* ed. Max Brod (New York: Schocken Books, 1951), p. 569.

9. Jacques Derrida, *Writing and Difference,* trans. Alan Bass (Chicago: University of Chicago Press, 1978), chap. 8, "The Theater of Cruelty and the Closure of Representation," p. 236.

10. Roland Barthes uses this term to suggest that the reader of pornography participates in the translation process (image / program / text / practice / program / fantasy, and so on) inscribed within the novels of Sade. *Sade / Fourier / Loyola,* trans. Richard Miller (New York: Hill & Wang, 1976), p. 164.

11. Charles Neider, *The Frozen Sea* (Oxford: Oxford University Press, 1948), p. 81.

4. NIETZSCHE'S *ECCE HOMO:* BEHOLD THE BEAST

1. Michael Ryan, "The Act," in *Glyph 2: Johns Hopkins Textual Studies* (Baltimore: The Johns Hopkins University Press, 1977), pp. 64–89.

2. This is both Ryan's contention and that of Rodolphe Gasché's complex philosophical argument in "Autobiography as *Gestalt:* Nietzsche's *Ecce Homo,*" *Boundary 2,* 9, no. 3, and 10, no. 1 (Spring / Fall 1981): 271–287: "I will try to argue in what follows that not only is the figure of Zarathustra, as Heidegger has demonstrated, a *Gestalt,* but Nietzsche's self-

representation in *Ecce Homo* as well. Yet if in a first moment Nietzsche obeys the logic of the *Gestalt* to elaborate a conception of being as *Typus,* as great personality, in a second he also subverts this same representation of being, and with it the notion of subjectivity and self-reflexivity. With this second movement, Nietzsche not only breaks away from the romantic heritage, but, more radically, from the modern representation of being, from the form of autobiography in which being is represented, and from representation itself, i.e., from representation as *Vorstellung*" (p. 274). However, Gasché essentially occludes Nietzsche's physiological emphasis in *Ecce Homo,* whereas I intend to restore the suppressed biology as the subversive agent in Nietzsche's reversal of autobiographical strategies and aims.

3. My text, both in this and in the next chapter, will attempt to distinguish both the basic Darwinian principles that remain operative in Nietzsche's physiologism and the cruxes of their conflict. But it is important to remember that as late as *The Gay Science,* Nietzsche calls Darwinism the last great scientific movement ("zur letzten grossen wissenschaftlichen Bewegung") in Europe (2, *GS,* 500).

4. David Friedrich Strauss, *Der Alte und der Neue Glaube: Ein Bekenntnis* (Bonn: Emil Strauss Verlag, 1904). Although Strauss does not surrender teleology altogether, he abandons the clockmaker—"The intelligent architect of the organism, the personal implanter of the instincts was, of course, not to be retained in the modern thought shaped by progressive natural science"—and accepts a physiological basis for reason and consciousness.

5. Heinrich Schipperges, *Am Leitfaden des Leibes: Zur Anthropologik und Therapeutik Friedrich Nietzsches* (Stuttgart: Ernst Klett Verlag, 1975), p. 86. Schipperges writes of Nietzsche's reading of the body, "The language of the body is, as we saw, in its grammar and dialectic as superior to the spirit as algebra to the multiplication tables."

6. Erich F. Podach, "Die Krankheit Friedrich Nietzsches," Sonderdruck, *Deutsches Aerzteblatt—Aerztliche Mitteilungen* (Köln: Deutschen Aerzte Verlag, 1964), 1: 43–48; 2: 99–104.

7. Podach summarizes the various diagnostic positions. P. J. Möbius, who had access to Nietzsche's medical records in Basel and Jena, and Max Kesselring, a Swiss psychiatrist, maintained the syphilitic origin of Nietzsche's illness, although Kesselring argued for a concomitant schizophrenic condition, a diagnosis Podach essentially supports. Nietzsche's sister, Elisabeth Förster-Nietzsche, arguing that Nietzsche had for years chronically abused chloral hydrate as a sedative, diagnosed Nietzsche's breakdown as an overdose of an exotic Javanese

drug identified by P. Cohn as *cannabis indica,* and suggesting a "hashish-paralysis" (ibid.).

8. I deliberately stress the literal residue of the idiomatic expression.

9. Ryan, "The Act," p. 64.

10. In the Dionysian dithyramb, "Ruhm und Ewigkeit," Zarathustra's curse is invested in meteorological imagery to indicate its lack of object, its aimlessness, and in physiological imagery (*geschwürig, Eingeweide*) to mark its zoomorphic character.

> Suspicious, swollen, sinister,
> Long, lying low,
> But suddenly, lightning
> Bright, terrible, a crash
> Against the heavens out of the abyss:
> —The mountain's entrails
> quiver. . . .
>   (3, 706)

11. In *Ecce Homo,* Nietzsche is much more relaxed and light-hearted in his procreative imagery. After meticulously tallying the period of *Thus Spake Zarathustra*'s gestation at precisely eighteen months ("so ergeben sich achtzehn Monate für die Schwangerschaft"), he goes on to conclude, "This number of exactly eighteen months might well suggest, at least among Buddhists, that I am fundamentally an elephant cow" (3, *EH,* 574).

12. Max Kesselring, "Nietzsches Kranken-Optik," Sonderdruck, *Deutsche Rundschau* (Darmstadt-Zürich: Montana Verlag, 1953), p. 176.

5. THE FATE OF THE HUMAN ANIMAL IN KAFKA'S FICTION

1. "In the Penal Colony" and the first chapter in *Amerika* are sometimes treated as companion pieces because of Kafka's diary entry of 9 February 1915: "If the two elements—most conspicuous in the 'Stoker' and in the 'Penal Colony'—don't merge, I am finished." Franz Kafka, *Gesammelte Werke: Tagebücher 1910-1923,* ed. Max Brod (New York: Schocken Books, 1951), p. 463.

2. Max Brod, *Franz Kafka: Eine Biographie* (Frankfurt am Main: S. Fischer Verlag, 1962), p. 65.

3. Gustav Janouch, *Gespräche mit Kafka* (Frankfurt am Main: S. Fischer Verlag, 1968), p. 180.

4. Kafka to Milena Jesenská, Franz Kafka, *Gesammelte Werke: Briefe an Milena,* ed. Max Brod (New York: Schocken Books, 1952), pp. 244, 230.

5. Franz Kafka, *In der Strafkolonie: Eine Geschichte aus dem Jahr 1914.* Mit Quellen, Abbildungen, Materialien aus der

Arbeiter-Unfall-Versicherungsanstalt, Chronik und Anmerkungen von Klaus Wagenbach (Berlin: Verlag Klaus Wagenbach, 1975), pp. 65–94.

6. Brod, *Franz Kafka*, p. 214.

7. Lionel Trilling, "The Fate of Pleasure" in *Beyond Culture* (New York: Harcourt Brace Jovanovich, 1965), p. 63. (Trilling borrows "unpleasure" from Freud.) Sokel acknowledges his debt to Trilling in his work *Franz Kafka—Tragik und Ironie* (München: Albert Langen Georg Müller Verlag, 1964), p. 534.

8. Sokel, *Franz Kafka*, p. 121.

9. Franz Kafka, *Der Heizer, In der Strafkolonie, Der Bau,* intro. and notes by J.M.S. Pasley (Cambridge: Cambridge University Press, 1966), p. 17.

10. Patrick Bridgwater, *Kafka and Nietzsche* (Bonn: Bouvier Verlag, 1974), pp. 41–46.

11. Ibid., p. 42.

12. Entry for 1 February 1922, Kafka, *Tagebücher*, p. 569.

13. Gilles Deleuze and Felix Guattari, *Kafka: Pour une Littérature mineure* (Paris: Les Editions de Minuit, 1975) contains no comparison of the two Kafka stories examined in this chapter.

14. Barthes writes, "Throughout his life, the Marquis de Sade's passion was not erotic (eroticism is very different from passion); it was theatrical." Roland Barthes, *Sade / Fourier / Loyola,* trans. Richard Miller (New York: Hill & Wang, 1976), p. 181.

15. Ibid., p. 36.

16. Ibid., p. 27.

17. Masoch has a novel of that title.

18. Barthes, *Sade / Fourier / Loyola*, p. 31.

19. Ibid., pp. 148, 164.

20. Entry for 31 January 1922, Kafka, *Tagebücher*, p. 568.

21. Ibid.

22. "Jenseits des Lustprinzips," Sigmund Freud, *Gesammelte Werke* (London: Imago Publishing Co., 1948), 13: 3–69.

23. Kafka to Grete Bloch, 18 November 1913, Franz Kafka, *Gesammelte Werke: Briefe an Felice,* ed. Erich Heller and Jürgen Born (New York: Schocken Books, 1967), p. 478.

24. Franz Kafka, *Letter to His Father / Brief an den Vater,* bilingual edition (New York: Schocken Books, 1966), p. 122.

25. Ibid., p. 7.

26. Entry for 9 August 1917, Kafka, *Tagebücher*, p. 527.

27. "Ein Kind wird geschlagen," Freud, *Gesammelte Werke*, 12: 97–226. For a discussion of the grammatical transformations of the fantasy see Jean Laplanche, *Life and Death in Psychoanalysis,* trans. Jeffrey Mehlman (Baltimore: The Johns Hopkins University Press, 1976), pp. 97–102.

28. Entry for 8 August 1917, Kafka, *Tagebücher*, p. 526.

29. Deleuze explains the appearance of the Greek at the end of Masoch's *Venus in Furs* via the mechanism of "foreclosure."
30. Max Brod to Felice, 22 November 1912. *Briefe an Felice*, p. 115.
31. Kafka to Felice 14 August 1913, *Briefe an Felice*, p. 444.
32. Clemens Heselhaus, "Kafkas Erzählformen," *Deutsche Vierteljahresschrift für Literaturwissenschaft und Geistesgeschichte* 26, no. 3 (1952): 353–76.
33. Deleuze accuses Kafka of epistolary vampirism: "Il y a un vampirisme des lettres, un vampirisme proprement épistolaire. Dracula, le végétarien, le jeûneur qui suce le sang des humains carnivores, a son château pas loin. Il y a du Dracula dans Kafka, un Dracula par lettres, les lettres sont autant de chauves-souris." Deleuze and Guattari, *Kafka*, p. 53.
34. Kafka to Milena, n.d., *Briefe an Milena*, p. 237.
35. Entry for May 4, 1913, Kafka, *Tagebücher*, p. 305. A variant of this fantasy with a female "cutter" appears in a February 1913 letter to Felice: "To be a rough piece of wood, and to be braced against her body by the cook, who from the edge of this stiff piece of wood (approximately in the place of my hip) draws the knife toward her with both hands and powerfully slices off kindling for starting the fire." Kafka to Felice, 21–22 February 1913, *Briefe an Felice*, p. 310.
36. Kafka to his father, November 1919, *Brief an den Vater*, p. 45. Kafka writes of the family dynamic, "Mother unconsciously played the role of a driver in the hunt."

6. KAFKA'S "JOSEFINE": THE ANIMAL AS THE NEGATIVE SITE OF NARRATION

1. Max Brod's postscript to the first edition of *The Trial*, which reproduces Kafka's correspondence on the disposition of his work, is reprinted in Franz Kafka, *The Trial*, trans. Willa and Edwin Muir (New York: Vintage Books, 1969), pp. 326–35.
2. Ibid., p. 330.
3. Kafka to Milena Jesenská, n.d., Franz Kafka, *Gesammelte Werke: Briefe an Milena*, ed. Max Brod (New York: Schocken Books, 1952), p. 80. References to *Der arme Spielmann* run like a theme through Kafka's correspondence with Grete Bloch. On 15 April 1914 he wrote to her, "Isn't *Der arme Spielmann* beautiful?" He then described to her an inspired reading of the story he had performed for his sister Ottla: "I was blissful over every word I uttered." Franz Kafka, *Gesammelte Werke: Briefe an Felice*, ed. Erich Heller and Jürgen Born (New York: Schocken Books, 1967), p. 551.

4. Friedrich Nietzsche, "Vom Nutzen und Nachteil der Historie für das Leben," 1, *UM*, 211.

5. Sigmund Freud, "Aus der Geschichte einer infantilen Neurose," *Gesammelte Werke* (London: Imago Publishing Co., 1947), 12: 155.

6. Jacques Derrida, *Writing and Difference,* trans. Alan Bass (Chicago: University of Chicago Press, 1978), chap. 7, "Freud and the Scene of Writing," p. 226. Derrida, following Freud, posits the perceptual erasure or repression of writing as occurring at intervals. I would postulate that, for the preverbal or nonverbal organism, this periodicity of erasure would be reduced to simultaneity.

7. Lacan explicates Hugo's line about Boaz, "His sheaf was neither miserly nor spiteful," in just this way. "So *his* generosity, affirmed in the passage, is yet reduced to *less than nothing* by the munificence of the sheaf which, coming from nature, knows neither our reserve nor our rejections, and even in its accumulation remains prodigal by our standards." Jacques Lacan, *Ecrits,* trans. Alan Sheridan (New York: W. W. Norton & Co., 1977), chap. 5, "The Agency of the Letter in the Unconscious or Reason since Freud," p. 157. Kobs argues for another register of meaning when he points out that "die Macht des Gesanges" is the verbatim title of Schiller's elegy. Jörgen Kobs, *Kafka: Untersuchungen zu Bewusstsein und Sprache seiner Gestalten* (Bad Homburg v. d. H. : Athenäum Verlag Gmb H, 1970), p. 62.

8. Wilhelm Emrich, *Franz Kafka* (Frankfurt am Main: Athenäum Verlag, 1961), p. 124.

9. Kafka to Felice, 18 November 1912, *Briefe an Felice,* p. 103.

10. Franz Kafka, "Das Schweigen der Sirenen," *Sämtliche Erzählungen*, ed. Paul Raabe (Frankfurt am Main: Fischer Bücherei, 1970), p. 304.

11. Ibid., p. 304.

12. Alexandre Kojève, *Introduction to the Reading of Hegel,* ed. Allan Bloom, trans. James H. Nichols, Jr. (New York: Basic Books, 1969), p. 16.

13. For interpretations that explore the question of the status of art in "Josefine" see: Heinz Politzer, *Franz Kafka: Parable and Paradox* (Ithaca: Cornell University Press, 1962), p. 311; John Hibberd, *Kafka in Context* (London: Studio Vista, 1975), p. 136. Wilhelm Emrich (*Franz Kafka*) treats "Josefine" as a critique of art as the mystique of genius, while Walter Sokel sees Josefine's art as the promise for a reconciliation of the proletariat (*Franz Kafka—Tragik und Ironie: Zur Struktur seiner Kunst* [München / Wien: Albert Langer / George Müller Verlag, 1964], p. 509). Patrick Bridgwater in *Kafka and Nietzsche* (Bonn: Bouvier Verlag, 1974), p. 143, sees Josefine's song as

Dionysian *Rausch-Kunst* scorned by an Apollonian public. Many other interpretations of "Josefine" read the story as allegory of the Jews of the Diaspora, and a number identify Josefine with specific Yiddish performers such as Mrs. Tshisik (Woodring) and Yitskhok Levi (Beck). See Carl R. Woodring, "Josephine the Singer, or the Mouse Folk," in *Franz Kafka Today,* ed. Angel Flores and Homer Swander (Madison: University of Wisconsin Press, 1958), pp. 71–76; Evelyn Torton Beck, *Kafka and the Yiddish Theater* (Madison: University of Wisconsin Press, 1971), pp. 205–7; Herbert Tauber, *Franz Kafka: Eine Deutung seiner Werke* (Zürich: Verlag Oprecht, 1941), pp. 184–85.

14. See Jacques Lacan, *The Language of the Self,* trans. Anthony Wilden (Baltimore: The Johns Hopkins University Press, 1968), chap. 1, "The Empty Word and the Full Word," pp. 9–28.

15. Michael Feingold, preface to Michael Mc Clure, *Josephine: The Mouse Singer* (New York: New Directions Publishing Corp., 1980).

7. MAX ERNST: THE RHETORICAL BEAST OF THE VISUAL ARTS

1. The essays of Read and Davies particularly trace the influence of British Romanticism in Surrealist art. See Herbert Read, ed., *Surrealism* (New York: Praeger Publishers, 1971). See Anna Balakian, *Surrealism: The Road to the Absolute* (New York: E. P. Dutton & Co., 1970) for another idealist reading of Surrealist art. Balakian writes, "What Freud took in dream interpretation for symbols of the conscious life, Breton and his colleagues wanted to grasp as naked realities, significant and even downright essential to the better and more complete knowledge of existence" p. 133.

2. "An Informal Life of M. E. (as told by himself to a young friend)" in *Max Ernst: The Museum of Modern Art, New York,* ed. William S. Lieberman (Garden City, N.Y.: Doubleday & Co., 1961), p. 9. Ernst describes his early educational ambitions as "a degree in philosophy at the University of Bonn with the intention of specializing in psychiatry."

3. John Russell, *Max Ernst: Life and Work* (New York: Harry N. Abrams, 1967), p. 20.

4. For a discussion of the complex mechanism of "foreclosure" in the Lacanian etiology of psychosis, see J. Laplanche and J.-B. Pontalis, *The Language of Psychoanalysis,* trans. Donald Nicholson-Smith (New York: W. W. Norton & Co., 1973), pp. 166–68. Lacan, it should be remembered, contributed to *Minotaure,* and to Surrealist discourse in general, with particular influence on Dali's paranoiac-critical method.

5. Ernst illustrated Carroll's *Hunting of the Snark* in 1946, painted *For Alice's Friends* in 1957, and in 1944 sculpted a plaster *White Queen*, which is a hybrid of the stacked-disc White Queen of Tenniel's drawings and the White Rabbit.

6. The three most important of the original collage novels are *La Femme 100 têtes* (1929), *Rêve d'une petite fille qui voulut entrer au Carmel* (1929), and *Une Semaine de bonté ou les sept éléments capitaux* (1934).

7. Loni and Lothar Pretzell, "Impressions of Max Ernst from His Homeland," in *Homage to Max Ernst*, special issue of the *XXe Siècle Review*, ed. G. di San Lazzaro (New York: Tudor Publishing Co., 1971), p. 8.

8. Spies lists among Gothic influences upon Ernst and his colleagues Walpole's *Castle of Otranto*, Maturin's *Melmoth*, Lewis's *Monk*, and the works of Radcliffe, Borel, Bertrand, and, of course, Sade. Werner Spies, *Max Ernst-Collagen: Inventar und Widerspruch* (Köln: Verlag M. Du Mont Schauberg, 1974), pp. 174, 178, 194.

9. Jacques Derrida, "White Mythology: Metaphor in the Text of Philosophy," *New Literary History* 6, 1 (Autumn 1974): 11.

10. Russell, *Max Ernst*, p. 9.

11. Yvon Taillandier, "The Fauna in Paradise Regained," in di San Lazzaro, ed., *Homage to Max Ernst*, p. 122.

12. "An Informal Life," p. 8.

13. Balakian, *Surrealism*, p. 138.

14. Whitney Chadwick, "Eros or Thanatos—The Surrealist Cult of Love Reexamined," *Artforum* 14, no. 3 (November 1975): 52.

15. Spies, *Max Ernst*, "Dokumentationsbilder."

16. Max Ernst, "Beyond Painting," trans. Dorothea Tanning, in *Max Ernst: Beyond Painting and Other Writings by the Artist and His Friends* (New York: Wittenborn, Schultz, Inc., 1948), p. 19.

17. Spies, *Max Ernst*, p. 11.

18. Jacques Damase, *Marc Chagall* (New York: Barnes and Noble, 1963), p. 12.

19. André Breton, "Max Ernst," trans. Ralph Manheim, in *Beyond Painting*, p. 179.

20. Roland Barthes, *Sade / Fourier / Loyola*, trans. Richard Miller (New York: Hill & Wang, 1976), p. 127.

21. Max Ernst, *The Hundred Headless Woman*, trans. Dorothea Tanning (New York: George Braziller, 1981), p. 235.

22. Ibid., pp. 17, 41.

23. Spies, "Dokumentationsbilder."

24. Ernst, *Hundred Headless Woman*, p. 219.

25. Ibid., p. 239.

26. Ibid., p. 305.

27. Jacques Derrida, "Structure, Sign, and Play in the Discourse of the Human Sciences," in *The Languages of Criticism and the Sciences of Man: The Structuralist Controversy*, ed. Richard Macksey and Eugenio Donato (Baltimore: The Johns Hopkins University Press, 1970), p. 264.

28. Russell, *Max Ernst*, p. 146.

29. Schneede quotes *Der Spiegel* as having written, "And indeed the blasphemy did not lie in the Christ Child being beaten; all that was shocking was the fact that the halo rolls down." Uwe M. Schneede, *Max Ernst*, trans. R. W. Last (New York: Praeger Publishers, 1973), p. 86.

30. Ibid., p. 56.

31. In an earlier version of this chapter ("Deconstruction in the Works of Max Ernst," *Structuralist Review* 1, no. 1 [Spring 1978]) I argued that the bride was not masked but represented a bird-headed hybrid of the sort recurring throughout "Oedipe" in *Une Semaine de bonté*. I have since seen the original painting in the Peggy Guggenheim Gallery in Venice and discovered a third eye, barely perceptible in most reproductions, peering through the mask.

32. The Douanier Rousseau painted *View of the Pont de Sèvres* in 1908, in which a balloon, a dirigible, and a biplane hang suspended like stars in the daytime sky over the little town. The aerial machines clearly enchanted Rousseau almost as much as the exotic jungle flora he had seen at the Paris World's Fair in 1889. Franz Kafka, Ernst's literary counterpart in the use of animal imagery, wrote one of his earliest works about his first encounter with the flying machines, "The Aeroplanes at Brescia," in 1909. In Guillaume Apollinaire's "Zône," published in 1911, real and mythical birds escort a stunt plane that is identified with Christ. "Christ surpasses pilots in his flight / He holds the record of the world for height." Ernst, much impressed by the poem, refers to it when he writes that in 1941, Loplop, the Bird Superior, followed the airplane that brought him to America. "An Informal Life," p. 20.

33. Ernst wrote, "Voracious gardens in turn devoured by a vegetation which springs from the debris of trapped airplanes." Ibid., p. 18.

34. Gilbert Lascault, "Traps and Lies in Max Ernst's Work," in di San Lazzaro, ed., *Homage to Max Ernst*, pp. 111–12.

35. In 1959 Ernst painted the nonrepresentational *A Web of Lies*.

36. Lucy R. Lippard, "Max Ernst: Passed and Pressing Tensions," *Art Journal* 33, no. 1 (Fall 1973): 16.

37. Ernst's point of reference is an enormous (72-foot by 36-foot) sandstone sculpture mounted in the cliffs below the fortification of Belfort, France, by Bartholdi (1834–1904), the French

Notes to Pages 148–57

sculptor of the Statue of Liberty. It commemorates Colonel Denfert-Rochereau's successful defense of the city during a ten-day siege of the 1870–71 war.

38. *Une Semaine de bonté* was not paginated in its original edition. Reference here is to volume and plate number.

39. Renée Riese Hubert, "The Fabulous Fiction of Two Surrealist Artists: Giorgio de Chirico and Max Ernst," *New Literary History* 4, no. 1 (Autumn 1972): 165.

8. THE ONTOLOGY OF D.H. LAWRENCE'S *ST. MAWR*

1. D. H. Lawrence, *Reflections on the Death of a Porcupine* (Bloomington: Indiana University Press, 1963), title essay, p. 210. Although the essays in this volume, with the exception of "The Crown" (1915), were written after *St. Mawr,* in the summer of 1925, they elaborate the Nietzschean philosophical foundation of the novella.

2. Mitzi Brunsdale, in *The German Effect on D. H. Lawrence and His Works, 1885–1912* (Bern: Peter Lang Publishers, 1978), pp. 126–140, explores at some length Jessie Chambers's clue that Lawrence acquired his knowledge of Nietzsche at the Croydon public library in the winter of 1908–9. See also John B. Humma's provocative argument, "D. H. Lawrence as Friedrich Nietzsche," *Philological Quarterly* 53 (January 1974): 110–20.

3. D. H. Lawrence, *St. Mawr & The Man Who Died* (New York: Vintage Books, 1953), p. 80. All citations from *St. Mawr* refer to this edition.

4. Sigmund Freud, "Das Unheimliche," *Gesammelte Werke* (London: Imago Publishing Co., 1947), 12: 227–68.

5. See Graham Hough, *The Dark Sun: A Study of D. H. Lawrence* (New York: Macmillan Co., 1957), pp. 182–83. Hough diagnoses *St. Mawr* as a failed realistic fiction ("not an authentic piece of work") because the characters' disaffection with England is marred by cultural implausibilities.

6. Lawrence suggested to Curtis Brown "Two Ladies and a Horse" as a possible alternative title to *St. Mawr.* Keith Sagar, *D. H. Lawrence: A Calendar of His Works* (Manchester: Manchester University Press, 1979), p. 139.

7. Although Cowan does invoke Jung to infer that "the horse in Lawrence's work usually connotes the instinctual life of the body," he is careful to detail the variety of its typological manifestations in the *oeuvres.* James C. Cowan, *D. H. Lawrence's American Journey* (Cleveland: Press of Case Western Reserve University, 1970), p. 88. Inniss regards St. Mawr as a "fairly conventional emblem only slightly touched with the sense of 'otherness.'" Kenneth Inniss, *D. H. Lawrence's Bestiary* (The Hague: Mouton, 1971), p. 169.

8. Cavitch, who reads the novella as a self-betraying allegory of sexual ambivalence, sees St. Mawr as representing both sexual potency and its rejection. "The stallion's conventional association with sexual power is meaningful to Lou because as a symbol St. Mawr also expresses her fear of catastrophe in sexual contact, revealing her sense of doom or fatality in the sexual impulse itself." David Cavitch, *D. H. Lawrence and the New World* (New York: Oxford University Press, 1969), p. 154.

9. Lawrence, *Porcupine*, "The Novel," p. 105.

10. F. R. Leavis, *D. H. Lawrence: Novelist* (New York: Simon & Schuster, 1969), pp. 225–45.

11. Lawrence, "The Novel," p. 110.

12. Ibid.

13. Lawrence, *Porcupine*, ". . . Love Was Once a Little Boy," p. 187.

14. Freud, "Das Unheimliche," p. 247.

15. Kingsley Widmer, *The Art of Perversity: D. H. Lawrence's Shorter Fictions* (Seattle: University of Washington Press, 1962), pp. 70–71.

16. Lawrence, "The Novel," p. 112.

17. Lawrence, ". . . Love Was Once a Little Boy," p. 188.

18. Lawrence, "Reflections on the Death of a Porcupine," *Porcupine*, p. 200.

19. D. H. Lawrence, *Phoenix: The Posthumous Papers (1936)*, ed. Edward Mc Donald (New York: Viking Press, 1968), pp. 32–34.

20. Lawrence, *Porcupine*, "Blessed are the Powerful," p. 145.

21. Lawrence, ". . . Love Was Once a Little Boy," p. 184.

22. The goatish artist who presents the company with the Pan theory is not Dean Vyner, as Inniss is misled to suppose (Inniss, *D. H. Lawrence's Bestiary*, p. 170) by the ambiguity of the text, but rather a separate guest later identified by the name of Cartwright.

23. Lawrence to Edward Garnett, from Lerici, per Fiascherino, Italy, 5 June 1914, *The Collected Letters of D. H. Lawrence,* Vol. 1, ed. Harry T. Moore (London: William Heinemann, 1962), p. 282.

24. D. H. Lawrence, *Apocalypse* (New York: Viking Press, 1966), p. 144. Inniss, *D. H. Lawrence's Bestiary*, p. 170, also discusses the dragon tropes in *St. Mawr.*

25. Lawrence, *Porcupine*, "Aristocracy," p. 224.

26. Ibid., p. 230.

27. Lawrence, "Novel," p. 110.

28. Lawrence, "Aristocracy," p. 227.

29. I am indebted for this line of thinking to Philippe Hamon, *Introduction à l'analyse du descriptif* (Paris: Hachette, 1981), chap. 1, "Rhetorical Status of the Descriptive," trans. Patricia Baudoin.

30. Freud, "Das Unheimliche," p. 259. Freud's analysis of the function of the mother in the uncanny and in homesickness, while not entirely germane to *St. Mawr,* is worth repeating. "It often happens that neurotic men claim to find the female genitals uncanny. But this uncanny thing is the entrance to the old abode of the human child, the site we all once inhabited. 'Love is homesickness' declares the old adage, and when the dreamer in addition thinks of a locale or landscape in dream, 'This is familiar to me; I have been here before,' then its meaning may refer to the genitals or body of the mother."

9. THE ANIMAL AND VIOLENCE IN HEMINGWAY'S *DEATH IN THE AFTERNOON*

1. Larry Collins and Dominique Lapierre, *Or I'll Dress You in Mourning* (New York: Simon & Schuster, 1968), p. 8.
2. Waldmeir's theory that Hemingway intends the bullfight to fulfill a religious function—"It assumes the stature of a religious sacrifice by means of which a man . . . can purify and elevate himself in much the same way that he can in any sacrificial religion"—is rendered ironic by Hemingway's own rather grisly and blasphemous transformation of Crucifixion imagery into that of the *corrida*—"A crucifixion of six carefully selected Christs will take place at five o'clock in the Monumental Golgotha of Madrid, government permission having been obtained. The following well-known, accredited and notable crucifiers will officiate, each accompanied by his cuadrilla of nailers, hammerers, cross-raisers and spade-men, etc." (204). Joseph Waldmeir, "Confiteor Hominem: Ernest Hemingway's Religion of Man," in Robert P. Weeks, ed., *Hemingway, A Collection of Critical Essays,* (Englewood Cliffs, N.J.: Prentice-Hall, 1962), p. 165. I will argue that Hemingway shares with orthodox religions the repression of the body and the sublimation of violence.
3. Dos Passos to Hemingway, February 1932, *The Fourteenth Chronicle,* ed. Townsend Ludington (Boston: Gambit, 1973), pp. 402–3.
4. Hemingway's reply to Robert M. Coates's review was published in *The New Yorker* 8 (Nov. 5, 1932): 74–75.
5. Jacques Derrida, *Writing and Difference*, trans. Alan Bass (Chicago: University of Chicago, 1978), chap. 8, "The Theater of Cruelty and the Closure of Representation," pp. 232–50.
6. Scott Donaldson, *By Force of Will* (New York: Penguin Books, 1977), p. 91.
7. Nemi D'Agostino, "The Later Hemingway," *Hemingway: A Collection of Critical Essays,* p. 153.

8. Norman Mailer, *The Bullfight: A Photographic Essay with Text* (New York: CBS Records / Macmillan Co., 1967). The work is not paginated, but the quotation appears on the fifth page of text. Although his text is entitled "Footnote to *Death in the Afternoon*," Mailer corroborates Lawrence's report of the squalor of the Mexican corrida and insists somewhat more than Hemingway does on the materiality of the violence. "The bull-fight always gets back to the blood. It pours in gouts down the forequarters of the bull, it wells from the hump of the morillo, and moves in waves of bright red along the muscles of his chest and the heaving of his sides. If he has been killed poorly and the sword goes through his lung, then the animal dies in vomit-ings of blood."

9. Roland Barthes, *Mythologies*, trans. Annette Lavers (New York: Hill & Wang, 1972), "The World of Wrestling," pp. 15–25.

10. Ibid., p. 20.

11. In a similar maneuver, Hemingway imputes a corrupt senti-mentality (pity for animals, exploitation of servants) to Kan-disky (Hans Koritschoner) (*GHA*, 25–31).

12. Marks, who repeats many of Hemingway's arguments without attribution, parrots this one as well when he writes of the bull, "The wounds he suffers are in hot blood; they are more bear-able for that reason." John Marks, *To the Bullfight Again* (New York: Alfred A. Knopf, 1967), p. 13. I am not prepared to accept this argument on faith without some physiological explanation of the phenomenon. We are not told (by Hemingway or Marks) whether "hot blood" refers to a somatic state, like excitation or exertion, or an emotional one, like fear or aggression, and whether the blockage of pain consequently has a neurological or a psychological etiology.

13. Scott Donaldson's discussion of Hemingway's homophobia in "The Mincing Gentry" (*By Force of Will*, chap. 7, pp. 182–88) amply reveals in Hemingway's comportment a Lacanian phallo-logocentrism, that is, an interpretation of the phallus as a signi-fier of a signifier, a signifier of all value. This supports my argument here that Hemingway's dominant concern is pres-tige, not animal vigor, and suggests that the sexual realm (like the battlefield, the safari, and the corrida) was for Hemingway not a site of libidinal experience but an explicitly social arena in which hierarchies of status and mastery are forged.

14. Marks, *To the Bullfight Again*, p. 14.

15. *Pundonor*, as we see in Pedro Romero in *The Sun Also Rises*, makes for perfectly interesting novelistic characters, and I have no quarrel with Hemingway's fiction. My quarrel is with his generic confusion, his translation of nonfiction into fiction, of

256

life into art, of violence into spectacle, and with his insistence on mimetic living, on living as though one were a character in a book with the obligation to enact—and internalize—heroic conventions. This insistence spells a denigration of life and a contempt for Nature as inferior kinds of reality, an inferiority Hemingway freely admits in his foreword to *Green Hills of Africa*. "The writer has attempted to write an absolutely true book to see whether the shape of a country and the pattern of a month's action can, if truly presented, compete with a work of the imagination."

16. Lawrence R. Broer, *Hemingway's Spanish Tragedy* (University, Ala.: University of Alabama Press, 1973), p. 69.

Index

Index

Index

265

About the Author

Margot Norris is professor of English at the University of Michigan. She is the author of *The Decentered Universe of "Finnegans Wake,"* also from Johns Hopkins.

The Johns Hopkins University Press

Beasts of the Modern Imagination

This book was composed in Garamond #49 text and display by BG Composition, Inc., from a design by Chris L. Smith. It was printed on Glatfelter 50-lb. offset paper and bound in GSB S/535 #11 by Thomson-Shore, Inc.